HOUSES of HORROR

HOUSES of HORROR

HANS HOLZER

FALL
RIVER
PRESS

Book design by Lundquist Design, New York

Fall River Press
122 Fifth Avenue
New York, NY 10011

ISBN-13: 978-0-7607-8384-9
ISBN-10: 0-7607-8384-5

Printed and bound in the United States of America

10 9 8 7 6 5 4 3 2

CONTENTS

INTRODUCTION

$\mathcal{H}$ave you ever come home and wondered what might be lurking up the stairs, in the dark of the corridor where the lights don't reach and the soft footfalls of the visitor disappear into the thick carpet?

If your house were devoid of all unseen presences, then you would not think along those lines. But thousands of people who live in old houses and even some who live in comparatively modern homes have come face to face with something that wasn't in their lease or purchasing contract.

The presence lets you know it is its house and not yet yours, and the disturbances to attract your attention to make sure you realize that you're never really alone—those are the earmarks of the haunted house, and if you're only a little bit psychic, sooner or later you will have to come to grips with the problem.

Across the nation and all over the world, sane respectable people report experiences with ghosts, or what for want of a better and less frightening term is called spectral. These people don't go about telling the newspapers, for they do not wish to be made the butt of cheap jokes, nor do they tell their ministers and doctors, for the men of religion and science instinctively fear the reality of ghostly phenomena as representing a threat to their preconceived notion of what the universe is all about.

Finally, these people turn to people like me, who are experts in such matters, and ask for advice and comfort: the comfort of knowing they are not alone in their predicament and their experiences with the world of the uncanny.

I cannot always come and lay the ghost, nor is it necessarily desirable to do so. Often the matter is complex and involves both the living and the dead in a mutually entwining relationship that cannot exist one without the other, and to sever arbitrarily that which nature has evidently ordained somehow, would be as wrong as not heeding the cry for help from those who desperately want help and release.

Man's inhumanity to man has created countless remnants of tragic events that persist in the areas of their demise and even the walls seem to be able to talk at times and tell posterity what has happened in them.

Wherever stark human emotions are involved there is no boundary of time or expiration, for these emotions cling to the surroundings forever. It does not really matter if you step into such whirlpools of feelings today or a hundred years hence, they will still be there and you will relive, the moments as if the time in between had never passed.

The events reported here are but a fraction of those in my files awaiting disposition or perhaps only a word of understanding. People keep having parallel experiences and they are the ones for whom I write especially, so that they may know theirs is not a unique world but one fashioned by an unsentimental nature in a rather routine way that has occurred elsewhere and will recur to the end of time. If this is not exactly comforting to those caught up in the turmoil of the experience, on both sides of the veil, it is at least a finger pointing to a better understanding of what hauntings are all about. Many of these cases remind one of the Gothic novels of the nineteenth century, for even though the surroundings are modern, the problems are like the sufferings of the Gothic tragedies, equally beyond real help. I am telling the stories from the point of view of the victims, for they are the ones who create the Gothic character of these true accounts.

The very fact that these are not cases easily resolved in the way many other ghost cases are resolved through trance investigations, points at the tragic character of the stories: for neither victim nor ghost escapes the consequences of their being put in each other's way. The victims may move on and find new surroundings, without, however, ever forgetting the imprint of what they have experienced previously. The ghost will keep re-enacting his final compulsion until the house is pulled down around him, or even beyond.

I have not intruded myself into these accounts other than to verify them as best I could. For one reason or another, dispatching the restless ghosts herein reported was neither possible nor desirable, and the introduction of a medium was neither required nor desired by those most concerned.

What we present then are ghost stories that have the touch of the tragic, but above all, are true!

THE SOMERSET SCENT

*S*omerset was one of those small towns that abound in rural Pennsylvania and that boast nothing more exciting than a few thousand homes, a few churches, a club or two and a lot of hardworking people whose lives pass under pretty ordinary and often drab circumstances. Those who leave may go on to bigger and better things in the big cities, and those who stay have the comparative security of being among their own and living out their lives peacefully. But then there are those who leave not because they want to but because they are driven, driven by forces greater than themselves that they cannot resist.

The Manners were middle-aged people with two children, a fourteen-year-old son and a six-year-old daughter. The husband ran a television sales and repair shop which gave them an average income, neither below middle-class standards for a small town, nor much above it. Although Catholic, they did not consider themselves particularly religious. Mrs. Manner's people originally came from Austria, so there was enough European background in the family to give their lives a slight continental tinge, but other than that, they were a typical Pennsylvania people without the slightest interest in, or knowledge of, such sophisticated matters as psychic research. But, the occult was never unknown to Mrs. Manner. She was born with a veil over her eyes, which to many means the Second Sight. Her ability to see things before they happened was not "precognition" to her, but merely a special talent she took in her stride. One night she had a vivid dream about her brother, then miles away in the army. She vividly saw him walking down a hall in a bathrobe, with blood running down his leg. Shortly after she awakened the next day, she was notified that her brother had been attacked by a rattlesnake and, when found, was near death. One night she awoke to see an image of her sister standing beside her bed. There was nothing fearful about the apparition, but she was dressed all in black.

The next day that sister died.

But these instances did not frighten Mrs. Manner; they were glimpses into eternity and nothing more.

As the years went by, the Manners accumulated enough funds to look for a more comfortable home than they one they were occupying, and as luck—or fate—would have it, one day in 1966 they were offered a fine old house in one of the better parts of town. The house seemed in excellent condition; it had the appearance of a Victorian home with all the lovely touches of that bygone era about it. It had stood empty for two years, and since it belonged to an estate, the executors seemed anxious to finally sell the house. The Manners made no special inquiries about their projected new home simply because everything seemed so right and pleasant. The former owners had been wealthy people, they were informed, and had lavished much money and love on the house.

When the price was quoted to them, the Manners looked at each other in disbelief. It was far below what they had expected for such a splendid house. "We'll take it," they said, almost in unison, and soon the house was theirs.

"Why do you suppose we got it for such a ridiculously low price?" Mr. Manner mused, but his wife could only shrug. To her, that was not at all important. She never believed one

6

should look a gift horse in the mouth.

It was late summer when they finally moved into their newly acquired home. Hardly had they been installed when Mrs. Manner knew there was something not right with the place.

From the very first, she had felt uncomfortable in it, but being a sensible person, she had put it down to being in a new and unaccustomed place. But as this feeling persisted, she realized that she was being watched by some unseen force all of the time, day and night, and her nerves began to tense under the strain.

The very first night she spent in the house, she was aroused at exactly two o'clock in the morning, seemingly for no reason. Her hair stood up on her arms and chills shook her body. Again, she put this down to having worked so hard getting the new home into shape.

But the "witching hour" of two A.M. kept awakening her with the same uncanny feeling that something was wrong, and instinctively she knew it was not her, or someone in her family, who was in trouble, but the new house.

With doubled vigor, she put all her energies into polishing furniture and getting the rooms into proper condition. That way, she was very tired and hoped to sleep through the night. But no matter how physically exhausted she was, at two o'clock the uncanny feeling woke her.

The first week somehow passed despite this eerie feeling, and Monday rolled around again. In the bright light of the late summer day, the house somehow seemed friendlier and her fears of the night had vanished.

She was preparing breakfast in the kitchen for her children that Monday morning. As she was buttering a piece of toast for her little girl, she happened to glance up toward the doorway. There, immaculately dressed, stood a man. The stranger, she noticed, wore shiny black shoes, navy blue pants, and a white shirt. She even made out his tie, saw it was striped, and then went on to observe the man's face. The picture was so clear she could make out the way the man's snowy white hair was parted.

Her immediate reaction was that he had somehow entered the house and she was about to say hello, when it occurred to her that she had not heard the opening of a door or any other sound—no footfalls, no steps.

"Look," she said to her son, whose back was turned to the apparition, but by the time her children turned around, the man was gone like a puff of smoke.

Mrs. Manner was not too frightened by what she had witnessed, although she realized her visitor had not been of the flesh and blood variety. When she told her husband about it that evening, he laughed.

Ghosts, indeed!

The matter might have rested there had it not been for the fact that the very next day something else happened. Mrs. Manner was on her way into the kitchen from the backyard of the house, when she suddenly saw a woman go past her refrigerator. This time the materialization was not as perfect. Only half of the body was visible, but she noticed her shoes, her dress up to the knees, and the fact that the figure seemed in a hurry.

This still did not frighten her, but she began to wonder. All those eerie feelings seemed to add up now. What had they gotten themselves into by buying this house? No wonder it was so cheap. It was haunted!

Mrs. Manner was a practical person, the uncanny experiences notwithstanding, or perhaps because of them. They had paid good money for the house and no specters were going to dislodge them!

But the fight had just begun. A strange kind of web began to envelop her frequently, as if some unseen force were trying to wrap her into a wet, cold blanket. When she touched the "web," there was nothing to be seen or felt, and yet, the clammy, cold force was still with her. A strange scent of flowers

8

manifested itself out of nowhere and followed her from room to room. Soon her husband smelled it too, and his laughing stopped. He, too, became concerned: their children must not be frightened by whatever it was that was present in the house.

It soon was impossible to keep doors locked. No matter how often they would lock a door in the house, it was found wide open soon afterwards, the locks turned by unseen hands. One center of particular activities was the old china closet, and the scent of flowers was especially strong in its vicinity.

"What are we going to do about this?" Mrs. Manner asked her husband one night. They decided to find out more about the house, for starters. They had hesitated to mention anything about their plight out of fear of being ridiculed or thought unbalanced. In a small town, people often don't like to talk about ghosts.

The first person Mrs. Manner turned to was a neighbor who had lived down the street for many years. When she noticed that the neighbor did not pull back at the mention of weird goings-on in the house, but, to the contrary, seemed genuinely interested, Mrs. Manner poured out her heart and described what she had seen.

In particular, she took great pains to describe the two apparitions. The neighbor nodded gravely.

"It's them, all right," she said, and started to fill Mrs. Manner in on the history of their house. This was the first time Mrs. Manner had heard of it and the description of the man she had seen tallied completely with the appearance of the man who had owned the house before.

"He died here," the neighbor explained. "They really loved their home, he and his wife. The old lady never wanted to leave or sell it."

"But what do you make of the strange scent of flowers?" Mrs. Manner asked.

"The old lady loved flowers, had fresh ones in the house every day."

Relieved to know what it was all about, but hardly happy at the prospect of sharing her house with ghosts, Mrs. Manner then went to see the chief of police in the hope of finding some way of getting rid of her unwanted "guests."

The chief scratched his head.

"Ghosts?" he said, not at all jokingly. "You've got me there. That's not my territory."

But he promised to send an extra patrol around in case it was just old-fashioned burglars.

Mrs. Manner thanked him and left. She knew otherwise and realized the police would not be able to help her.

She decided they had to learn to live with their ghosts, especially as the latter had been in the house before them. Perhaps it wouldn't be so bad after all, she mused, now that they knew who it was that would not leave.

Perhaps one could even become friendly, sort of one big, happy familyæhalf people, half ghosts? But she immediately rejected the notion. What about the children? So far, they had not seen the ghosts, but they knew of the doors that wouldn't stay shut and the other uncanny phenomena.

Fortunately, Mrs. Manner did not fully understand the nature of poltergeists: had she realized that the very presence of her teen-age son was in part responsible for the physical nature of the happenings, she would no doubt have sent him away. But the phenomena continued unabated, day and night.

One night at dinner, with everyone accounted for, an enormous crash shook the house. It felt as if a ton of glass had fallen on the kitchen floor. When they rushed into the kitchen, they found everything in order, nothing misplaced.

At this point, Mrs. Manner fell back on her early religious world. "Maybe we should call the minister?" she suggested, and no sooner said than done. The following day, the minister came to their house. When he had heard their story, he nodded quietly and said a silent prayer for the souls of the disturbed ones.

He had a special reason to do so, it developed. They had been among his parishioners when alive. In fact, he had been to their home for dinner many times, and the house was familiar to him despite the changes the present owners had made. If anyone could, surely their own minister should be able to send those ghosts away.

Not by a long shot.

Either the couple did not put much stock into their minister's powers, or the pull of the house was stronger, but the phenomena continued. In fact, after the minister had tried to exorcise the ghosts, things got worse.

Many a night, the Manners ran out into the street when lights kept going on and off by themselves. Fortunately, the children slept through all this, but how long would they remain unaffected?

At times, the atmosphere was so thick Mrs. Manner could not get near the breakfast nook in the kitchen to clear the table. Enveloped by the strong vibrations, she felt herself tremble and, on two occasions, she fainted and was found thus by her family.

They were seriously considering moving now, and let the original "owners" have the house again. They realized now that the house had never been truly "empty" for those two years the real estate man had said it was not in use.

It was 2 A.M. when they finally went up to bed.

Things felt worse than ever before. Mrs. Manner clearly sensed three presences with her now and started to cry.

"I'm leaving this house," she exclaimed. "You can have it back!" Her husband had gone ahead of her up the stairs to get the bedding from the linen closet. She began to follow him and slowly went up the stairs. After she had climbed about half way up, something forced her to turn around and look back.

What she saw has remained with her ever since, deeply impressed in her mind with the acid of stark fear.

Down below her on the stairway, was a big, burly man, trying to pull himself up the stairs. His eyes were red with torture as he tried to talk to her. Evidently he had been hurt, for his trousers and shirt were covered with mud. Or was it dried blood?

He was trying to hang on to the banister and held his hands out towards her.

"Oh, God, it can't be true," she thought and went up a few more steps. Then she dared look down again.

The man was still holding out his hand in a desperate move to get her attention. When she failed to respond, he threw it down in a gesture of impatience and frustration.

With a piercing scream, she ran up the stairs to her husband, weeping out of control.

The house had been firmly locked and no one could have gained entrance. Not that they thought the apparitions were flesh and blood people. The next morning, no trace of the nocturnal phenomenon could be found on the stairs. It was as if it had never happened.

But that morning, the Manners decided to pack and get out fast. "I want no more houses," Mrs. Manner said firmly, and so they bought a trailer. Meanwhile, they moved into an apartment.

But their furniture and all their belongings were still in the house, and it was necessary to go back a few more times to get them. They thought that since they had signed over the deed to the house, it would be all right for them to go back. After all, it was no longer their house.

As Mrs. Manner cautiously ascended the stairs, she was still trembling with fear. Any moment now, the specter might confront her again. But all seemed calm. Suddenly, the scent of flowers was with her again and she knew the ghosts were still in residence.

As if to answer her doubts, the doors to the china closet flew open at that moment.

Although she wanted nothing further to do with the old house, Mrs. Manner made some more inquiries. The terrible picture of the tortured man on the stairs did not leave her mind. Who was he, and what could she have done for him?

Then she heard that the estate wasn't really settled—the children were still fighting over it. Was that the reason the parents could not leave the house in peace? Was the man on the stairs someone who needed help, someone who had been hurt in the house?

"Forget it," the husband said, and they stored most of their furniture. The new house trailer would have no bad vibrations and they could travel wherever they wanted, if necessary.

After they had moved into the trailer, they heard rumors that the new owners of the house had encountered problems, too. But they did not care to hear about them and studiously stayed away from the house. That way, they felt, the ghosts would avoid them, now that they were back in what used to be—their beloved home!

But a few days later, Mrs. Manner noticed a strange scent of flowers wafting through her brand-new trailer. Since she had not bought any flowers, nor opened a perfume bottle, it puzzled her. Then, with a sudden impact that was almost crushing, she knew where and when she had smelled this scent before. It was the personal scent of the ghostly woman in the old house! Had she followed her here into the trailer?

When she discussed this new development with her husband that night, they decided to fumigate the trailer, air it, and get rid of the scent, if they could. Somehow, they thought, they might be mistaken—it was just coincidence. But the scent remained, clear and strong, and the feeling of a presence that came with it soon convinced them that they had not yet seen the last of the Somerset ghosts.

They sold the new trailer and bought another house, a fifty-seven-year-old, nice rambling home in a nearby

Pennsylvania town called Stoystown, far enough from Somerset to give them the hope that the Unseen Ones would not be able to follow them there.

Everything was fine after they had moved their furniture in and for the first time in many a month, the Manners could relax. About two months after they had moved to Stoystown, the scent of flowers returned. Now it was accompanied by another smell, that resembling burned matches.

The Manners were terrified. Was there no escape from the Uncanny? A few days later, Mrs. Manner observed a smoky form rise up in the house. Nobody had been smoking. The form roughly resembled the vague outlines of a human being.

Her husband was home, fortunately, and experienced the smells also, so she was not alone in her plight. But the children, who had barely shaken off their terror; were now faced with renewed fears. The Manners could not keep running. Running away from what?

They tried every means at their command. Holy water, incense, a minister's prayer, their own prayers, curses and commands to the Unseen; but the scent remained.

Gradually, they learned to live with their psychic problems. For a mother possessed of definite mediumistic powers from youth and a young adult in the household were easy prey to those among the restless dead who desire a continued life of earthly activities. With the physical powers drawn from these living people, they play and continue to exist in a world of which they were no longer a part.

As the young man grew older, the available power dwindled and the scent was noticed less frequently. But the tortured man on the stairs of the house in Somerset will have to wait for a more willing medium to be set free.

THE HOUSE OF EVIL

*P*arker Keegan was a practical man not much given to daydreaming or speculation. That was as it should be. For Parker made his living, if you can call it that, driving a truck with high explosives, tanks containing acetylene, oxygen, nitrogen, and other flammable substances for a welding company in upstate New York.

So you see, he had to have his mind on his work all the time—if he wants to get old.

His wife Rebecca was a more emotional type. That, too, was as it should be. She was an artist, free-lancing, and now and again making sales. There was some Native American blood in her and she had had an occasional bout with the supernatural. But these were mainly small things, telepathy or dream experiences and anything that really worried her. Neither she nor her husband had any notions that such things as haunted houses really existed, except, of course, in Victorian novels.

Now the Keegans already had one child and Rebecca was expecting her second, so they decided to look for a larger place. As if by the finger of fate, an opportunity came their way just about then. Her young cousin Jane telephoned Rebecca at her parents' home to tell them of a place they might possibly rent. It developed she did this not entirely out of the goodness of her heart, but because she didn't like being alone nights in the big place she and her husband lived in. He worked most of the night in another city.

"There are two halves to this house," Jane explained, and she made it so enticing that Parker and Rebecca decided then and there to drive over and have a look at it.

Even though they arrived there after dark, they saw immediately that the house was attractive, at least from the outside. Built in pre-Civil War days, it had stood the test of time well. As is often the case with old houses, the servant quarters were in a separate unit and parallel, but do not intrude upon the main section of the house. So it was here, and it was the former servant quarters that Jane and Harry occupied. As the visitors had not spoken to the landlord about their interest, they entered the unused portion of the building from their cousin's apartment. This was once the main house and contained eight rooms, just what they needed.

The ground floor consisted of a large front room with two windows facing the road and two facing the other way. Next to it was an old-fashioned dining room, and branching off from it, a narrow kitchen and a small laundry room. In the dim light they could make out a marvelous staircase with a lovely, oiled banister. It was at this point that the two apartments that made up the house connected, and one could be entered into from the other.

Underneath the front stairway was a closet and the door leading to the other side of the house, but they found another, enclosed, stairway leading from the bedroom at the top of the front stairs into the dining room. Exactly below this enclosed staircase were the cellar stairs leading into the basement. There were three cellars: one under the servant quarters, one underneath the front room, and one below the dining room.

As Rebecca stepped into the cellar under the dining room, which had apparently served as a fruit cellar, she grew panicky

16

for a moment. She immediately dismissed her anxiety with a proper explanation: they had seen the thriller *Psycho* the night before and this cellar reminded her of one of the gruesome incidents in that movie. But later she was to learn that the feeling of panic persisted whenever she came down into this particular part of the basement, even long after she had forgotten the plot of that movie.

For the present, they inspected the rest of the house. The upstairs portion contained two large bedrooms and two smaller ones. Only the larger rooms were heated. There was an attic but nobody ever investigated it during their entire stay in the house.

They decided the house was just what they wanted and the next morning they contacted the owner.

George Jones turned out to be a very proper, somewhat tight-lipped man. He inquired what they did for a living and then asked, "Are you religious people?"

Rebecca thought this an odd question, but since she had told him she was an artist, she assumed he considered artists somewhat unreliable and wanted to make sure he had responsible and "God-fearing" tenants. Only much later did it occur to her that Jones might have had other reasons.

It was a cold, miserable day in December of 1964 when the Keegans moved into their new home. They were happy to get into a home full of atmosphere, for Rebecca was an avid amateur archaeologist who read everything on antiques she could get her hands on. At the same time they were doing a good deed for her cousin, keeping her company on those long nights when her husband was away at work. It all seemed just right and Rebecca did not even mind the difficulties the moving brought them. For one thing, they couldn't afford professional moving men, but had turned to friends for help. The friends in turn had borrowed a truck that had to be back in the garage by nightfall, so there was a lot of shoving and pushing and bad tempers all around. On top of that, the stinging cold and snow made things even more uncomfortable, and Rebecca could do little to help matters, being pregnant with their second child at the time.

Late that first night, they finally climbed the stairs to the large bedroom. They were both exhausted from the day's work and as soon as they fell into bed, they drifted off into deep sleep.

But even though they were very tired, Rebecca could not help noticing some strange noises, crackling sounds emanating seemingly from her cousin's side of the house. She put them down to steam pipes and turned to the wall.

When the noises returned night after night, Rebecca began to wonder about them. Parker also worked nights now and she and Jane sat up together until after the late show on television was over, around 1:30 A.M. All that time, night after night, they could hear the steam pipes banging away. Nobody slept well in the house and Jane became jumpier and jumpier as time went on. Her mood would change to a certain sullenness Rebecca had not noticed before, but she dismissed it as being due to the winter weather, and of no particular significance.

Then one night, while she was lying awake in bed thinking about some of the events of the recent past, Rebecca heard heavy footsteps coming up the stairs. They were the steps of a heavy man, and since she had not heard the characteristic clicking of the front door lock, she knew it could not be her husband.

Alarmed, and thinking of burglars, she got out of bed and called out to her cousin. She then went to the top of the stairs and was joined by Jane coming through the connecting door, and standing at the foot of the stairs. What the two women saw from opposite ends of the staircase was far from ordinary. They could hear someone walking up the stairs and the stairs bending with each step as if a heavy person were actually stepping upon them!

Only there was no one to be seen. They did not wait until the footsteps of the invisible man reached the top of the stairs. Rebecca dove back into her bedroom banging the door shut after her. Just before she did, she could still hear her young cousin downstairs screaming, before she, too, ran back into the assumed safety of her bedroom.

The experience on the stairs made Jane even moodier than before and it was not long afterwards that she took her little girl and left her husband. There had been no quarrel, no apparent reason for her sudden action. He was a handsome young man who had treated her well, and Jane loved him. Yet, there it was—she could not stand the house any longer and did what her panicky mind told her to do.

Rebecca was now left alone nights with the noisy wraith on the stairs and she scarcely welcomed it. Soon after the incident, Jane's abandoned husband sold his belongings and moved away, leaving the former servant quarters empty once again.

It was then that Rebecca kept hearing, in addition to the heavy footsteps, what seemed to be someone crying in the empty side of the house. She convinced herself that it wasn't just a case of nerves when the noises continued at frequent intervals while she was fully awake. Her time was almost at hand, and as sometimes happens with approaching motherhood, she grew more and more apprehensive. It did not help her condition any when she heard a loud banging of the cupboards in the dining room at a time when she was all alone in the house. Someone was opening and closing the doors to the cupboard in rapid succession soon after she had retired for the night. Of course she did not run downstairs to investigate. Who would?

Fortunately, Parker came home a little earlier that night, because when he arrived he found Rebecca in a state of near hysteria. To calm her fears as much as to find out for himself, he immediately went downstairs to investigate. There was no one there and no noise. Getting into bed with the assurance of a man who did not believe in the supernatural, he was about to tell his wife that she must have dreamed it all, when he, too, clearly heard the cupboard doors open and close downstairs.

He jumped out of bed and raced down the stairs. As he took the steps two at a time, he could clearly hear the doors banging away louder and louder in the dining room. It must be stated to Parker's eternal credit, that not once did he show fear or worry about any possible dangers to himself: he merely wanted to know what this was all about.

The noise reached a crescendo of fury, it seemed to him, when he stood before the dining room door. Quickly he opened the door and stepped into the dark expanse of the chilly dining room.

Instantly, the noise stopped as if cut off with a knife.

Shaking his head and beginning to doubt his own sanity, or at least, power of observation, Parker got into bed once more and prepared to go to sleep. Rebecca looked at him anxiously, but he did not say anything. Before she could question him, the ominous noise started up again downstairs.

Once more, as if driven by the furies, Parker jumped out of bed and raced down the stairs. Again the noise stopped the moment he opened the dining room door.

He slowly went up the stairs again and crawled into bed. Pulling the covers over his ears, he cursed the ghosts downstairs, but decided that his badly needed sleep was more important than the answer to the puzzle.

Shortly after, their son was born. When they returned from the hospital, they were greeted by a new couple, the Winters, who had just moved into the other half of the house.

Although friendly on the surface, they were actually stern and unbending and, as they were also much older than the

Keegans, the two families did not mingle much. Mrs. Winters was a tough and somewhat sassy old woman who did not look as if anything could frighten her. Her husband worked as a night watchman, and there were no children. It was not long before Mrs. Winters knocked at Rebecca's door in fear.

"Someone is trying to break in," she whispered, and asked to be let in. Rebecca knew better but did not say anything to frighten the old woman even further.

It seemed as if winter would never yield to spring, and if you have ever lived in the cold valleys of upstate New York, you know how depressing life can be under such circumstances.

To brighten things a little, the Keegans acquired a female German shepherd dog, and also for use as a watchdog.

All this time Rebecca made sure she was never alone in the house. There was someone watching her, night and day. Her husband no longer scoffed at her fears, but could do little about them. The strange noises in the walls continued on and off and it got so that Rebecca no longer felt fear even when she saw the doorknob of a perfectly empty room turn slowly by its own volition. By now she knew the house was haunted, but as yet she did not realize the nature of the uncanny inhabitants.

One day she left the baby securely strapped in his seat while she ran to catch her little girl who was climbing the front stairs and was in immediate danger of falling off. Just at that precise moment, the strap broke and the baby fell to the floor, fracturing his skull.

It seemed that all during their stay at the house, someone was always having accidents or becoming unaccountably ill. Their debts increased as their medical expenses grew higher, so it was decided that Rebecca should go to work and earn some money. In addition, Parker started working extra shifts. But far from helping things, this only served to incite the landlord to raise their rent, on the theory that they were earning more and could pay more. To make things even more difficult for them, Rebecca could riot find a proper baby-sitter to stay with the children while she was at work. Nobody would stay very long in the house, once they got to know it.

She turned to her mother for help, and her mother, after a short stay, refused to spend any more time in the house, but offered to take the children to her own home. There was no explanation, but to Rebecca it seemed ominous and obvious. Finally, her teenage sister Mary consented to become a baby-sitter for them. She could use the money for school, but soon her enthusiasm waned. She began to complain of a closed-in feeling she experienced in the old house and of course she, too, heard all the strange noises. Each day, Mary became more and more depressed and even ill, whereas she had been a happy-go-lucky girl before.

"There are prowlers about," she kept saying, and one day she came running to Rebecca in abject fear. On a moonless night she happened to be glancing out of a living room window when she saw what appeared to be a face. Rebecca managed to calm her by suggesting she had seen some sort of shadow, but the incessant barking of the dog, for no apparent reason, made matters worse. Added to this were incidents in which objects would simply fly out of their hands in broad daylight. The end of the rope was reached one day when they were all in the front room. It was afternoon and Mary was holding a cup in her hand, about to fill it with tea. That instant it flew out of her hands and smashed itself at Parker's feet. Without saying another word, the young girl went up the stairs to her room. Shortly after, her things all packed, she came down again to say goodbye.

Once again they were without help, when Rebecca's sister-in-law Susan saved the day for them. A simple and quite unimaginative person, she had put no stock into all the tales of goings-on she had heard and was quite willing to prove her point.

Within a day after her arrival, she changed her tune.

"Someone is watching me," she complained, and she refused to stay alone in the house. She, too, complained of things flying off the shelves seemingly by their own volition and of cupboard doors opening and closing as if someone were looking into the drawers for something or other.

The footsteps going up the stairs continued and. Susan heard them many times. She took the dog into the house with her but that was of little use: the dog was more afraid than all of the people together.

Incredible though it seemed to the Keegans, two years had passed since they had come to the "House of Evil." That they still had their sanity was amazing, and that they had not moved out, even more amazing. But they simply could not afford to, and things were difficult enough in the physical world to allow the unseen forces to add to their problems. So they stuck it out.

It was the night before Christmas of 1966, and all through the house a feeling of ominous evil poisoned the atmosphere. They were watching television in order to relax a little. Rebecca suddenly saw a presence out of the corner of her eye, a person of some kind standing near the window in back of the sofa where her sister-in-law was sitting. Without raising her voice unduly or taking her eyes off the spot, she said, "Susan, get the rifle!" They had a rifle standing ready in the corner of the room.

Only then did Susan take a sharp look at the face peering into the window. It was a man's face, and so unspeakably evil it took her breath away. Scowling at them with hatred, the face remained there for a moment, while Susan grabbed the gun. But when she pointed it towards the window, the face had disappeared.

Immediately, they rushed outside. The ground was frozen hard, so footprints would not have shown, had there been any.

But they could not see anyone nor hear anyone running away.

The dog, chained at a spot where an intruder would be visible to her, evidently did not feel anything. She did not bark. Was she in some strange way hypnotized?

Shortly after Christmas, Susan had to leave and the Keegans no longer could afford a baby-sitter. Rebecca quit her job, and things were rough financially again.

To help matters, they invited a young couple with a small child to move in with them and help share expenses. The husband did not believe in the supernatural and the wife, on being told of their "problems," showed herself open-minded, even interested, although skeptical.

What had appeared to be a sensible arrangement soon turned out a disaster and additional burden to an already over-burdened family. The Farmers weren't going to contribute to the household, but spend what money they earned on liquor arid racing. The tension between the Keegans and the Farmers mounted steadily. But the monetary problems were not the sole cause. The Farmers, too, noticed the noises and the unbearable, heavy atmosphere of the house and instinctively blamed the Keegans for these things. Then there was a quilt with an early American eagle and ship motif printed on it. Soon the wife had noticed that someone had turned the quilt around after she had put it away safely for the night. In the morning, the motif would face the opposite way. They could not blame the Keegans for that, since the quilt had been stored out of anyone's reach, and they dimly realized that the house was indeed haunted.

As the tension grew, the two couples would scarcely speak to each other even though they naturally shared the same quarters. Rebecca began to realize that no matter how cheery a person might have been on the outside, once such a person moved into the House of Evil, there would be changes of personality and character. Although far from superstitious, she began to believe that the house itself was dangerous and that prolonged life in it could only destroy her and her loved ones.

One night early in April, Rebecca and Parker were in the bedroom upstairs when they saw a form cross from where their telephone was, over their bed, and then down the stairs. At it crossed past the telephone, the phone rang. An instant later, as the form reached the bottom of the stairs, the downstairs telephone also rang.

This brought the Farmers out screaming and demanding to know what was going on! For once, there was unison in the house as the four adults gathered together soberly downstairs to discuss what they just witnessed and compare impressions.

They agreed there was a blue-white light around the form, a light so intense it hurt the eyes. They all had felt an icy chill as the form passed them. Only Parker bravely insisted it might have been lightning. But nobody had heard any thunder.

For the Farmers, this was the ghost that broke their patience's back. They moved out the next day.

Left once again to themselves, Rebecca and her husband decided it was time for them to look elsewhere, too.

Tired from the long struggle with the Uncanny, they moved soon afterwards.

As soon as they had settled in a new house, life took on a different aspect: where ominous presences had dampened their spirits, there was now good spirits and a zest for life they had not known for four years. Nobody in the family was feeling sick after their move, and they no longer had problems getting and keeping babysitters.

The House of Evil still stands on lonely Route 14, and there have been people living in it since. But whenever Parker had occasion to pass Route 14 in his car, he stepped on the gas and drove just a little bit faster. No sense taking chances!

COUNTRY HOUSE GHOSTS

On May of 1964, I received a telephone call from a lady who identified herself as Doris A. She had read my book *Ghost Hunter*, and wanted to invite me to a house at Rehoboth, Massachusetts, where a poltergeist had taken up residence.

I asked her to give me a detailed account of her experiences.

"My husband and I purchased the house sometime around 1940. It was purported to be more than 200 years old. We have never heard that it was haunted or that any violent death had occurred in it, but the legend has persisted that this was the house that had a fortune buried somewhere in a stone wall, and we treated this story as an old-time tale.

"We have had many odd happenings at the house during the years, but the noises heard in the kitchen are what concern me. The original house was a regular Cape Cod consisting of four rooms downstairs and an attic upstairs. One hundred years after the original house was built, a kitchen ell was added, consisting of the kitchen, a small room off the kitchen, and a large back hall. Our current postmaster in town lived in the house at one time and he added dormers upstairs. We put a porch along the ell. There was also a small barn used as a garage. These constitute the physical plan of the house. We own about 100 acres on both sides of the street.

"Shortly after we moved in, the first event happened. My husband and I were eating supper in the kitchen when a sound like an explosion made us both bound from our chairs. We found that a glass dish in the kitchen cupboard on the top shelf had shattered. We decided that maybe a change of temperature had made the dish break and left it at that. However, this particular noise has been the only one where we found physical evidence of breakage.

"About two years after this, my husband joined the Navy in World War II and his aunt came to stay with me for a week or two. The first night as we sat down to supper in the kitchen, my dog Dusty sat beside my chair, and all of a sudden he started to growl very deeply. The hackles rose on his back, he bared his teeth, and scared me half to death, because I had never seen him do this unless he thought my husband or I was threatened. He was staring at an empty chair to my left, but I thought his growl meant someone was around the house. I went out and looked around, but no one was there.

"My aunt went home to her own house after a week or so and I lived alone in the house with the dog and some assorted cats. One night I was reading in bed, with the dog at my feet. I reached up to put off the bed lamp when I heard a tremendous crash and the sound of dishes banging, crashing, and shattering. I knew immediately that the dish cupboard in the kitchen had fallen loose from the wall and that it had hit the counter beneath it and just spewed all the hundreds of dishes across the floor and smashed them to smithereens. The dog and I flew into the kitchen only to find everything was intact. I took a flashlight and went all over the house from cellar to attic, knowing all the while that the only big quantity of dishes were in that kitchen cupboard.

"We decided to make a three-room apartment upstairs for a girlfriend of ours who had lost her husband a few years before. She moved in, and the years went by, eighteen years, in fact.

"One evening at 5 P.M., she came home from work, and walked upstairs to her apartment. She had her foot on the last step when she just stood there unable to believe that horrible crashing and clattering of dishes being broken.

"Naturally, she expected to see the three-shelved kitchen cupboard torn away from the wall, figured it had hit the counter beneath it, and that every dish had fallen, breaking and rolling along the floor. She stood there in amazement when she found nothing was disturbed.

"We went home the next weekend, and as we compared noises, we found we had both had the same impression of what had happened, and the noises were identical. This happened about two years ago.

"About two months ago, a neighbor and myself were singing, and also playing the piano in the dining room, and were also tape recording our efforts. My husband was in the room behind the kitchen, and my sister was reading in the living room. At the end of a song we heard a crash of dishes or glasses and we all converged on the kitchen. I thought our Siamese cat had climbed onto a shelf on the hutch and possibly knocked off three or four plates that had then broken. Once again we all looked at each other and couldn't believe that nothing was broken. I then thought of the fact that the crash was on the tape, and we played it back and sure enough, we heard it loud and clear."

Immediately after I received Mrs. A.'s report, I telephoned her at her weekday residence in Connecticut. The house at Rehoboth, Massachusetts, where the uncanny phenomena had taken place, was a weekend retreat. I offered to come out to have a look at the house on my next trip to Boston.

"Everything is quiet for the moment," she replied, "but you're welcome any time."

Somehow the trip never occurred, and it was not until April, 1965, when I finally got around to reaching the A.s again. I had no staff to help me, and cases just piled up until I can get around to them myself. This time my note was answered by Doris' husband, Richard A.. His wife had passed away in January of 1965. Under the circumstances, I decided not to trouble him, hoping that Mrs. A. herself might have discovered what or who it was who caused the uncanny noises in the Rehoboth house—from her side of the veil.

Charles D., who described himself as a combat veteran and unafraid of anything, lived with his family in an old house in Hampstead, New Hampshire. He bought the house in 1959. His two older girls—he had three children—slept upstairs in a finished room at the rear of the attic. Right away, they complained about noises in the attic. When he went to investigate, he himself heard the footsteps of a heavy person walking across the floor, night after night, at 10 P.M. The two children were moved downstairs, and Mr. D. himself took the room in the attic.

"I have stared death in the eye many times, Mr. Holzer," D. said, "and I was not afraid. I listened hard and sure enough, *it* was coming to the door of the bedroom. I gently slid out of bed and turned on the light, waiting. The ghost was just outside the door. I looked at the door knob, and *it was being turned slowly.* I did not panic, but nothing further was heard."

No footsteps going down, for instance.

Another New Hampshire case concerned a certain Mrs. V., who had been subject to the uncanny all her life. On more than one occasion she had seen an apparition of her own father, especially when she was in some sort of difficulty. The house she and her husband occupied in a small town in New

Hampshire was very old. There was a little door leading up to the attic. A narrow staircase ascended to the attic, and for no apparent reason, the door kept opening by itself. Someone walking about in the attic, softly, as if in stocking feet, had become an almost daily occurrence. Finally, she asked around, and found out that the house had once belonged to an old man who had been abused and put into the attic. The man finally cut his throat, and was buried in the family cemetery nearby. It was his house once, but his people apparently took it away. And now he was back in command once more.

Mae R. was a widow in her late thirties, with three children, who lived in a small town in the Cape Cod area. I talked to her on the telephone at length and she struck me as pretty levelheaded, although she seemed scared of ghostly visitations. Small wonder, with the ones she had.

There was a certain young man her father disliked very much. She stopped seeing him when she got married, but after her divorce many years later, she took up with him again.

Her father had died in the late 1940s, and Mrs. R. left Massachusetts soon after, only to return in 1954. Shortly after she had placed some flowers on her father's grave after her return to Cape Cod, she woke one night from deep sleep with the fearful feeling that she was not alone in the room. Groping for some matches she had put near her bed, she was unable to find them. In the semi-darkness her eyes fell upon the left side of her pillow where she distinguished the outline of a man. Finally she overcame her fears, and sat up in bed. Before her stood her late father, dressed in dark clothes, looking directly at her. Without saying a word, he left slowly and quietly.

"I heard the steps," Mrs. R. said, "but when he reached the stairs, he did not go down, *but through the wall.* Afterwards I went downstairs, and checked the doors, looked in closets, and there was no one there."

After she stopped seeing the young man her father had disapproved of, the ghost of her father never returned.

Jane Morgan had a house in Kennebunkport, Maine, that was full of ghosts. I had talked to her time and again, offering my services and those of Sybil Leek to help her get relief. But she didn't want to free her house from its ghosts. To begin with, her brother, who shared ownership in the house with the talented singer, had for years insisted that there was nothing to the story.

"You may have discussed the hauntings in my house with my sister," he said cheerily, "but I live here and I assure you there ain't none!"

I thanked Mr. Currier—Currier was Jane Morgan's real name—and forgot all about it, for, let's face it: I've got more unsolved hauntings to take care of than an army of parapsychologists could handle. But the whole controversy—was there or wasn't there a ghost at Jane Morgan's place—was brought to mind again when the *New York Daily News*, November 16, 1964, quoted the singer as saying:

"I don't want to have them exorcised. That would be cruel. They might have no other place to go ... and besides, I'd miss these friendly spirits."

Having read *Ghost Hunter*, Miss Morgan knew perfectly well what happens to a freed ghost, and that the "place" they are helped to reach is infinitely more joyous than a musty New England mansion.

Because of an exciting séance I held with Ethel Johnson Meyers in a New York apartment, a piece appeared in the *New York World Telegram* in which columnist Norton Mockridge described the procedure we used. He was swamped with mail from people with similar problems, he says, although I never saw the letters. But he did manage to follow up his first piece with an interview with Jane Morgan in which she unburdened herself of the whole story of her ghosts.

Ned, a revolutionary soldier, had killed his girlfriend Nellie's other lover, and since that time, he and his lady-love had cavorted in the old house, kept there, presumably, by their guilty feelings. Their laughing and moaning had been heard by many. Doors opened and closed by themselves at night and spectral figures had been seen flitting from room to room. Visitors, it was alleged, had spoken of a "lady in gray" in the hall who did not return their greetings, and there was a sealed coffin in the cellar of the house.

"I had a medium at the house," Miss Morgan told me, but when she mentioned her name, I confessed I had never heard of her.

"She refused to stay at the house," Jane Morgan continued, and explained that for that reason anyone else would not be likely to succeed either. I patiently explained the rather considerable difference between a successful parapsychologist and a timid medium who runs at the first chilly sign of a *real* ghost!

All the same, Jane Morgan refused to allow us to have a go at it. Meanwhile, Norton Mockridge reported that playgoers at the nearby Kennebunkport Playhouse frequently saw a man in Colonial uniform and a woman framed in the window of the haunted house across the road. They usually took them for actors rehearsing for the next week's play.

The Curriers finally, however, abandoned the house for another place not far away. The new tenants didn't complain about any ghostly visitations. But then Ned and Nellie may have needed some time to get used to their new keepers.

The John Jay House near Bedford Village, Westchester, New York, is a museum maintained by the county. Restored exactly as it was when one of America's founding fathers, Chief Justice John Jay, lived in it, it had the reputation of being haunted. "Was there anything to it?" I asked the curator, Lewis Rubenstein.

"According to family tradition," the curator explained, "Mrs. William Jay, wife of the second of the Jays to live permanently at Bedford, saw the ghost of her mother-in-law in one of the bedrooms. Two guests at widely spaced intervals are also reported to have seen the apparition. Although he personally did not put stock in such stories, Mr. Rubenstein extended a cordial invitation for me to visit the house.

"We know that discovery of a ghost would be good for business," he said, "but we would prefer that people came to see the site for its real historic value rather than for its other somewhat tenuous merit."

When I finally got around to making an appointment to see the house in the company of a good medium, Mr. Rubenstein got cold feet, it seems. Retracting his invitation, he referred the decision to the trustees. Otto Koegel, board chairman, informed me curtly that I was not welcome. Maybe the ghostly mother-in-law was afraid I'd dislodge her.

PROPER BOSTONIAN GHOSTS

The proper Bostonian ghosts here are not the political skeletons rattling in many a Back Bay closet. In Boston, a ghost is a ghost. But make no mistake, something of their English forebears has rubbed off on many a Bostonian. They take their specters with grim pride and a matter of nature—it is part of the regional scenery, so to speak, and really all terribly chic, but the Bostonian prefers to pretend it's nothing much. Far from it. New England ghosts can be pretty exciting stuff.

Sometimes New Englanders take the memories of their ghosts with them even when they move to other states. A Mrs. C. E. Foster once wrote me from Indianapolis about her grandmother, who seems to have been buried alive. At the time her grandmother, Louisa Wallace, was lowered into her grave in Revere, Massachusetts, Mrs. Foster had a vision of her in the casket ... and heard her cough. The dead don't do that, and Mrs. Foster thinks her grandmother tried to tell her that she wasn't quite ready yet. Unfortunately, nothing was done about it at the time, so she went, ready or not.

Many of my contacts were made through a Boston radio

34

program called "Contact," with Bob Kennedy, on Station WBZ. I appeared on it many times and always found it most rewarding. After one of my radio stints in the fall of 1963, I was approached by a young lady with the appealing name of Aimee Violante, a nurse who had a most interesting and rather touching experience she wanted to tell me about.

"In 1957, my boyfriend took me to Lake Quannapowette outside of Boston. We rented a rowboat and rowed to the other side of the lake to go swimming, as swimming was prohibited there.

"In the boat, I sat facing the opposite shore. We were heading for a strip of beach with a few benches on it. There were three benches. It was nearing dusk. Sitting on these benches were elderly people all dressed in white. The ladies were dressed in silky dresses, wearing big picture hats and gloves. The men wore white suits. They were just sitting watching us. They weren't frightening, so I didn't pay too much attention to them, but I was angry that my boyfriend was pulling in there, as I thought they would say something about us going swimming. He didn't see them, as his back was toward them, and when we pulled up, they were gone.

"When we rowed back, I was wondering where they all went to, so I asked him. When I told him about the people I saw, he got frightened and hurried me back to the car. There he told me that on the side we were on was a cemetery, and there was no way any people could get to the benches once the gates were closed."

The Peter Hofmann family consisted of husband, wife Pennie, and baby—then about three or four years old. The parents were articulate, well-educated people making their home in Harvard. Not Harvard University, but Harvard near Ayer, Massachusetts, about an hour's ride from the university.

An automobile accident in 1956 had left Mrs. Hofmann partially paralyzed, but her keen gift of observation was not impaired. She had always had a peculiar liking for graveyards, and her first psychic experience, in 1951, consisted of a vision of a horse-drawn hearse that had passed near a cemetery. One could argue that lots of such hearses used to pull into cemeteries, but the fact remains that Mrs. Hofmann's was not a real one.

Their house stood next to a house built by Mrs. Hofmann's father, a well-known physician, and it seemed that both houses were haunted. The larger house, owned by Mrs. Hofmann's father, was built in 1721 "on the bounty received from an Indian scalp."

From the first moment she saw it, Pennie Hofmann had odd sensations about it. In 1960 or 1961, she and her husband were spending the night there, when at about two in the morning they both woke up for no apparent reason.

"I spoke to what I thought was Pete," she said, "as I could see someone by the front window, but it turned out that Pete was *behind* me. Needless to say, we left right away."

Peter Hofmann nodded and added: "I myself have been in the house at night a few times alone, and I've always had the feeling I was being watched."

Then in late October, 1963, Pennie Hofmann phoned me in New York. Could I please come to Boston and tell her if she was *seeing things?*

What sort of things, I asked.

"Well," she replied, somewhat upset, "we'd been staying over in my father's house again a week ago. I saw a soldier in the bedroom. He was dark and had a noose around the neck; the rope was cut and his face seemed almost luminous. I swear I saw him."

I hurried to Boston and they met me at radio station WBZ.

What about the ghostly soldier? Any clues?

Both Hofmanns nodded.

"We've checked in Nourse's *History of the Town of Harvard*," Mrs. Hoffman said gravely, "and there was a Colonial drummer named Hill who was hanged in this area … for some misdeeds."

I remembered her telling me of a ghost in their own house on Poor Farm Road, and Mrs. Hofmann filed me in on this far gentler wraith.

"During the summer months," she explained, "there is what appears to be a Quaker lady that walks across our front lawn, usually during the afternoon. This person often appears many times a day."

Her husband added that she had given him many details of the ghost's dress, which he checked for authenticity. He found that they were indeed worn by the Quaker women of the eighteenth century.

Why a member of so gentle a persuasion as the Quakers would turn into a ghost we may never know, but perhaps someday there will be an explanation of the Quaker lady's walks.

There is said to be the ghost of a pirate near the water's edge in old Boston, where so many secret passages existed in the days when Massachusetts was British. The Black Lady of Warren Island, out in the bay, has been seen by a number of people. She was executed during the Civil War for helping her husband, a Yankee prisoner, break out of prison.

Boston's emotional climate was fine for special activities. There may not be any medieval castles, but Beacon Hill can look pretty forbidding, too—especially on a chilly November night when the fog drifts in from the sea.

In September of 1963 I appeared on WBZ-TV on Mike Douglas's television show, discussing my ever-present interest in haunted houses. As a consequence, there was an avalanche of letters, many of which contained leads to new cases.

One came from a Mrs. Anne Valukis, of South Natick, near Boston, Massachusetts. She wrote me of an old house she lived in where the stairs creaked unaccountably at odd times, as if someone were walking up and down them; of the strange behavior her little boy showed whenever he was in a certain room of the house; and of an overall atmosphere of the uncanny prevailing throughout the house, as if an unseen force were always present.

I wrote for additional data about herself and the background of the house. Meanwhile, the public television station in Boston, Channel 2, took an interest in my work, and the station and I decided to join forces for an expedition to the haunted house in South Natick. Fred Barzyk, the director, undertook the preliminary task of additional research. My visit was scheduled for the last week of October. Mrs. Valukis wasn't long in answering me.

"The stairs haven't creaked for over a week, but my four year old woke up Saturday night four times, and was really scared, so much so he would not go back upstairs to his room … Years ago this house was kind of a speakeasy, connected to a dance hall that was on the Charles River. Probably anything could have happened here. Who knows?"

Not because of the spooky stairs, but for other reasons, the Valukis family decided to move to Anne's parents' house. This made our visit problematical, until Fred Barzyk discovered that the house belonging to Mrs. Valukis' parents was even more haunted than Anne Valukis' place.

Mrs. Rose Josselyn, Anne's mother, was a Canadian Indian, and, like many of her people, had had psychic experiences all her life.

About forty years before I met her, Mrs. Josselyn was living in Annapolis Royal, Canada, in what was purported to be a haunted house. Frequently she awoke in the middle of the night and found it difficult to breathe. Her arms seemed to be pinned down by an unseen force and she was unable to move even so much as a finger!

"It felt as if someone were choking me," she said to me later. "I tried to scream, but could not move my lips."

This had gone on for about a year. Finally Rose told her mother, who was mediumistic herself, and Rose was forbidden ever to sleep again in "that room." Twenty years later, Mrs. Josselyn still remembered the stark terror of those nights in Canada, but nothing like it had happened to her since—nothing, that is, until she moved into this house.

The house itself was a gray-white, medium-sized early American house, built in the stately manner of early Georgian architecture and very well preserved. It was set back from the road a bit, framed by tall, shady trees, and one had the feeling of being far from the bustle of the big city. Built about 150 years earlier, the house had an upper story and a total of eight rooms. Bordering on the lawn of the house was a cemetery, separated from the Josselyn house by an iron gate and fence.

When the Josselyns moved in with their family, Mrs. Josselyn had no thoughts of anything psychic or uncanny. She soon learned differently.

Upstairs, there were two bedrooms separated only by a thin wall. The larger one belonged to Mrs. Josselyn; the smaller one, to the rear of the house, to her husband Roy. It was in her bedroom that Mrs. Josselyn had another attack of the terrible feeling she had experienced in her Canadian youth. Pinned down on her bed, it was as if someone were upon her, holding her.

"Whose bedroom was this before you took it?" I inquired.

"Well, my daughter-in-law slept here for awhile," Mrs. Josselyn confided, "that is, before she died."

I asked further questions about this daughter. At the age of 21, she had fallen ill and suffered her last agonies in this very room, before being taken off to a hospital, never to return. Her only child, to whom she was naturally very

39

attached, was reared by Mrs. Josselyn and Mrs. Valukis.

I walked across the floor to a small room belonging to David Josselyn, then 17, the brother of Mrs. Valukis. Here I was shown a handmade wooden chair that was said to creak at odd moments, as if someone were sitting in it. David himself had been awakened many times by this unearthly behavior of his chair, and Anne had also observed the noise. I tried the chair. It was sturdy enough, and only strong efforts on my part produced any kind of noise. It could not have creaked by itself.

"Who gave you this chair?" I asked.

"The same man who made our clock downstairs," David said. I recalled seeing a beautiful wooden grandfather clock in the corner of the downstairs room. The odd thing about that clock was it sometimes ticked and the hands moved, even though it no longer had any works or pendulum!

The clock, chair, and a desk in David's room were the work of a skilled craftsman named Thomas Council, who was a well-liked house guest of the Josselyns and gave them these things to show his gratitude for their hospitality. He was a lonely bachelor and the Josselyns were his only close friends. David in particular was the apple of his eye. Thomas Council's body rested comfortably, it was hoped, across the way in the cemetery, and the Josselyns made sure there were always fresh flowers on his grave.

I decided to return to Mrs. Josselyn's room.

"Outside of your nightmarish experiences here and in Canada, " said, "have you had any other psychic incidents?"

Mrs. Josselyn, a serious, quiet woman of about 60, thought for a moment.

"Yes, frequently. Whenever my children are in some sort of trouble, I just know it. No matter how trifling. You might say we have telepathic contact."

"Did you also hear those stairs creak at your daughter's house across the road?"

"Yes, many times."

"Was that after or before your daughter-in-law passed away?"

"After."

"I clearly heard those steps upstairs, and there wasn't anyone but me and the baby in the house," added Anne Valukis for corroboration.

They all had been visited, it seemed to me, except the father, Roy Josselyn. It was time I turned my attention in his direction.

Mr. Josselyn sat on the bed in his room, quietly smoking a pipe. I had been warned by Fred Barzyk that the man of the house was no particular believer in the supernatural. To my relief, I discovered Mr. Josselyn at least had an open mind. I also discovered that a great-aunt of his in Vermont had been a spiritualistic medium.

I asked if he had seen or heard anything unusual.

"Well," he said, "about a year ago I started to hear some moans and groans around here ..." he pointed toward the wall adjoining the bedroom occupied by his wife. "At first I thought it was my wife, but there was no one in her room at the time. I looked."

"This moaning ... was it a human voice?"

"Oh yes, very human. Couldn't sleep a wink while it lasted."

"When did you last hear it?"

"Yesterday," he said laconically.

"How did you and your daughter-in-law get along?" I suddenly felt compelled to ask.

"Very well," he said. "As a matter of fact, she took more to me than to anyone else. You know how women are—a bit jealous. She was a little on the possessive side as far as her baby was concerned. I mean, she was very much worried about the child."

"But she wasn't jealous of you?"

"No, not of me. We were very close."

I thought of the 21-year-old woman taken by death without being ready for it, and the thoughts of fear for her child that must have gone through her mind those dreadful last hours when her moaning filled the air of the room next to Roy Josselyn's.

I also thought about Mrs. Roy Josselyn's background—the fact that she was Princess of the Micmac Tribe. I remembered how frequent psychic experiences were among Native Americans, who are so much closer to nature than we city-dwellers.

Perhaps the restless spirit of the 21-year-old woman wanted some attention. Perhaps her final moments had only impressed themselves on the atmosphere of the upstairs room and were relived by the psychically sensitive members of the family. Perhaps, too, Thomas Council, the family friend, roamed the house now and then to make sure everything was all right with his favorite family.

When we drove back to Boston late that night, I felt sure I had met a haunted family, for better or worse.

THE LADY OF THE GARDEN

*G*ardening is one of the finest expressions of man's cultural heritage, for it stems back to the early Greek and Roman cultures, and even beyond that into Babylonian and Chaldean realms. The hanging gardens of Nineveh were far more elaborate than anything modern man can dream up no matter how green his thumb, and the rose gardens of Emperor Diocletian at Salonae, among which he spent his declining years, were a great deal more elaborate than the gardens we were apt to have for our own.

Gardening is also a health measure for it serves two purposes admirably well: it provides humans with physical exercise, and cleanses the air around them through the chemical process of photosynthesis, the miraculous arrangement whereby carbon dioxide is changed into oxygen naturally.

Americans in the Eastern states often find gardening a hard-to-find pleasure, especially if they live in the cities. But in the sunny West, it comes as a natural adjunct to one's house and is often the most desirable feature of it. Many of the citizens of the small communities of California have gone there, usually from the East or Midwest, to have an easier life in their later years. To them, having a garden to putter in is perhaps one of the chief attractions of this unhurried way of life.

The western climate is very kind to most forms of flowers, to fruit trees and almost all the plants usually found in both moderate and tropical climates, so it is small wonder that some of the California gardens turn into veritable show places of color and scent for their loving owners.

Naomi S. was a widow who has lived in California most of her life. Since the passing of her second husband, she has lived quietly in the southern California community of Huntington Park, and nothing of great importance was happening to her at this time. That as it should be, for she had had a glimpse into a world that has at once amazed and frightened her and she preferred that the excursion into it remain a veiled memory that will eventually be indistinguishable from the faded pictures of other past experiences in her busy and full life.

At one time, in the 1950s, she and her husband had been house hunting in Lynwood for a suitable place to live. She did not care for the run-of-the-mill houses one often finds in American communities and when they both saw this strangely attractive old house on Lago Avenue, they knew at once that that was *it*.

It was almost as if the house had *invited* them to come and get it, but so eager were they to investigate its possibilities, they never thought of this until much, much later.

The house was built in Norman style, almost European in its faithful copying of such old houses, and it was covered with all kinds of greens and vines going up and down the stone walls. Since it was surrounded by shrubbery and trees in the manner of a fence, it was most secluded, and one had the feeling of complete privacy. There was sufficient land around it to make it even more remote from the surrounding community, and as the zoning laws in Lynwood were quite careful, chances of a new building going up next door to them were remote. They immediately went past the shrubbery and looked around, possibly to see if

44

anyone could show them the house. The sign outside had read "For Sale" and given the name of a real estate firm, but it did not state whether or not the house was currently inhabited. As they approached the house across the soft lawn they came to realize immediately that it could not be. All around them were signs of neglect and apparently long periods of no care at all. What had once been a beautifully landscaped garden was now a semi-wilderness in which weeds had overgrown precious flowers and the shrubbery grew whichever way it chose.

The paths, so carefully outlined by a previous owner, were hardly recognizable now. The rains had washed them away, and birds had done the rest.

"Needs lot of work," her husband mumbled apprehensively, as they observed the earmarks of destruction all around them. But they continued toward the house. They did not enter it but walked around it at first in the manner in which a wild animal stalks it prey. They wanted to take in all of the outside, and the grounds, first, before venturing inside.

On the other side of the house was a fine patio that had apparently served as a breakfast and dining patio at one time. A forlorn broken cup and a rusty spoon lay on the ground, but otherwise the patio was empty and still.

"Boy, they sure let this place run downhill," Mr. S. remarked and shook his head. He was a businessman used to orderly procedures and this was anything but good sense. Why would anyone owning so lovely a place let it to go pot? It didn't make sense to him.

All over the neighborhood, down Elm Street, the houses were aristocratic and well kept. It would seem *someone* would care enough to look after this little jewel of a house, too. Why hadn't the real estate man sent someone around to clean things up once in a while? He decided to question the man about it.

From the patio on down to the end of the property, clearly marked by the shrubbery, was almost nothing but rose bushes.

Or rather, there had been at one time. One could still see that some loving hand had planted rows upon rows of rose bushes, but only a few had grown up and what there was left of the roses needed careful and immediate pruning, his knowledgeable eyes told him at once. Still, there was hope for the roses if a lot of work were to be put in on them.

They entered the house through the patio door, which was ajar. Inside they found further proof of long neglect. The furniture was still there, so it was a furnished house for sale. This was a pleasant surprise for it would make things a lot easier for them, financially speaking, even if some of the things they might buy with the house had to be thrown out later.

The dust covering the inside and an occasional spider's web drove home the fact that no one had lived there for years. But this did not disturb them, for there were lots of nice houses in California standing empty for years on end until someone bought them. They felt a strange sensation of being at home now, as if this had already been their house and they had just now re-entered it only after a long summer vacation.

Immediately, they started to examine each room and the gray, almost blackened windows. No doubt about it, it would take months of cleaning before the house would be livable again. But there was nothing broken or inherently beyond repair in the house and their courage rose, especially when they realized that most of the Victorian furniture was in excellent condition, just dirty.

After a prolonged stay in the house, during which they examined every one of the rooms, every nook and cranny, and finally went out into the garden again, they never doubted for a moment that this would be their future home. It never occurred to them that perhaps the sign had been out there for months even though someone had already bought the place or that it might be available, but priced beyond their means.

Somehow they knew immediately that the house was right

for them, just the size they wanted—they had no children—not too big to manage, but yet spacious and above all quiet, as it sat in the midst of what might once again become a fine garden.

"Well, what do you say, Naomi?" Mr. S. inquired. It was more of a rhetorical question since he, and she, knew very well what they were to do next.

"Yes, it will do," she nodded and smiled at him. It was a good feeling to have found one's home.

They carefully closed the patio door and locked it as best they could—after all, it was *their* home now, practically, and not just a neglected, empty old house for sale. As they walked up the garden path towards Elm Street, they had the distinctive feeling of being followed by a pair of eyes. But they were so preoccupied with thoughts of how to make this place into a livable home, that they paid no heed. They didn't even turn around when they heard a rustling in the leaves that covered the path. It was the kind of sound the wind would make, had there *been* a wind.

After they left the place, they immediately drove down to the real estate office.

Yes, the place was still for sale. They sighed with relief, too noticeably to escape the glance of the real estate man. It bemused him, since he was only too glad to unload the white elephant the house on Lago Avenue represented to him. After some small talk, they agreed on a price and a move-in date, and then Mrs. S. began to wonder about the people who had lived there before.

But the real estate man, either by design or ignorance, could not tell them much. The house had been there for about thirty years or so, but even that was not certain. It might have been sixty years, for all he knew. It could not be more than that, for Lynwood wasn't much older. Who had built it? He didn't know their names, but a couple had built it and lived in it orig- inally, and after them a number of other people had either bought or rented it, but somehow nobody stayed very long. His company had just recently taken over its sale, he believed, in the name of some absentee heir, across the country somewhere, but he really could not tell them more than that.

"It's just an old house, you know," he finally said and looked at them puzzled. "Why do you want to know more?"

Why indeed? The man was right. Resolutely, they signed the contract and a few weeks later, when their affairs elsewhere had been wound up, they moved into the house.

The first few days were grim. They reminded one of the pioneering days of early Americans as the S.'s worked from early to late to get their bedroom into livable condition. After that, the kitchen, and so forth until gradually, with much sweat and effort, the house changed. In the spring, they turned their attention to the garden, and since Mr. S. had meanwhile gone into semi-retirement from his business he had a little more time on his hands to help. Now and then they used the services of a local gardener, but by and large, it was their own effort that made the garden bloom again. Carefully pruning the roses, and whenever they found a gap, replanting a rose bush, they managed to bring back a new life to the beautiful place. Inside the house the old furniture had been dusted and repaired where necessary, and they had augmented the pieces with some of their own, interspersing them where suitable. So the house took on a strange look of mixture of their old house and what must have been the former owner's own world, but the two did not seem to clash, and intermingled peacefully for their comfort.

They never tried to change anything in either house or garden just for change's sake: if they could find what had stood on the spot, they would faithfully restore it, almost as if driven by a zeal to turn the clock back to where it had stood when the house had first been built. They felt themselves motivated by the same loyalty a museum curator displays in restoring a priceless masterpiece to its original appearance. Their efforts paid off, and the house became a model of comfortable, if somewhat Victorian, living.

As they became acquainted with their garden, they became aware of the fact that it contained lots more than roses or ordinary flowers. Apparently the previous owners liked rare plants for there were remnants of unusual flowers and green plants they had never seen before outside of museums or arboretums. With some of them, the original label had remained, giving the name and origin. Whenever they were able to, they fixed these labels so that much of the old flavor returned to the garden. They even went to the local florist and asked him to explain some of the rare plants, and in turn they bought some replacements for those that had died of neglect, and put them where they would have been before.

With all this work taking up most of their time, they found no opportunity to make friends in the community. For a long time, they knew no one except the real estate man and the gardener who had occasionally worked for them, neither person of social acquaintance status.

But one morning Mrs. S. noticed a nice lady pass her as she was working in the front garden, and they exchanged smiles. After that, she stopped her in the street a day or so later and inquired about shops in the area and it turned out the lady was a neighbor living across the street from them, a certain Lillian G., who had been a longtime resident of the area. Not a young woman any longer, Mrs. G. knew a great deal about the community, it appeared, but the two women never talked about anything but current problems of the most mundane nature—on the few occasions that they did meet again. It was almost as if Naomi did not *want to* discuss the story of her house-any longer, now that she owned it.

A year went by, and the S.'s were finally through with all their restorations in the house and could settle back to a comfortable, and well-earned rest. They liked their home and knew that they had chosen well and wisely. What had seemed at the time a beckoning finger from the house itself to them, now appeared merely as an expression of horse sense upon seeing the place and they prided themselves on having been so wise.

It was summer again and the California sky was blue and all was well with the house and themselves. Mr. S. had gone out and would not be back until the afternoon. Mrs. S. was busy working in the rose garden, putting some fine touches on her bushes. Despite the approaching mid-day, it was not yet too hot to work.

Naomi had just straightened out one of the tea roses, when she looked up and realized she had a visitor. There, on the path no more than two yards away, stood a rather smallish lady. She was neatly dressed in a faded house dress of another era, but in California this was not particularly unusual. Lots of retired people like to dress in various old-fashioned ways and no one cares one way or another. The lady was quite elderly and fragile, and Naomi was startled to see her there.

Her surprise must have been obvious, for the visitor immediately apologized for the intrusion. "I didn't mean to scare you," she said in a thin, high-pitched voice that somehow went well with her general appearance and frailty.

"You didn't," Naomi bravely assured her. She was nothing if not hospitable. Why should a little old lady scare her?

"Well, then," the visitor continued tentatively, "would it be all right if I looked around a bit?"

This seemed unusual, for the place was scarcely a famous show place, and Naomi did not feel like turning it into a public park. Again, her thoughts must have shown on her face, for *the* lady immediately raised her hand and said, "You see, my husband and I originally built this place."

Naomi was flabbergasted. So the owners had decided to have a look at their house after all these years. At the same time, a sense of accomplishment filled her heart. Now they could see how much had been done to fix up the house!

"It's a beautiful place," Naomi said and waved her visitor to come with her.

"Yes, isn't it?" the lady nodded. "We took great pride in it, really."

"Too bad it was in such bad shape when we bought it, though," Naomi said succinctly. "We had to put a lot of work into it to bring it back to its old state."

"Oh, I can see that," the lady commented and looked with loving eyes at each and every shrub.

They were on the garden path in the rear now.

"Oh, you've put pink roses where the tea roses used to be," she suddenly exclaimed. "How thoughtful."

Naomi did not know that the tea roses had been on that spot, for there had been nothing left of them. But she was glad to hear about it. The visitor now hopped from flower to flower almost like a bird, inspecting here, caressing a plant there, and pointing out the various rare plants to Naomi, as if *she* were the hostess and Naomi the visitor.

"I am so glad you have brought life back into the house, so glad," she kept repeating.

It made Naomi even happier with her accomplishment. Too bad her husband couldn't be here to hear the lady's praise. Mr. S. had sometimes grumbled about all the hard work they had had to put in to make the place over.

"The begonia over there ... oh, they are still missing, too bad. But you can fix that sometime, can you not?" she said and hurried to another pan of the garden, as if eager to take it all in whatever time Naomi allowed her to visit with her.

"Wouldn't you like to have a look at the inside of the house, too?" Naomi finally suggested. The lady glowed with happiness at the invitation.

"Yes, I would like that very much. May I?" Naomi pointed at the garden door and together they stepped inside the house. The cool atmosphere inside was in sharp contrast to the pleasant, but warm air in the garden.

"Over there, that's where the grandfather clock used to be.

I see you've moved it to the den."

Naomi smiled. They had indeed. The lady surely must have an excellent memory to remember all that, for they had not yet entered the den. It never occurred to Naomi that the visitor knew the clock had been moved prior to seeing it in the den. So much at home was the little old lady in what used to be her house, that it seemed perfectly natural for her to know all kinds of things about it.

"The table is nice, too, and it fits in so well," she now commented. They had brought it with them from their former home, but it did indeed blend in with the furniture already in the house. The visitor now bounced cheerfully to the other end of the long room that they were using as a day room or parlor.

"That chair," she suddenly said, and pointed at the big, oaken chair near the fireplace, and there was a drop in her voice that seemed to indicate a change in mood.

"What about the chair?" Naomi inquired and stepped up to it.

The visitor seemed to have difficulty in holding back a tear or two, but then composed herself and explained— "My husband died in that chair."

There was a moment of silence as Naomi felt compassion for the strange lady.

"He was raking leaves one morning … it was a nice summer day just like today … just like today … he always liked to do a little work around the garden before breakfast. I was still in bed at that hour, but I was awake and I heard him come into the house when he had finished his chores in the garden."

Naomi had not said anything, but her eyes were on the lady with interest. She noticed how frail and ethereal she looked, and how old age had really rendered her thin and somehow tired. And yet, her eyes had an unusual, bright sparkle in them that belied her frail and aged appearance. No, this woman was all right, despite her advanced age. Probably lived alone somewhere in the area, too, now that her husband was dead, Naomi mused.

"My husband came into the house and a little later I got up to fix him breakfast as I always did," the visitor continued, all the while holding the back of the chair firmly with one hand.

"When I called out to him to come and get it, I received no reply. Finally I thought this odd and went into the room—this room—and there, in this chair, I found him. He was dead."

The account had given Naomi a strange chill. It suddenly occurred to her how little she knew about the former owners. But the icy hush that had settled over the two women was broken when the lady let go of the chair and turned towards the door.

"I'd like another look at the patio, if I may," she said and as if she wanted to make up for her seriousness before, now she chattered interminably and lightly about the pleasures of living in such a house as this.

They had arrived at the rose beds again and the visitor pointed at a particularly full-blown dark red bush Naomi had fancied all along more than any other rose bush in the garden.

"They were always my favorites," the lady said, almost with a whisper.

"Then let me give you some to take home with you," Naomi offered and since the visitor did not protest her offer, she turned around to reach for the scissors, which she kept at the foot of the patio.

Her back was not turned more than a second. But when she looked up at her visitor again, the little lady was gone.

That's rude of her, Naomi thought immediately. Why had she suddenly run away? Surely, the offer of roses from her former home was no reason to be offended. But then it occurred to Naomi that perhaps the lady's emotions at being back in her old home, yet no longer mistress of it, might have gotten the upper hand with her and she simply could not face getting roses from *her* favorite bush by a stranger.

"I wonder which way she went, though," Naomi said out loud. She heard no car drive off, so the lady must have come on foot. Perhaps she could still catch her, for surely she could not have gotten far. It was plain silly of her not to take the proffered roses.

Naomi quickly went down the garden path and looked and then the driveway and looked there but the woman was not on the property any longer. She then ran out onto the street and even looked down Elm Street but the visitor was nowhere in sight.

"But this is impossible," Naomi thought. "She can't just disappear." So little time had elapsed between their last words and Naomi's pursuit that no human being could have disappeared without a trace.

Naomi, still puzzled, went back into the house. The whole episode took on a certain dreamlike quality after a while and she forgot about it. Surely, there must be some explanation for the lady's quick disappearance, but Naomi had other things to do than worry about it.

For reasons of her own, she felt it best not to tell her husband about the visit, for she was not at all sure herself now that she hadn't dreamed the whole thing. Of course, she hadn't. The lady's footprints were still visible in the soft soil of the lawn several days after the visit. Such small feet, too. But somehow she felt reluctant to discuss it further. Besides, what of it? A former tenant wants to visit the old home. Nothing special or newsworthy about that.

Several weeks later she happened to have tea with the neighbor across the street. Over tea and cookies, they talked about the neighborhood and how it had changed over all the years Mrs. G. had lived there. Somehow the visitor came to mind again, and Naomi felt free to confide in Mrs. G.

"I had a visitor the other day, only person I've talked to here except for you," Naomi began.

"Oh," Mrs. G. perked up. "Anyone I might know?"

"Perhaps ... it was the lady who built our house ... who lived there before us."

Mrs. G. gave Naomi a strange look but said nothing.

"She was a little lady with a faded pink dress and kind of sparkling eyes, and she told me she and her husband had built the house," Naomi said, and described what the visitor had looked like in minute detail. When she had finished, Mrs. G. shook her head.

"Impossible," she finally said. "That woman has been dead for years."

Naomi laughed somewhat uncertainly.

"But how could she be? I saw her as plainly as I see you. She looked just like any little old lady does."

"Maybe it was someone else," the neighbor said, half hoping Naomi would readily agree to her suggestion.

"I don't think so," Naomi said firmly, however. "You see she also pointed out the chair her husband died in. He had been raking leaves before breakfast, and when she called out to him to come and get it, he didn't answer, and then she went into the parlor and there he was, dead in that big oaken chair."

Mrs. G. had suddenly become very pale.

"That is absolutely true, I mean, the story of how he died," she finally managed to say. "But how would you know about it?"

Naomi shrugged helplessly.

"I didn't know it until the lady told me about it," she repeated.

"Incredible. But you've described her to a tee and he did die the way she said. They've both been dead for years and years, you know."

Naomi finally realized the implication.

"You mean I've been visited by a ghost?"

"Seems that way," Mrs. G. nodded gravely.

"But she seemed so very real ... so solid. I'd never have

known she was just a ghost. Why, we even shook hands and her hand felt fine to me."

The woman went over the experience once more, detail for detail. There was one thing that was odd, though. On recollection, Mrs. S. did recall that she had not *heard the woman* enter her garden. She had looked up from her chores, and there the woman stood, smiling at her from in front of the roses. No sound of footsteps on either entering or leaving. Then, too, her intimate knowledge of each and every plant in the garden.

"She even knew the Latin names of everyone of them," Naomi pointed out.

"No doubt she did," Mrs. G. explained, and added, "she and her hubby were great horticulturists and took enormous pride in creating a genuine arboretum in their garden."

But why had she visited her old home?

After some thought, Naomi felt she knew the answer. They had just finished restoring the house and garden to their original appearance and probably the same flavor they had had in the years when the original owners had the place. The ghostly lady felt they should be rewarded for their efforts by an approving gesture from *them.* Or had she simply been homesick for her old home?

Naomi was quite sure, now, that little lady had never really left it. In her mind's eye it had never fallen into disrepair, and the lovely roses never ceased to bloom even when the garden had become a wilderness.

She never discussed the matter again with her neighbor, or with anyone else for that matter. Her husband, whom she later divorced, never knew of the incident, for Mrs. G. also kept the secret well.

The house may still be there amid the roses, and the little lady in the faded dress no doubt has a ball skipping along its paths and enjoying her beloved flowers.

THE DEVIL IN THE FLESH

*I*f you live in Kansas City, and if you are a Bible student or churchgoer in a church that goes in for the hell and brimstone variety of preaching, you're bound to hear about the devil now and again. To some people, the devil is real, and they will give you an argument filled with fervor and Bible quotations to prove that he exists.

Mrs. G. wasn't one of those who were impressed by demonic outbursts, however, and she could not care less whether there was a devil or not. She had grown up in a well-to-do family and spent her adult years in the world of business. At age nineteen, she met and married Mr. G. and they had a happy life together ever since. There were no children, also no problems, and no difficulties whatever. She was always active in her husband's gasoline business, and only recently had she decided to slow down a little, and perhaps do other things, leisure-time things, or just plain nothing, when the mood would strike her.

At age 49 that was a pretty good way to do things she figured, and since she really did not have to work, it was just as well that she started to enjoy life a little more fully. Not that she was unhappy or frustrated in any way, but the gasoline business was not the most exciting activity in the world, and after thirty years of living by and with gas, she longed for some fresh air.

One day in the spring of 1964, a good friend suggested something new and different for them to do. She had read an advertisement in the local paper that had intrigued her. A Spiritualist church was inviting the general public to its message service. Why didn't they have a look?

"Spiritualist church?" Mrs. G. asked with some doubt. She really did not go for that sort of thing.

And yet, way back in her early years, she had had what are now called ESP experiences. When she talked to a person, she would frequently know what that person would answer before the words were actually spoken. It scared the young girl, but she refused to think about it. Her parents' home was a twelve-year-old house in a good section of Kansas City. It was just a pleasant house without any history whatever of either violence or unhappiness. And yet, frequently she would hear strange raps at night, raps that did not come from the pipes or other natural sources. Whenever she heard those noises she would simply turn to the wall and pretend she did not hear them, but in her heart she knew they were there.

Then one night she was awakened from deep sleep by the feeling of a presence in her room. She sat up in bed and looked out. There, right in front of her bed, was the kneeling figure of a man with extremely dark eyes in a pale face. Around his head he wore a black and white band, and he dressed in a toga-like garment with a sash, something from another time and place, she thought. She rubbed her eyes and looked again, but the apparition was gone.

Before long, she had accepted the phenomenon as simply a dream, but again she knew this was not so, and she was merely accommodating her sense of logic. But who had the stranger been? Surely, the house was not haunted. Besides, she did not believe in ghosts.

As a young woman, she once heard a friend in real estate talk about selling a haunted house very near them. She thought this extremely funny and kidded her friend about it often. Little did she know at the time how real this subject was to become in her later years!

The haunted house across the street was sold, incidentally, but nothing further was heard about it, so Mrs. G. assumed the new owners did not care, or perhaps weren't aware of whatever it was that was haunting the premises.

Her own life had no room for such matters, and when her friend suggested they attend the Spiritualist church meeting, she took it more as a lark than a serious attempt to find out anything about the hereafter.

They went the next night, and found the meeting absorbing, if not exactly startling. Perhaps they had envisioned a Spiritualist meeting more like a séance with dark windows and dim lights and a circle of hand-holding believers, but they were not disappointed in the quality of the messages. Evidently, some of those present did receive proof of survival from dear departed ones, even though the two women did not. At least, not to their satisfaction. But the sincere atmosphere pleased them and they decided to come back again on another occasion.

At the meeting they managed to overhear a conversation between two members.

"He came through to me on the Ouija board," one lady said, and the other nodded in understanding.

An Ouija board? That was a toy, of course. No serious-minded individual would take such a game at face value. Mrs. G. had more time than ever on her hands and the idea of "playing around" with the Ouija board tickled her fancy. Consequently she bought a board the following week and decided she would try it when she had a moment all to herself.

That moment came a few days later, when she was all by herself in the house. She placed her fingers lightly on the indicator. This was a plastic arrow designed to point at individual letters, and in that way, spell out entire words. Mrs. G. was positive that only her own muscle power could move the indicator but she was willing to be amused that afternoon and, so to speak, game for whatever might come through the board.

Imagine her surprise when the board began to throb the moment she had placed her hands upon it. It was a distinct, intense vibration, similar to the throbbing of an idling motor. As soon as she lifted her hands off the board, it stopped. When she replaced them, it began again after about a minute or two, as if it were building up energy again. She decided there was nothing very alarming in all this and that it was probably due to some natural cause, very likely energy drawn from her body.

After a moment, her hands began to move across the board. She assured herself that she was not pushing the indicator knowingly, but there was no doubt she was being compelled to operate the indicator by some force outside herself!

Now her curiosity got the upper hand over whatever doubts she might have had at the beginning of the "experiment," and she allowed the indicator to rush across the board at an ever-increasing speed.

As the letters spelled out words she tried to remember them, and she stopped from time to time to write down what had been spelled out on the board.

"Hello," it said, "this is John W."

She gasped and let the pencil drop. John W. was someone she knew well. She had not thought of him for many years, and if his name was still imbedded in her unconscious mind, it had been dormant for so long and so deeply, she could scarcely accuse her own unconscious of conjuring him up now.

John W. had worshiped her in the days before she was married. Unfortunately, she had not been able to return the feeling with the same intensity. Ultimately, they lost track of each other and in thirty years never saw each other again. She learned from mutual acquaintances, however, that he had also got married and settled down in a nice house not far from where she and Mr. G. lived. But despite this proximity, she never met him nor did she feel any reason to.

John W. was also in the gasoline business, so they did have that in common, but there had been difficulties between the two of them that made a marriage undesirable from her point of view. He was a good man, all right, but not her "type," somehow, and she never regretted having turned him down, although she supposed he did not take it lightly at the time. But so many years had passed that time would have healed whatever wounds there might have been then.

When John W. died of heart failure in 1964, he was in his late fifties. Over the years, he had developed a morbid personality and it had overshadowed his former cheerful self.

"Hello," the Ouija board communicator had said, "this is John W."

Could it be? she wondered. She put the board away in haste. Enough for now, she thought.

But, her curiosity made her try it again. As if by magic, the indicator flew over the board.

"I want to be with you, always," the board spelled out now. And then a very avalanche of words followed, all of them directed towards her and telling her how much he had always loved and wanted her.

Could this be something made up in her own unconscious mind? Why would she subject herself to this incursion? For an incursion it soon turned out to be. Every day, practically, she found herself drawn to the Ouija board. For hours, she would listen to the alleged John W. tell her how much he wanted to stay with her, now that he had found her again.

This was punctuated with bitter complaints that she had hurt him, that she had not understood his great devotion for her.

As the weeks went, by, her own personality changed and she began to take on more and more of his characteristic moods. Whereas she had been a light-hearted, cheerful person, she turned moody and morbid, and her husband could not fail to notice the change that had come over his wife.

But she did not feel she could tell him what had happened, partly because she did not really believe it herself yet, and partly because she felt it might harm their marriage. So, she pretended to be depressed and her husband understood, blaming her middle years for it.

By the winter of 1964, her life was no longer her own. In addition to the frequent Ouija board sessions, she now began to hear the man's voice *directly*.

"*I* am with you," he explained, fervently, and with her he was. There was never a moment where she could be sure he was not nearby. Her privacy was gone. She kept hearing his voice, sad, but nevertheless his voice as it had been in life, talking to her from somewhere outside, and yet seemingly inside her head at the same time. She could not understand any of this and she did not know how to cope with it at first.

She threw away the accursed Ouija board that had opened the floodgates to the invasion from the beyond. But it did not help much. He was there, always present, and he could communicate with her through her own psychic sense.

She found it difficult to fall asleep. About that time, she noticed she was no longer alone in bed. At first she thought it was her imagination, spurred on by fear that made her *think* the undesired one was with her. But she soon felt his physical presence close to her body.

One night she extended her hand and clearly felt *something* other than air above her own body! She let out a scream and turned on the light. But this merely woke her husband and she had to explain it as a bad dream, so that he would not be alarmed.

Night after night, she felt John W.'s ethereal body next to or on top of hers. There was no mistake about it. He was trying to make love to her from the shadowy world he was in, something he had been denied while in the flesh. She fought off his advances as best she could, but it did not deter him in the least.

At the beginning of their communication with the Ouija board's help, she had still felt a kind of compassion for the poor devil who had died so sadly and rather early in his life. But whatever positive feelings she still harbored for him soon went by the board and her attitude turned into one of pure hate.

Nothing mattered in her life but to rid herself of this nightmare and return to the placid life she had been leading prior to the incident with the Ouija board.

John W. added threats and intimidation to his arsenal of evil now. Threats as to what he would do to her and her husband, if she did not accept him willingly. Ultimately, she could not bear it any longer and decided to inform her husband of what she was going through.

At first she was fearful as to what he might say. Perhaps he would have her committed to an institution, or at best, subject her to the humiliating treatments of a private psychiatrist.

But her husband listened quietly and with compassion.

"Terrible," he finally commented, "we've got to get you out of this somehow."

She sighed with relief. He evidently believed her. She herself had moments now where she questioned her own sanity. Could such things be as the sexual invasion of a woman by a dead man? Was she not merely acting out her own suppressed desires due perhaps to her middle-aged change of life?

She went to seek the advice of a physician.

After a careful checkup, he found her physically sound but suggested a psychiatric examination and possibly an EEC—an electroencephalogram to determine brain damage, if any. None of these tests showed anything abnormal. After a while, she concluded that medicine men could not help her even if they should believe her story.

Meanwhile, the attacks became worse.

"You will always hear my voice," he promised her night and day, "You won't be able to get rid of me now."

She tried all sorts of things. Grabbing whatever books on the subject of possession she could find, she tried to learn whether others had suffered similar attacks. She tried her skill at automatic writing hoping it might give the accursed ghost a chance to express himself and perhaps she might reason with him that way. But though she became a proficient automatist, it did not do any good.

The handwriting she wrote in was not hers. What she wrote down made no sense to her, but it was he who was using her in still one more way, and so she stopped it.

That night, she felt him closer than ever. It was as if his body was entering hers, and suddenly she felt her heart being squeezed and she gasped for breath. For a few moments of agonizing fear, she felt herself dying of a heart attack. The next day she went to see her doctor again. Her heart was as sound as could be. But she knew then that she had just relived the very moment of his death. He had died of just such a heart failure!

Clearly John W. was a disturbed personality in the in-between world in which he now existed after a fashion. He could not distinguish right from wrong, nor indeed recognize his true status.

His hatred and love at once kept him glued to her body and her environment, it would appear, unwilling and unable to break what must have been his strongest desire at the time of death.

During their courtship, he had appeared as a good person, unselfish and kind. Now he seemed bitter and full of selfish desire to own her, unwilling to let her go or do anything she asked him to.

She enlisted the help of a local amateur hypnotist, but he failed to put her under hypnosis.

Discouraged, she was losing all desire to live, if it meant living on with this monstrous person inside her.

One day she saw a television program on which hypnotic treatment in parapsychological cases was the subject of discussion. Again encouraged, she asked for help, and went to New York for an attempt to dislodge the unwanted entity from her body and soul.

This time she did go under, although not very deeply. But it was enough for the personality of John W. to emerge and carry on a conversation of sorts with the hypnotist.

"I want her to go with me, she is all I have now," he said, speaking through Mrs. G.'s mouth in trance.

Later, she confirmed that she had been on the brink of suicide recently, and this had not been in a moment of panic but as if someone had actually made her attempt it. Luckily, she had managed to pull out of it just in time.

"Do you believe in a God?" the hypnotist asked.

"No," the entity replied and brushed the question aside. "I told her, she made life hell for me, now I'll make her life hell for her."

"But why do that?"

"No one wants me—I want to cry—you don't know what this is like—over here—nothing but darkness—"

Tears came down Mrs. G.'s cheeks now.

"It's me crying, not *her*," the voice of John W. said, and then, somewhat quieter, "No one wanted me as a child ... I came from an orphanage ... my grandparents never wanted me ... she could have made me happy but she didn't want to. She's the only woman who would have made me happy, only her, but she doesn't want me."

"Then why force yourself on her? What is the point?"

"I force myself on her because I can make her miserable."

"You can't force love'."

"I have no pride."

"Renounce her."

"I don't want to listen to you. She hates me now anyway. I'm going to take her with me ... I'll get her, one way or another, I'll get her all right."

The hypnotist, patiently, explained about the freedom of the Other Side and how to get there by wishing oneself with one's loved ones who have preceded one.

"This is all new to me," the confused entity replied, but seemed for a moment to be thinking it over.

But it was only a brief squint at The Light, then darkness took over once again.

"I've made her cry ... miserable ... she made me miserable. I don't like the way she's lived her life ..."

Suddenly, the personality seemed to squirm as if from guilt.

Was this his own private hell he was in?

"I'm not really that person ... I've been lying to her ... just so I can be around her, I tell her one thing and then another...."

"Then why not leave her and go on to the Other Side?"

"I want to, but don't know how—I can't go without *her.*"

The hypnotist tried again, explaining that other souls had been equally confused and had been helped "across" the Great Divide.

The voice of the possessing entity hesitated. He was willing to go, but could he see Mrs. G. now and again? Visiting privileges, the hypnotist thought, with a bitter sense of humor.

"Will I be able to come back and see her?" the voice asked again.

But then the demented mind emerged triumphant.'

"She hates me for what I've done to her. I'm not going to leave. I can do anything with her. Never could do it when living."

Now the hypnotist dropped the polite approach.

"You are to leave this woman," he intoned, "on pain of eternal damnation."

"I won't go."

"You will be in hell."

"She will be with me, then."

"I send you away, the psychic door is closed. You cannot return."

"I will."

A moment later, Mrs. G. awoke, somewhat dumbfounded and tired, but otherwise no worse off than she had been when she had been put under by the hypnotist.

After Mrs. G. returned to Kansas City, she had some hopes that the power of John W. had been broken. But the molesting continued. True, there had been conversation and the entity now knew at least that he was committing a moral offense. But evidently it did not matter to him, for the attacks continued.

Mrs. G. realized that her anxiety and abject fear were contributing factors to John W.'s unholy powers. She realized that negative emotions can create energies that become usable by entities such as John W. and when she realized this fact, her attitude began to undergo a change.

Where she had been waiting for his attacks to occur and counting the moments when she was totally free from his possession, she now deliberately disregarded all he did and treated his presence with utter indifference. She could still feel the rage within him when he wanted to possess her, but the rage was slowly cooling. Gradually, her compassion for the bedeviled soul returned and as it did, his hold upon her weakened. He had made his point, after all, and now the point no longer mattered. When last heard from, Mrs. G. was living quietly in Kansas City.

THE PHANTOM ADMIRAL

I had never heard of Goddard College until I received a letter from Jay Lawrence, a second-semester student at Goddard College in Plainfield, Vermont. Mr. Lawrence was serious about his interest in psychic phenomena and he had some evidence to offer. He did more than ask me to speak at the college on extrasensory perception; he invited me to come and have a look at a ghost he had discovered in Whiteheld, New Hampshire, about two hours' drive from Goddard.

The haunted house in Whitefield belonged to the Jacobsen family who used it as a summer home only. The younger Jacobsen, whose first name was Erlend—they're of Norwegian descent—invited us to come stay at the house, or at least have a look at it. The Goddard College boys offered to pick us up in Boston and drive us up through the scenic White Mountains to Whitefield.

We arrived at dusk, when the country tends to be peaceful and the air was almost still. The house was at the end of a narrow, winding driveway lined by tall trees, hidden away from the road. There was a wooden porch around three sides of the wooden structure, which rose up three stories.

We were welcomed by Erlend Jacobsen, his wife, Martha, and their little boy Erlend Eric, a bright youngster who had met the ghost, too, as we were to find out.

Inside the house with its spacious downstairs dining room and kitchen, decorated in a flamboyant style by the Jacobsens, we found Mr. and Mrs. Nelson, two friends of the owners, and Jeff Broadbent, a young fellow student of Jay Lawrence.

Sybil puttered around the house, indulging her interest in antiques. I mounted my tape recorder to hear the testimony of those who had experienced anything unusual in the house. We went upstairs, where Sybil Leek could not very well hear us, and entered a small bedroom on the second floor, which, I was told, was the main center of ghostly activities, although not the only one.

The house was called "Mis 'n Top" by its original owner and builder. I lost no time in questioning Erlend Jacobsen, a tall young man of thirty on the Goddard College faculty as an instructor, about his experiences in the old house.

"When my parents decided to turn the attic into a club room where I could play with my friends," Erlend Jacobsen began, "they cut windows into the wall and threw out all the possessions of the former owner of the house they had found there. I was about seven at the time.

"Soon after, footsteps and other noises began to be heard in the attic and along the corridors and stairs leading toward it. But it was not until the summer of 1956, when I was a senior in college and had just married, that I experienced the first really important disturbance."

"1955, Erlend," the wife interrupted. Wives have a way of remembering such dates. Mr. Jacobsen blushed and corrected himself.

"1955, you're right," he said. "That summer we slept here for the first time in this room, one flight up, and almost nightly we were either awakened by noises or could not sleep, waiting for them to begin. At first we thought they were animal noises, but they were too much like footsteps and heavy objects being moved across the floor overhead, and down the hall. We were

69

so scared we refused to move in our beds or turn on the lights."

"But you did know of the tradition that the house was haunted, did you not?" I asked.

"Yes, I grew up with it. All I knew is what I had heard from my parents. The original owner and builder of the house, an admiral named Hawley, and his wife, were both most difficult people. The admiral died in 1933. In 1935, the house was sold by his daughter, who was then living in Washington, to my parents. Anyone who happened to be trespassing on his territory would be chased off it, and I imagine he would not have liked our throwing out his sea chest and other personal possessions."

"Any other experience outside the footsteps?"

"About four years ago," Erlend Jacobsen replied, "my wife and I, and a neighbor, Shepard Vogelgesang, were sitting in the living room downstairs discussing interpretations of the Bible. I needed a dictionary at one point in the discussion and got up to fetch it from upstairs.

"I ran up to the bend here, in front of this room, and there were no lights on at the time. I opened the door to the club room and started to go up the stairs, when suddenly I walked into what I can only describe as a *warm, wet blanket*, something that touched me physically as if it had been hung from wires in the corridor. I was very upset, backed out, and went downstairs. My wife took one look at me and said, 'You're white.' 'I know,' I said. *'I think I just walked into the admiral.'*"

"I suppose he didn't enjoy your bumping into him in this fashion either," I commented. "Anything else?"

"I was alone in the house, in the club room, which is designed like a four-leaf clover—you can see into the section opposite you, but you can't see into the other two. I was lying there, looking out the window at sunset, when I heard someone breathing—rhythmically breathing in, out, in, out."

"What did you do?"

"I held my own breath, because at first I thought I might be doing it. But I was not. The breathing continued right next to me! I became terrified, being then only fifteen years of age, and ran out of the house until my parents returned."

I asked him again about the time *he touched the ghost.*

How did it feel? Did it have the touch of a human body?

"Nothing like it. It was totally dark, but it was definitely warm, and it resisted my passage."

"Has anything happened to you here recently?"

"About two and a half weeks ago, I walked into the house at dusk and I heard very faint crying for about fifteen or twenty seconds. I thought it might be a cat, but there was no cat in the house, and just as suddenly as it had started, the crying stopped. It sounded almost as if it were outside this window, here on the second floor."

"Is there any record of a tragedy attached to this house?"

"None that I know of."

"Who else has seen or heard anything uncanny here?"

"My parents used to have a friend who was psychic. She had her share of experiences here all right. Her name was Sarah Wheeler and she was about seventy-five now. The admiral had a reputation for disliking people, and she claimed that when she was in bed here, frequently the bedposts would move as if someone were trying to throw her out of bed. The posts would move off the floor and rock the bed violently, held by unseen hands, until she got out of bed, and then they would stop. She was a Catholic and went to the church the next day to fetch some Holy Water. That quieted things down. But the first night of each season she would come without her Holy Water and that was when things were worst for her."

"Poor Sarah," I said.

"She was psychic, and she had an Indian guide," Erlend Jacobsen continued. "I did not put much stock in some of the things she told us, such as there being treasure underneath the house, put there by the old admiral. But eight or nine years ago, I had occasion to recall this. The house has no cellar but rests on stone pillars. We used to throw junk under the house, where wooden steps led down below. I was cleaning up there with a flashlight, when I saw something shiny. It was a cement block with a silver handle sticking out of it. I chipped the cement off, and found a silver bowl, with 'A.H.' engraved on it."

I turned my attention to Mrs. Jacobsen. She had three children, but still gave the impression of being a college sophomore. As a matter of fact, she was taking courses at Goddard, where her husband was an instructor.

It was ten years to the day—our visit was on June 11—that the Jacobsens had come to this house as newlyweds.

"We spent one night here, then went on our honeymoon, and then came back and spent the rest of the summer here," Martha Jacobsen said. "The first night I was very, very frightened—hearing this walking up and down the halls, and we the only ones in the house! There was a general feeling of eeriness and a feeling that there was someone else in the house. There were footsteps in the hall outside our bedroom door. At one point before dawn, the steps went up the stairs and walked around overhead. But Erlend and I were the only ones in the house. We checked."

Imagine one's wedding night interrupted by unseen visitors—this could give a girl a trauma!

"Two weeks later we returned and stayed here alone," Mrs. Jacobsen continued, "and I heard these footsteps several times. Up and down. We've been coming here for the last ten years and I heard it again a couple of weeks ago."

"Must be unnerving," I observed.

"It is. I heard the steps overhead in the club room, and also, while I was downstairs two weeks ago, the door to the kitchen opened itself and closed itself, without anyone being visible. Then the front door did the same—thing opened and shut itself.

"Along with the footsteps I heard things being dragged upstairs, heavy objects, it seemed. But nothing was disarranged afterwards. We checked."

"Any other events of an uncanny nature?" I asked as a matter of record. Nothing would surprise me in *this* house.

"About ten years ago, when we first moved in, I also heard the heavy breathing when only my husband and I were in the house. Then there was a house guest we had, a Mrs. Anne Merriam. She had this room and her husband was sleeping down the hall in one of the single rooms. Suddenly, she saw a figure standing at the foot of her bed."

"What did she do?"

"She called out, 'Carol, is that you?' twice, but got no answer. Then, just as suddenly as it had come, the figure dissolved into thin air.

"She queried her husband about coming into her room, but he told her that he had never left his bed that night. When this happened on another night, she attempted to follow the figure, and found her husband entering through another door!"

"Has anyone else had an encounter with a ghost here?" I asked.

"Well, another house guest went up into the attic and came running down reporting that the door knob had turned in front of his very eyes before he could reach for it to open the door. The dog was with him, and steadfastly refused to cross the threshold. That was Frank Kingston and it all happened before our marriage. Then another house guest arrived very late at night, about five years ago. We had already gone to bed, and he knew he had to sleep in the attic since every other room was already taken. Instead, I found him sleeping in the living room, on the floor, in the morning. He knew nothing about the ghost. 'I'm not going back up there any more,' he vowed, and would not say anything further. I guess he must have run into the admiral."

What a surprise that must have been, I thought, especially if the admiral was all wet.

"Three years ago, my brother came here," Mrs. Jacobsen continued her report. "His name is Robert Gillman. In the morning he complained of having been awake all night. A former skeptic, he knew now that the tales of ghostly footsteps were true, for he, too, had heard them—all night long in fact."

Jeffrey Broadbent was a serious young man who accompanied Jay Lawrence to the house one fine night, to see if what they were saying about the admiral's ghost was true. They had sleeping bags and stayed up in the attic. It was a chilly November night in 1964, and everything seemed just right for ghosts. Would they be lucky in their quest? They did not have to wait long to find out.

"As soon as we entered the room, we heard strange noises on the roof. They were indistinct and could have been animals, I thought at first. We went off to sleep until Jay woke me up hurriedly around six in the morning. I distinctly heard human footsteps on the roof. They slid down the side to a lower level and then to the ground where they could be heard walking in leaves and into the night. Nothing could be seen from the window and there was nobody up on the roof. We were the only ones in the house that night, so it surely must have been the ghost."

Jay Lawrence added one more thing to this narrative.

"When we first turned out the flashlight up in the attic, I distinctly heard a high-pitched voice—a kind of scream or whine—followed by footsteps. They were of a human foot wearing shoes, but much lighter than the normal weight of a human body would require."

Jerry Weener also had spent time at the haunted house.

"In early March of 1965, Jay and I came over and had dinner at the fireplace downstairs. We decided to sleep downstairs and both of us, almost simultaneously, had a dream that night in which we met the admiral's ghost, but unfortunately on awakening, we did not recall anything specific or what he might have said to us in our dreams. A second time when I slept in the house, nothing happened. The third time I came over with friends, I slept in the attic, and I heard footsteps. We searched the house from top to bottom, but there was no one else who could have accounted for those steps."

Erlend Eric, age eight going on nine, was perhaps the youngest witness to psychic phenomena scientifically recorded, but his testimony should not be dismissed because of his age. He had heard footsteps going up and down and back up the stairs. One night he was sleeping in the room across the hall when he heard someone trying to talk to him.

"What sort of voice was it?" I asked. Children are frequently more psychic than adults.

"It was a man's," the serious youngster replied. "He called my name, but I forgot what else he said. That was three years ago."

Miriam Nelson was a petite young woman, the wife of one of Erlend Jacobsen's friends, who had come to witness our investigation that evening. She seemed nervous and frightened and asked me to take her to another room so I could hear her story in private. We went across the hall into the room where the figure had stood at the head of the bed and I began my questioning.

"My first experience was when Erlend and I brought a Welsh Corgi up here; Erlend's parents were here, too. I was downstairs in the library; the dog was in my lap. Suddenly I felt another presence in the room, and I could not breathe anymore. The dog started to bark and insist that I follow him out of the room. I distinctly felt someone there.

"Then on a cold fall day about four years ago, I was sitting by the stove, trying to get warm, when one of the burners lifted itself up about an inch and fell down again. I looked and it moved again. It could not have moved by itself. I was terrified. I was alone in the house."

I had heard all those who had had an encounter with the ghost and it was time to get back downstairs where the Jacobsens had laid out a fine dinner—just the right thing after a hard day's drive. A little later we all went up the stairs to the top floor, where Sybil stretched out on a couch near the window. We grouped ourselves around her in the haunted attic and waited.

"I had a feeling of a *midde* room upstairs," Sybil said, "but I don't feel anything too strongly yet."

Soon Sybil was in deep trance as we awaited the coming of the admiral—or whoever the ghost would be—with bated breath. The only light in the attic room was a garish fluorescent lamp, which we shut off, and replaced with a smaller conventional lamp. It was quiet, as quiet as only a country house can be. But instead of the ghost speaking to us directly and presumably giving us hell for trespassing, it was Sybil herself, in deep trance "on the other side," reporting what she saw—things and people the ordinary eye could not perceive.

"I'm walking around," Sybil said. "There is a man lying dead in the middle room. Big nose, not too much hair in front, little beard cut short now. There is a plant near him."

"Try to get his name, Sybil," I ordered.

"I'll have to go into the room," she said.

We waited.

"He is not in here all the time," she reported back. "He came here to die."

"Is this his house?"

"Yes, but there is another house also. A long way off. This man had another house. Hawsley … Hawsley."

Almost the exact name of the admiral, I thought. Sybil could not have known that name.

"He went from one house to another, in a different country. Something Indian."

"Is he still here and what does he want?"

"To find a place to rest because ... he does not know in which house it's in!"

"What is he looking for?"

"Little basket. Not from this country. Like a handle ... it's shiny ... silver ... a present. It went to the wrong house. He gave it to the wrong house. He is very particular not to get things confused. It belongs to Mrs. Gerard at the other house. He usually stays in the little room, one flight up. With the fern. By the bed."

"But what about Mrs. Gerard? How can we send the package to her unless we get her address?" I said.

"It's very important. It's in the wrong perspective, he says," Sybil explained.

"What did he have for a profession?" I tried again.

"He says he brought things ... seeds."

"What are his initials or first name?"

"A. J. H."

Sybil seemed to listen to someone we could not see.

"He's not troublesome," she said. "He goes when I get near to him. Wants to go to the other house."

"Where is the other house?"

"Liang ... Street ... Bombay."

"Does he know he is dead?"

"No."

I instructed her to tell him.

"Any family?"

"Two families ... Bombay."

"Children?"

"Jacob ... Martin."

It was not clear whether the ghost said Jacob or Jacobsen.

"He is shaking himself," Sybil now reported. "What upset him? He worries about names. A. J. A. name on something he is worried about. The names are wrong on a paper. He said Jacobsen is wrong. It should be Jacob Hawsley son."

Evidently the ghost did not approve the sale of his house by his executors, but wanted it to go to his son.

"Because of two houses, two families, he did not know what to do with the other."

"What does 'A' stand for in his name?"

"Aaron … Aaron Jacob."

"Does he have any kind of title or professional standing?"

"A-something … A-D-M … can't read … Administrator A-D-M … it's on the paper, but I can't read the paper."

Still, she did get the admiral's rank!

I promised to have the gift delivered to Mrs. Gerard, if we could find her, but he must not stay in this house any further.

"Who waters the plants, he asks," Sybil said.

I assured him the plants would be taken care of.

"But what about the other house, who waters the plants there?" the ghost wanted to know.

"How does he go there?" I asked in return.

"He sails," Sybil replied. "Takes a long time."

Again I promised to find the house in India, if I could.

"What about a date?" I asked. "How long ago did all this happen?"

"About 1867," Sybil replied.

"How old was he then?"

"Fifty-nine."

I implored the admiral not to cause any untidiness in the house by upsetting its inhabitants. The reply via Sybil was stiff.

"As a man with an administrative background, he is always tidy," Sybil reported. "But he is going now."

"He is going now," Sybil repeated, "and he's taking the ferns."

I called Sybil back to her own body, so as not to give some unwanted intruder a chance to stop in before she was back in the driver's seat, so to speak.

None the worse for her travels in limbo, Sybil sat up and smiled at us, wondering why we all stared at her so intently. She remembered absolutely nothing.

Erlend Jacobsen spoke up.

"That basket she mentioned," he said. "When my parents first bought the house, there was one hanging over the dining room, on a chain, a stuffed armadillo, which had been shellacked from the outside. It had straw handles and had been turned into a basket. It was around the house until about five years ago, but I have no idea where it is now. For all we know, it may still be around the house somewhere."

"Better find it," I said. "That is, if you want those footsteps to cease!

Just as we were leaving the house, the senior Jacobsens returned. Mr. Eric Jacobsen does not care for ghosts and I was told not to try to get him to talk about the subject. But his wife, Josephine, Erlend's mother, had been pushed down the stairs by the ghost—or so she claims. This was quite possible, judging by the way the admiral was behaving in his post-funeral days and nights.

Our job in Whitefield seemed finished and we continued on to Stowe, Vermont, where we had decided to stay at the famous Trapp Family Lodge. My wife had become interested in Mrs. Trapp's books, and from *The Sound of Music*, we both thought that the lodge would provide a welcome interlude of peace during a hectic weekend of ghost hunting.

The next morning we rested up from the rigors of our investigation and found the world around us indeed peaceful and promising. The following morning we would go down to Goddard College and address students and teachers on the subject of ghosts, which would leave us with a pleasant afternoon back at Stowe, before flying back to Manhattan. But we had reckoned without the commercial spirit at the lodge. Like most overnight lodgings, they wanted us out of our rooms by eleven o'clock Sunday morning, but finally offered to let us stay until two. I declined.

After my talk at the college, we were taken to one of the girls' dormitories where uncanny happenings had taken place. The college was situated on the old Martin farm, and the manor had been turned into a most elegant girl students' residence, without losing its former Victorian grandeur. Reports of a dead butler still walking the old corridors upstairs had reached my ears. Two students, Madeleine Ehrman and Dorothy Frazier, knew of the ghost. The phenomena were mainly footsteps when no one was about. A teacher who did not believe in ghosts set foot in the manor and later revealed that the name Dawson had constantly impressed itself on her mind. Later research revealed that a butler by that name did in fact live at the manor house long ago.

Sue Zuckerman was a New York girl studying at Goddard.

"One night last semester," she said, "I was up late studying when I heard footsteps approaching my room. After a few seconds I opened my door—there was nobody there. I closed the door and resumed studying. I then heard footsteps walking away from my door. I looked again, but saw nothing.

"During this time for a period of about three weeks, my alarm clock had been shut off every night. I would set it for about seven-thirty, but when I woke up much later than that, the alarm button was always off. I began hiding my clock, locking my door—but it still happened.

"Back in 1962, I was toying with a Ouija board I had bought more in fun than as a serious instrument of communication. I had never gotten anything through it that could not have come from my own mind, but that Friday afternoon in 1962, I worked it in the presence of three other friends, and as soon as we put our hands on it, it literally started to leap around. It went very fast, giving a message one of us took

80

down: 'I am dead … of drink. Are you here now in the Manor? One could speak of my presence here.' There was more, but I can't remember it now.

"Afterwards, a strange wind arose and as we walked past a tree outside, it came crashing down."

I don't know about a strange "wind," and Ouija boards are doubtful things at times, but the footfalls of the restless butler named Dawson must have been a most unusual extracurricular activity for the co-eds at Goddard College.

THE SOMERVILLE GHOST

I'm Mrs. Campano," the letter read in a large, clear handwriting, "and I've been living in this house for four months now." The woman had heard me on station WBZ, Boston, and wanted to report a haunted house.

I called her and found Mrs. Campano a reasonable, well-spoken lady in her middle years. Her elder daughter had recently married and her son was grown, and it made sense for the mother to move to a smaller house. But at the moment she was still at the haunted house on Washington Avenue in Somerville, Massachusetts.

The first impression that something strange went on in her house was when she noticed her dog's unusual behavior. The dog barked constantly and kept running up and down the stairs to the upper floor. When the daughter moved out, she took the dog with her, and Mrs. Campano's house became quiet, *except for the ghost.*

There was a light in the downstairs living room of the wooden house, so she found it unnecessary to turn on any additional lights when she wanted to mount the stairs. One night in 1964, when she passed the stairway, she heard someone crying. She entered the bathroom, and when she came out she still heard the sound of someone crying, as if hurt. She walked up the stairs, thinking it was one of her children having a nightmare, but when she got to the top of the stairs, the crying stopped.

She checked all the rooms upstairs, and the children were fast asleep. She went back to bed downstairs. Then, above her head, she distinctly heard the shuffling of feet, as if two people were fighting and struggling. She had a puppy, who started to act strangely, just as the larger dog had done.

The experience upset Mrs. Campano no end, and she talked it over with her elder daughter, Marsha, now married. The daughter was sympathetic, for she, too, had heard the crying and at one time footsteps of someone going up and down the stairs, with the crying continuing for about twenty minutes. It sounded like a woman.

They decided to do something about the noises. A group of young boys, friends of her son's, stayed overnight at the old house. They took the upstairs room where most of the disturbances centered. At first, everything was quiet. The youngest girl and some of her friends went to sleep in another room upstairs. Soon the boys heard tapping and crying, but thought the girls were trying to put over a practical joke. They jumped from their beds and raced across the hall only to find the girls fast asleep in their room.

Mrs. Campano turned to the church for relief, but the local priest refused to come. A friend supplied her with Holy Water but the relief was short lived. A week later, the noises started up again.

When Marsha, the elder daughter, had the bedroom upstairs to the right, she often heard the crying and felt as though someone were touching her. But she had kept quiet about these sensations. After she had moved out, the younger daughter, who had the room now, also reported that she felt a presence in her room, and something or someone unseen touching her feet as if to rouse her!

The eighteen-year-old son also had heard the footsteps

and crying and had decided to check on the source. When he had reached the hallway, the crying suddenly stopped, but the puppy, which had come with him, kept on growling. Ten minutes later the noises started up again, this time from the cellar.

One more thing Mrs. Campano found strange about the house: on the wall of the room upstairs there was a red spot that looked like blood.

I reached Jim Tuverson, of WBZ's "Contact" program, to arrange for a visit to the haunted house on Washington Avenue, Somerville.

There was a problem, though. Mrs. Campano had decided to move out on May 31, 1965, and our visit would be in June. We took it up with the landlord, Costa & Sons. This was not as easy as it sounds. How do you tell a real estate man one of his properties is haunted? You don't tell him, that's how. You do tell him you've got an interest in old New England houses and could you do a little historical research?

When we arrived at the house I realized immediately how funny the request must have sounded to Mr. Costa. The house was a ramshackle, run-down structure. Since Mrs. Campano had moved, we agreed to see her *after* the investigation and trance session.

It was a warm day for Boston when we met Jim Tuverson and Bob Kennedy of WBZ at Boston's Logan Airport. Sybil Leek had flown in directly from San Francisco—using an airplane of course—and joined us for the ride to the haunted house. She knew nothing whatever about the case, not even the location of the house. We left our cars in front of the house where a few curious people had gathered. They rarely saw two radio cars pull up in this unglamorous section of town.

Quickly we went inside the house where a lady from the real estate firm of Costa & Sons was expecting us. The house had been stripped of all its contents except the dirt, which was still around in generous quantities. The aroma was somewhat less than heavenly and it was my fondest wish to get out of there as soon as possible. It was about four in the afternoon and bright, but Sybil never lets such things bother her when we investigate a place.

We hastily borrowed a chair from the house across the street and assembled in the kitchen downstairs. Sybil took to the chair, and I began the session by asking for her impressions of this dismal house.

"As you know, I came in and walked right out again and got a drink next door—that's always a bad sign for me. I don't like this place at all, and I don't think we're in the right room. The upstairs room is the right place."

"What do you feel about the upstairs?"

"There is a strange smell in one of the rooms upstairs, not just a physical smell, but something beyond that. I always associate this smell with something quite evil and I don't think I'm in for a good time."

"What do you think has taken place in this house?" I asked.

"I think there has been some violence here," Sybil replied without hesitation, "the right hand room upstairs."

"Do you feel any presence in this house?"

"I feel a very bad head right now," Sybil said and touched the back of her own head as if she felt the pain herself. "My head is very bad. There is some lingering evil which pervades not only the inside of the house, but even the outside is not immune."

I then asked Sybil to relax as well as she could under these uncomfortable circumstances, and to allow whatever entity might be hovering about to communicate through her.

Outside, the warm air was filed with the distant noises of a bustling city, but inside the drab, dirty house, time seemed to stand still as we tried to wedge open a doorway into another dimension.

"Things are different today," Sybil finally said. "I'm looking in at the house—but nobody can speak through me."

We should have gone upstairs to the room Sybil thought was the center of the haunting, I thought. Still, one never knows. Sometimes just being in a house, any place within the walls, is sufficient to make contact.

I instructed Sybil to remain in trance and to report back anything she could find.

"Right hand side," Sybil said in a quiet, slow voice, different from her habitual speech. "There's someone in the house ... it's a girl."

"What do you see upstairs?"

"I see the girl on the bed. She's got long, wavy hair, she can't get up, her head is very bad."

"Is she injured?"

"Yes ... in the back. She's dead. There's a child or a dog, a child ... this is 1936 ... I keep going outside the house, you see, because there's someone around ... I can't find him."

"Can you speak to the woman on the bed?"

"She worries about the child."

I explained about her true status and where the child now was.

"She's getting angry," Sybil reported. "She does not believe you."

I told Sybil to instruct the woman how to call for her child. But the ghost was very confused. We tried to get her to follow Sybil out of the house. I kept explaining what had happened to her.

"She won't leave until she finds the child," Sybil explained and I kept thinking of the scurrying footsteps on those stairs, the crying it all fitted in with a mother trying to find her baby!

"What is her name?" I asked.

There was silence as we waited for more evidence from Sybil's lips.

"Linda Mathews," Sybil said, clearly and distinctly.

"And the child's name?"

"Margaret."

I had never heard these names before in connection with this case, nor had anyone else in the room. Mrs. Campano had not mentioned them to me either.

I instructed Linda to call for her child and then leave the house. But she wouldn't budge.

"She's waiting for someone ... Robert Shaw was here, she says."

"Did *he* hurt her?"

"She'll kill him, because she hates him enough. He hurt her. He hit her."

"Did he kill her?"

"She doesn't know."

"Did her husband kill her?"

"She doesn't know."

Again Sybil, on my urging, explained her situation to the ghost.

"She's coming a little closer now," Sybil reported. "I think she's Scots. Country type. She's moving now, off the bed. I'm with her. She's very weak."

I told Sybil to withdraw as soon as the ghost was safely outside the house. Quickly I brought her out of trance.

"Quite an ordeal, somehow," Sybil said, although she didn't remember anything that had come through her while in trance. I sent her and my wife on to the radio station with Bob Kennedy, while Jim Tuverson and I drove in his car to Mrs. Campano's new house, a few blocks down Washington Avenue.

The new house was much smaller and the Campanos occupied only a part of it, but it was brighter and much more cheerful than the house we had just left.

A sudden idea struck me. I walked into the Campano living room, and shot a question at Mrs. Campano—"Have you ever heard of Linda Mathews?"

"Yes," Mrs. Campano replied with surprise. "I used to get her mail at the old house all the time, and always sent it back. She used to live in the house. In fact, she died there. But I don't know any more than that."

Here we had immediate corroboration of a name—not such a common name like Jones or Smith, but a definite name not easily guessed—and information concerning this name had not been known to anybody in the haunted house while we were there!

Thus Sybil could not have gotten the name from the unconscious minds of any of us in the house, not indeed from me, since I only learned of the Mathews matter this minute. Jim Tuverson was visibly impressed. Here was proof of the kind that would stand up in any court of law. Sybil had really done a superb job.

I questioned Mrs. Campano about her experiences at the house. Was there anything she had not told me prior to my coming to Somerville?

"It was like a woman crying as if she had been hurt," she reiterated. "Then one night I was the last one to go to bed and everything seemed perfectly normal. In the morning, however, I discovered a series of pictures, which I have in the room between bookends, placed on the floor as if by human hands. Nobody could have done this."

I thought perhaps the unfortunate woman ghost had been trying to get her attention.

"What about your husband?" I asked. "Has he ever heard anything unusual?"

"Yes. One morning we came in around 3 A.M., and we were in the kitchen downstairs cooking, when we both heard someone coming down the stairs. He thought one of the children had smelled the food and was about to join us, but, of course, nobody appeared."

"What about you and your son hearing those footsteps coming up from the cellar?" I asked.

"It sounded like someone in heavy boots coming up the cellar steps," Mrs. Campano explained, "and then we heard the noise of someone handling pots and pans in the kitchen."

"Were they actually moved around?"

"Yes. The next morning we found the kitchen in disorder, but nobody had been in who could have done this. No burglars, either."

I began to wonder if the cellar at the Washington Avenue house did not hold the bodies of two murdered people.

"Did you check the cellar?" I asked.

"The next day," Mrs. Campano replied, "but we found nothing."

Mrs. Campano's father, Peter Cagliano, then 73 years old, was a mystic and probably psychic. He came to the house, and for a while things became quiet after that.

Evidently, Mrs. Campano also had inherited some of her family's psychic talents. Her first psychic experience took place when she was seventeen years old. She then lived in a house where a murder had been committed and witnessed the noises and physical phenomena accompanying the haunting. Seven years ago, she saw the apparition of a woman known to have died, by the name of Jehasses, but no communication ensued.

"What do you know about a murder committed in the house you just left?" I finally asked her.

"The husband killed his wife and baby, and then himself," she replied, "with an ax, up in one of the rooms."

Exactly what Sybil had said in trance!

There was one more witness I wanted to question: Mrs. Campano's married daughter, Marsha Parmesano, who used to sleep in the haunted room upstairs.

"When I was asleep," she said, "I used to feel someone

breathing over me, but when I turned around there was nobody there. At the edge of my bed I felt someone sitting there, like getting up and sitting down, but there was no one there. That was the room to the right, upstairs. I felt it a couple of times."

After all, she was occupying Linda Mathews' bed—and adding discomfort to the ghost's unhappy state.

We left the Somerville ghost house with the conviction that the next tenant would have nothing to worry about. No more footsteps, no more crying. That is, unless there is something—or somebody—buried in the cellar that needs to be discovered.

But I doubt it even then. Sybil Leek managed to lead the murdered woman out of her self-imposed prison to join her child. Unless the allegedly guilt-laden husband was still outside the walls of the old house, unable to leave the place of his crimes, everything should have become peaceful on Washington Avenue.

A REVOLUTIONARY COROLLARY: PATRICK HENRY, NATHAN HALE, ET AL.

Nathan Hale, as every schoolboy knows, was the American spy hanged by the British. He was captured at Huntington Beach and taken to Brooklyn for trial. How he was captured is a matter of some concern to the people of Huntington, Long Island. The town was originally settled by colonists from Connecticut who were unhappy with the situation in that colony. There were five principal families who accounted for the early settlement of Huntington, and to this day their descendants were the most prominent families in the area. They were the Sammes, the Downings, the Busches, the Pauldings, and the Cooks. During the Revolutionary War, feelings were about equally divided among the town people: some were Revolutionaries and some remained Tories. The consensus of historians is that members of these five prominent families, all of whom were Tories, were responsible for the betrayal of Nathan Hale to the British.

All this was brought to my attention by Mrs. Geraldine P. of Huntington. Mrs. P. grew up in what she considered the oldest house in Huntington, although the Huntington Historical Society claims that theirs was even older. Be that as it may, the house was there when the Revolutionary War started. Local legend had it that an act of violence took place on the corner of the street, which was then a crossroads in the middle of a rural area. The house in which Mrs. P. grew up, stands on that street. Mrs. P. suspected that the capture—or, at any rate, the betrayal—of the Revolutionary agent took place on that crossroads. When she tried to investigate the history of her house, she found little cooperation on the part of the local historical society. It was a conspiracy of silence, according to her, as if some people wanted to cover up a certain situation from the past.

The house had had a "strange depressing effect on all its past residents," according to Mrs. P. Her own father, who studied astrology and white magic for many years, had related an incident that occurred several years ago in the house. He awoke in the middle of the night in the master bedroom because he felt unusually cold. He became aware of "something" rushing about the room in wild, frantic circles. Because of his outlook and training, he spoke up, saying, "Can I help you?" But the rushing about became even more frantic. He then asked what was wrong and what could be done. But no communication was possible. When he saw that he could not communicate with the entity, Mrs. P.'s father finally said, "If I can't help you, then go away." There was a snapping sound, and the room suddenly became quiet and warm again, and he went back to sleep. There had been no other recorded incidents at the house in question. But Mrs. P. wonders if some guilty entity wanted to manifest, not necessarily Nathan Hale, but perhaps someone connected with his betrayal.

At the corner of 44th Street and Vanderbilt Avenue, Manhattan, one of the busiest and noisiest spots in all of New York City, there is a small commemorative plaque explaining that the British executed Nathan Hale, the Revolutionary spy, on that spot. I doubt that too many New Yorkers were aware of this, or could accurately pinpoint the location of the tragedy. It was even less likely that a foreigner would know about it. When I suggested to my good friend Sybil Leek that she accompany me to a psychically important spot for an experiment, she readily agreed. Despite the noises and the heavy traffic, the spot being directly across from Grand Central Station, Sybil bravely stood with me on the street corner and tried to get some sort of psychic impression.

"I get the impression of food and drink," Sybil said. I pointed out that there were restaurants all over the area, but Sybil shook her head. "No, I was thinking more of a place for food and drink, and I don't mean in the present. It is more like an inn, a transit place, and it had some connection with the river. A meeting place, perhaps, some sort of inn. Of course, it is very difficult in this noise and with all these new buildings here."

"If we took down these buildings, what would we see?"

"I think we would see a field and water. I have a strong feeling that there is a connection with water and with the inn. There are people coming and going—I sense a woman, but I don't think she's important. I am not sure … unless it would mean foreign. I hear a foreign language. Something like *Verchenen*. I can't quite get it. It is not German."

"Is there anything you feel about this spot?"

"This spot, yes. I think I want to go back two hundred years at least, it is not very clear, 1769 or 1796. That is the period. The connection with the water puzzles me."

"Do you feel an event of significance here at any time?"

"Yes. It is not strong enough to come through to me completely, but sufficiently *drastic* to make me feel a little nervous."

"In what way is it drastic?"

"Hurtful, violent. There are several people involved in this violence. Something connected with water, papers connected with water, that is part of the trouble."

Sybil then suggested that we go to the right to see if the impressions might be stronger at some distance. We went around the corner and I stopped. Was the impression any stronger?

"No, the impression is the same. Papers, violence. For a name, I have the impression of the letters P.T. Peter. It would be helpful to come here in the middle of the night, I think. I wish I could understand the connection with water, here in the middle of the city."

"Did someone die here?"

Sybil closed her eyes and thought it over for a moment. "Yes, but the death of this person was important at that time and indeed necessary. But there is more to it than just the death of the person. The disturbance involves lots of other things, lots of other people. In fact, two distinct races were involved, because I sense a lack of understanding. I think that this was a political thing, and the papers were important."

"Can you get anything further on the nature of this violence you feel here?"

"Just a disturbed feeling, an upheaval, a general disturbance. I am sorry I can't get much else. Perhaps if we came here at night, when things are quieter."

I suggested we get some tea in one of the nearby restaurants. Over tea, we discussed our little experiment and Sybil suddenly remembered an experience she had had when visiting the Hotel Biltmore before. (The plaque in question was mounted on the wall of what was then the Biltmore Hotel.) "I receive many invitations to go to this particular area of New

York," Sybil explained, "and when I go I always get the feeling of repulsion to the extent where I may be on my way down and get into a telephone booth and call the people involved and say, 'No, I'll meet you somewhere else.' I don't like this particular area we just left; I find it very depressing. *I feel trapped.*"

I was indebted to R. M. Sandwich of Richmond, Virginia, for an intriguing account of an ESP experience he had connected to Patrick Henry. Mr. Sandwich stated that he had had only one ESP experience and that it took place in one of the early estate-homes of Patrick Henry. He admitted that the experience altered his previously dim view of ESP. The then-owner of the estate had said that Mr. Sandwich had not been the only one to experience strange things in that house.

The estate-home where the incident took place was called Pine Flash and was presently owned by E. E. Verdon, a personal friend of Mr. Sandwich. It was located in Hanover County, about fifteen miles outside of Richmond. The house was given to Patrick Henry by his father-in-law. After Henry had lived in it for a number of years, it burned to the ground and was not rebuilt until fifteen years later. During that time Henry resided in the old cottage, which was directly behind the house, and stayed there until the main house had been rebuilt. This cottage was frequently referred to in the area as the honeymoon cottage of young Patrick Henry. The new house was rebuilt exactly as it had been before the fire. As for the cottage, which was still in excellent condition, it was thought to be the oldest wood frame dwelling in Virginia. It may have been there even before Patrick Henry lived in it.

On the Fourth of July, 1968, the Sandwiches had been invited to try their luck at fishing in a pond on Mr. Verdon's land. Since they would be arriving quite early in the morning, they were told that the oars to the rowboat, which they were

95

to use at the pond, would be found inside the old cottage. They arrived at Pine Flash sometime around 6 A.M. Mrs. Sandwich started unpacking their fishing gear and food supplies, while Mr. Sandwich decided to inspect the cottage. Although he had been to the place several times before, he had never actually been inside the cottage itself.

Here then is Mr. Sandwich's report.

"I opened the door, walked in, and shut the door tight behind me. Barely a second had passed after I shut the door when a strange feeling sprang over me. It was the kind of feeling you would experience if you were to walk into an extremely cold, damp room. I remember how still everything was, and then I distinctly heard footsteps overhead in the attic. I called out, thinking perhaps there was someone upstairs. No one answered, nothing. At that time I was standing directly in front of an old fireplace.

"I admit I was scared half to death. The footsteps were louder now and seemed to be coming down the thin staircase toward me. As they passed me, I felt a cold, crisp, odd feeling. I started looking around for something, anything that could have caused all this. It was during this time that I noticed the closed door open very, very slowly. The door stopped when it was half opened, almost beckoning me to take my leave, which I did at great speed! As went through that open door, I felt the same cold mass of air I had experienced before. Standing outside, I watched the door slam itself, almost in my face! My wife was still unpacking the car and claims she neither saw nor heard anything."

Revolutionary figures have a way of hanging on to places they like in life. Ms. Candy Bosselmann of Indiana had had a long history of psychic experiences. She was a budding trance medium and not at all ashamed of her talents. In 1964 she happened to be visiting Ashland, the home of Henry Clay, in

Lexington, Kentucky. She had never been to Ashland before, so she decided to take a look at it. She and other visitors were shown through the house by an older man, a professional guide, and Candy became somewhat restless listening to his historical ramblings. As the group entered the library and the guide explained the beautiful ash paneling taken from surrounding trees (for which the home is named), she became even more restless. She knew very well that it was the kind of feeling that forewarned her of some sort of psychic event. As she was looking over toward a fireplace, framed by two candelabra, she suddenly saw a very tall, white-haired man in a long black frock coat standing next to it. One elbow rested on the mantel, and his head was in his hand, as if he were pondering something very important.

Ms. Bosselmann was not at all emotionally involved with the house. In fact, the guided tour bored her, and she would have preferred to be outside in the stables, since she had a great interest in horses. Her imagination did not conjure up what she saw: she knew in an instant that she was looking at the spirit imprint of Henry Clay.

In 1969 she visited Ashland again, and this time she went into the library deliberately. With her was a friend who wasn't at all psychic. Again, the same restless feeling came over her. But just as she was about to go into trance, she decided to get out of the room in a hurry.

Rock Ford, the home of General Edward Hand, was located four miles south of Lancaster, Pennsylvania, and commanded a fine view of the Conestoga River. The house was not a restoration, but a well-preserved eighteenth-century mansion, with its original floors, railings, shutters, doors, cupboards, panelings, and window glass. Even the original wall painting could be seen. It was a four story brick mansion in the Georgian style, with the rooms grouped around a center hall in the design popular during the latter part of the eighteenth century. The rooms were furnished with antiquities of the period, thanks to the discovery of an inventory of General Hand's estate that permitted the local historical society to supply authentic articles of daily usage wherever the originals had disappeared from the house.

Perhaps General Edward Hand was not as well known as a hero of the American Revolution as others are, but to the people of the Pennsylvania Dutch country he was an important figure, even though he was of Irish origin rather than German. Trained as a medical doctor at Trinity College, Dublin, he came to America in 1767 with the Eighteenth Royal Irish Regiment of Foote. However, he resigned British service in 1774 and came to Lancaster to practice medicine and surgery. With the fierce love of liberty so many of the Irish possess, Dr. Hand joined the Revolutionaries in July of 1775, becoming a lieutenant colonel in the Pennsylvania Rifle Battalion. He served in the army until 1800, when he was discharged as a major general. Dr. Hand was present at the Battle of Trenton, the Battle of Long Island, the Battle of White Plains, the Battle of Princeton, the campaign against the Iroquois, and the surrender of Cornwallis at Yorktown. He also served on the tribunal that convicted Major John André, the British spy, and later became the army's adjutant general. He was highly regarded by George Washington, who visited him in his home toward the end of the war. When peace came, Hand became a member of the Continental Congress and served in the Assembly of Pennsylvania as representative of his area. He moved into Rock Ford when it was completed in 1793 and died there in September 1802.

Nowadays, hostesses from a local historical society serve as guides for the tourists who come to Rock Ford in increasing numbers. Visitors were taken about the lower floor and basement and were told of General Hand's agricultural experiments, his medical studies, and his association with George Washington. But unless you ask specifically, you were not likely to hear about what happened to the house after General Hand died. To begin with, the General's son committed suicide in the house. Before long the family died out, and eventually the house became a museum since no one wanted to live in it for very long. At one time, immigrants were contacted at the docks and offered free housing if they would live in the mansion. None stayed. There was something about the house that was not as it should be, something that made people fear it and leave it just as quickly as they could.

Mrs. Ruth S. lived in upstate New York. In 1967 a friend showed her a brochure concerning Rock Ford, and the house intrigued her. Since she was traveling in that direction, she decided to pay Rock Ford a visit. With her family, she drove up to the house and parked her car in the rear. At that moment she had an eerie feeling that something wasn't right. Mind you, Mrs. S. had not been to the house before, had no knowledge about it, nor any indication that anything unusual had occurred in it. The group of visitors was quite small. In addition to herself and her family, there were two young college boys and one other couple. Even though it was a sunny day, Mrs. S. felt icy cold.

"I felt a presence before we entered the house and before we heard the story from the guide," she explained. "If I were a hostess there, I wouldn't stay there alone for two consecutive minutes." Mrs. S. had been to many old houses and restorations before but had never felt as she did at Rock Ford.

It was not surprising that George Washington should be the subject of a number of psychic accounts. Probably the best known (and most frequently misinterpreted) story concerns General Washington's vision which came to him during the encampment at Valley Forge, at a time when the fortunes of war had gone heavily in favor of the British, and the American army, tattered and badly fed, was just about falling to pieces. If there ever was a need for divine guidance, it was at Valley Forge. Washington was in the habit of meditating in the woods at times and saying his prayers when he was quite alone. On one of those occasions he returned to his quarters more worried than usual. As he busied himself with his papers, he had the feeling of a presence in the room. Looking up, he saw opposite him a singularly beautiful woman. Since he had given orders not to be disturbed, he couldn't understand how she had gotten into the room. Although he questioned her several times, the visitor would not reply. As he looked at the apparition, for that was what it was, the General became more and more entranced with her, unable to make any move. For a while he thought he was dying, for he imagined that the apparition of such unworldly creatures as he was seeing at that moment must accompany the moment of transition.

Finally, he heard a voice, saying, "Son of the Republic, look and learn." At the same time, the visitor extended her arm toward the east, and Washington saw what to him appeared like white vapor at some distance. As the vapor dissipated, he saw the various countries of the world and the oceans that separated them. He then noticed a dark, shadowy angel standing between Europe and America, taking water out of the ocean and sprinkling it over America with one hand and over Europe with the other. When he did this, a cloud rose from the countries thus sprinkled, and the cloud then moved westward until it enveloped America. Sharp flashes of lightning became visible at intervals in the cloud. At the same time, Washington thought he heard the anguished cries of the American people underneath the cloud. Next, the strange visitor showed him a vision of what America would look like in the future, and he saw villages and towns springing up from one coast to the other until the entire land was covered by them.

"Son of the Republic, the end of the century cometh, look and learn," the visitor said. Again Washington was shown a dark cloud approaching America, and he saw the American people fighting one another. A bright angel then appeared wearing a crown on which was written the word Union. This angel bore the American Flag, which he placed between the divided nation, saying, "Remember, you are brethren." At that instant, the inhabitants threw away their weapons and became friends again.

Once more the mysterious voice spoke. "Son of the Republic, look and learn." Now the dark angel put a trumpet to his mouth and sounded three distinct blasts. Then he took water from the ocean and sprinkled it on Europe, Asia, and Africa. As he did so, Washington saw black clouds rise from the countries he had sprinkled. Through the black clouds, Washington could see red light and hordes of armed men, marching by land and sailing by sea to America, and he saw these armies devastate the entire country, burn the villages, towns, and cities, and as he listened to the thundering of the cannon, Washington heard the mysterious voice saying again, "Son of the Republic, look and learn."

Once more the dark angel put the trumpet to his mouth and sounded a long and fearful blast. As he did so, a light as of a thousand suns shone down from above him and pierced the dark cloud that had enveloped America. At the same time the angel wearing the word Union on his head descended from the heavens, followed by legions of white spirits. Together with the inhabitants of America, Washington saw them renew the battle and heard the mysterious voice telling him, once again, "Son of the Republic, look and learn."

For the last time, the dark angel dipped water from the ocean and sprinkled it on America; the dark cloud rolled back and left the inhabitants of America victorious. But the vision continued. Once again Washington saw villages, towns, and cities spring up, and he heard the bright angel exclaim, "While the stars remain and the heavens send down dew upon the earth, so long shall the Union last." With that, the scene faded, and Washington beheld once again the mysterious visitor before him. As if she had guessed his question, the apparition then said:

"Son of the Republic, what you have seen is thus interpreted: Three great perils will come upon the Republic. The most fearful is the third, during which the whole world united shall not prevail against her. Let every child of the Republic learn to live for his God, his land, and his Union." With that, the vision disappeared, and Washington was left pondering over his experience.

One can interpret this story in many ways, of course. If it really occurred, and there were a number of accounts of it in existence that lead me to believe that there is a basis of fact to this, then we were dealing with a case of prophecy on the part of General Washington. It was a moot question whether the third peril has already come upon us, in the shape of World War II, or whether it is yet to befall us. The light that was stronger than many suns may have ominous meaning in this age of nuclear warfare.

Washington himself was said to have appeared to Senator Calhoun of South Carolina at the beginning of the War Between the States. At that time, the question of secession had not been fully decided, and Calhoun, one of the most powerful politicians in the government, was not sure whether he could support the withdrawal of his state from the Union. The question lay heavily on his mind when he went to bed one hot night in Charleston, South Carolina. During the night, he thought he awoke to see the apparition of General George Washington standing by his bedside. The General wore his presidential attire and seemed surrounded by a bright outline, as if some powerful source of light shone behind him. On the senator's desk lay the declaration of secession, which he had not yet signed. With Calhoun's and South Carolina's support, the Confederacy would be well on its way, having closed ranks. Earnestly, the spirit of George Washington pleaded with Senator Calhoun not to sign the declaration. He warned him against the impending perils coming to America as a divided nation; he asked him to reconsider his decision and to work for the preservation of the Union. But Calhoun insisted that the South had to go its own way. When the spirit of Washington saw that nothing could sway Senator Calhoun, he warned him that the very act of his signature would be a black spot on the Constitution of the United States. With that, the vision was said to have vanished.

One can easily explain the experience as a dream, coming as it did at a time when Senator Calhoun was particularly upset over the implications of his actions. On the other hand, there was this to consider: Shortly after Calhoun had signed the document taking South Carolina into the Confederacy, a dark spot appeared on his hand, a spot that would not vanish and for which medical authorities had no adequate explanation.

Mrs. Margaret Smith of Orlando, Florida, had had a long history of psychic experiences. She had personally seen the ghostly monks of Beaulieu, England; she had seen the actual lantern of Joe Baldwin, the famous headless ghost of Wilmington, North Carolina. She took takes her "supernatural" experiences in stride the way other people feel about their musical talents or hobbies. When she was only a young girl, her grandmother took her to visit the von Steuben house in Hackensack, New Jersey. (General F. W. A. von Steuben was a German supporter of the American Revolution who aided General Washington with volunteers who had come over from Europe because of repressions, hoping to find greater freedom in the New World.) The house was old and dusty, the floorboards were creaking, and there was an eerie atmosphere about it. The house had been turned into an historical museum, and there were hostesses to take visitors through.

While her grandmother was chatting with the guide downstairs, the young girl walked up the stairs by herself. In one of the upstairs parlors she saw a man sitting in a chair in the corner. She assumed he was another guide. When she turned around to ask him a question about the room, he was gone. Since she hadn't heard him leave, that seemed odd to her, especially as the floorboards would creak with every step. But being young, she didn't pay too much attention to this peculiarity. A moment later, however, he reappeared. As soon as she saw him, she asked the question she had on her mind. This time he did not disappear but answered her in a slow, painstaking voice that seemed to come from far away. When he had satisfied her curiosity about the room, he asked her some questions about herself, and finally asked the one which stuck in her mind for many years afterward—"What is General Washington doing now about the British?"

Margaret was taken aback at this question. She was young, but she knew very well that Washington had been dead for many years. Tactfully, she told him this, and added that Harry Truman was now president and that the year was 1951. At this information, the man looked stunned and sat down again in the chair. As Margaret watched him in fascinated horror, he faded away.

THE VINDICATION OF AARON BURR

*V*ery few historical figures have suffered as much from their enemies or have been as misunderstood and persistently misrepresented as the onetime Vice-President of the United States, Aaron Burr, whose contributions to American independence were frequently forgotten while his later troubles were made to represent the man.

Burr was a lawyer, a politician who had served in the Revolutionary forces and who later established himself in New York as a candidate of the Democratic-Republican Party in the elections of 1796 and 1800. He didn't get elected in 1796, but in 1800 he received exactly as many electoral votes as Thomas Jefferson. When the House of Representatives broke the tie in Jefferson's favor, Burr became Vice-President.

Burr soon realized that Jefferson was his mortal enemy. He found himself isolated from all benefits, such as political patronage, normally accruing to one in his position, and he was left with no political future at the end of his term. Samuel Engle Burr, a descendant of Theodosia Barstow Burr, Aaron's first wife, and the definitive authority on Aaron Burr himself, calls him "the American Phoenix," and truly he was a man who frequently rose from the ashes of a smashed career.

Far from being bitter over the apparent end of his career, Burr resumed his career by becoming an independent candidate for governor of New York. He was defeated, however, by a smear campaign in which both his opponents, the Federalists, and the regular Democratic-Republican Party took part.

"Some of the falsehoods and innuendoes contained in this campaign literature," writes Professor Burr in his namesake's biography, "have been repeated as facts down through the years. They have been largely responsible for much of the unwarranted abuse that has heaped upon him since that time."

Aside from Jefferson, his greatest enemies were the members of the Hamilton-Schuyler family, for in 1791 Burr had replaced Alexander Hamilton's father-in-law, General Philip Schuyler, as the senator from New York. Hamilton himself had been Burr's rival from the days of the Revolutionary War, but the political slurs and statements that had helped to defeat Burr in 1804, and that had been attributed to Hamilton, finally led to the famed duel.

In accepting Burr's challenge, Hamilton shared the illegality of the practice. He had dueled with others before, such as Commodore Nicholson, a New York politician, in 1795. His own son, Philip Hamilton, had died in a duel with New York lawyer George Eacker in 1801. Thus neither party came to Weehawken, New Jersey that chilly July morning in 1804 exactly innocent of the rules of the game.

Many versions have been published as to what happened, but to this day the truth is not clear. Both men fired, and Burr's bullet found its mark. Whether or not the wound was fatal was difficult to assess today. The long voyage back by boat, and the primitive status of medicine in 1804 may have been contributing factors to Hamilton's death.

That Alexander Hamilton's spirit was not exactly at rest

I proved a few years ago when I investigated the house in New York City where he had spent his last hours after the duel. The house belonged to his physician, but it has since been torn down to make room for a modern apartment house. Several tenants have seen the fleeting figure of the late Alexander Hamilton appear in the house and hurry out of sight, as if trying to get someplace fast. I wonder if he was trying to set the record straight, a record that saw his opponent Burr charged with *murder* by the State of New Jersey.

Burr could not overcome the popular condemnation of the duel; Hamilton had suddenly become a martyr, and he, the villain. He decided to leave New York for a while and went to eastern Florida, where he became acquainted with the Spanish colonial system, a subject that interested him very much in his later years. Finally he returned to Washington and resumed his duties as the Vice-President of the United States.

In 1805 he became interested in the possibilities of the newly acquired Louisiana Territory, and tried to interest Jefferson in developing the region around the Ouachita River to establish there still another new state.

Jefferson turned him down, and finally Burr organized his own expedition. Everywhere he went in the West he was cordially received. War with Spain was in the air, and Burr felt the United States should prepare for it and, at the right time, expand its frontiers westward.

Since the government had shown him the cold shoulder, Burr decided to recruit a group of adventurous colonists to join him in establishing a new state in Louisiana Territory and await the outbreak of the war he felt was sure to come soon. He purchased four hundred thousand acres of land in the area close to the Spanish-American frontier and planned on establishing there his dream state, to be called Burrsylvania.

In the course of his plans, Burr had worked with one General James Wilkinson, then civil governor of Louisiana

Territory and a man he had known since the Revolutionary War. Unfortunately Burr did not know that Wilkinson was actually a double agent, working for both Washington and the Spanish government.

In order to bolster his position with the Jefferson government, Wilkinson suggested to the President that Burr's activities could be considered treasonable. The immediate step taken by Wilkinson was to alter one of Burr's coded letters to him in such a way that Burr's statements could be used against him. He sent the document along with an alarming report of his own to Jefferson in July of 1806.

Meanwhile, unaware of the conspiracy against his expedition, Burr's colonists arrived in the area around Natchez, when a presidential proclamation issued by Jefferson accused him of treason. Despite an acquittal by the territorial government of Mississippi, Washington sent orders to seize him.

Burr, having no intention of becoming an insurrectionist, disbanded the remnants of his colonists and returned east. On the way he was arrested and taken to Richmond for trial. The treason trial itself was larded with paid false witnesses, and even Wilkinson admitted having forged the letter that had served as the basis for the government's case. The verdict was "not guilty," but the public, inflamed against him by the all-powerful Jefferson political machine, kept condemning Aaron Burr.

Under the circumstances, Burr decided to go to Europe. He spent the four years from 1808 to 1812 traveling abroad, eventually returning to New York, where he reopened his law practice with excellent results.

The disappearance at sea the following year of his only daughter Theodosia, to whom he had been extremely close, shattered him; his political ambitions vanished, and he devoted the rest of his life to an increasingly successful legal practice. In 1833 he married for the second time—his first wife, Theodosia's mother, also called Theodosia, having died in

1794. The bride was the widow of a French wine merchant named Stephen Jumel, who had left Betsy Jumel a rich woman indeed. It was a stormy marriage, and ultimately Mrs. Burr sued for divorce. This was granted on the 14th of September 1836, the very day Aaron Burr died. Betsy never considered herself anything but the *widow* of the onetime Vice-President, and she continued to sign all documents as Eliza B. Burr.

Burr had spent his last years in an apartment at Port Richmond, Staten Island, overlooking New York Harbor. His body was laid to rest at Princeton, the president of which for many years had been Burr's late father, the Reverend Aaron Burr.

I had not been familiar with any of this until after the exciting events of June 1967, when I was able to make contact with the person of Aaron Burr through psychic channels.

My first encounter with the name Aaron Burr came in December of 1961. I was then actively investigating various haunted houses in and around New York City as part of a study grant by the Parapsychology Foundation. My reports later grew into a popular book called *The Ghost Hunter.*

One day a publicist named Richard Mardus called my attention to a nightclub on West Third Street then doing business as the Cafe Bizarre. Mr. Mardus was an expert on Greenwich Village history and lore, and he pointed out to me that the club was actually built into remodeled stables that had once formed part of Richmond Hill, Aaron Burr's estate in New York City. At the time of Burr's occupancy this was farm-land and pretty far uptown, as New York City went.

But Mardus did not call to give me historical news only: Psychic occurrences had indeed been observed at the Burr stables, and he asked me to look into the matter. I went down to have a look at the edifice. It was located on a busy side street in the nightclub belt of New York, where after dark the curious and the tourists gather to spend an evening of informal fun. In the daytime, the street looks ugly and ordinary, but after dark it seems to sparkle with an excitement of its own.

The Cafe Bizarre stood out by its garish decor and posters outside the entrance, but the old building housing it, three stories high, was a typical early nineteenth-century stone building, well preserved and showing no sign of replacement of the original materials.

Inside, the place had been decorated by a nightmarish array of paraphernalia to suggest the bizarre, ranging from store dummy arms to devil's masks, and colorful lights played on this melee of odd objects suspended from the high ceiling. In the rear of the long room was a stage, to the left of which a staircase led up to the loft; another staircase was in back of the stage, since a hayloft had occupied the rear portion of the building. Sawdust covered the floor, and perhaps three dozen assorted tables filled the room.

It was late afternoon and the atmosphere of the place was cold and empty, but the feeling was nevertheless that of the unusual—uncanny, somehow. I was met by a pretty, dark-haired young woman, who turned out to be the owner's wife, Mrs. Renée Allmen. She welcomed me to the Cafe Bizarre and explained that her husband, Rick, was not exactly a believer in such things as the psychic, but that she herself had indeed had unusual experiences here. On my request, she gave me a written statement testifying about her experiences.

In the early morning of July 27, 1961, at 2:20 A.M., she and her husband were locking up for the night. They walked out to their car when Mrs. Allmen remembered that she had forgotten a package inside. Rushing back to the cafe, she unlocked the doors again and entered the deserted building. She turned on the lights and walked toward the kitchen, which was about a third of the way toward the rear of the place. The cafe was quite empty, and yet she had an eerie sensation of not being alone. She hurriedly picked up her package and walked toward the front door again. Glancing backward into the dark recesses of the cafe, she then saw the apparition of a man, staring at her with piercing black eyes. He wore a ruffled shirt of the kind nobody wears in our time, not even in colorful Greenwich Village. He seemed to smile at her, and she called out to him, "Who is it?"

But the figure never moved or reacted.

"What are you doing here?" Renée demanded, all the while looking at the apparition.

There was no answer, and suddenly Renée's courage left her. Running back to the front door, she summoned her husband from the car, and together they retuned to the cafe. Again unlocking the door, which Renée had shut behind her when she fled from the specter, they discovered the place to be quite empty. In the usual husbandly fashion, Mr. Allmen tried to pass it off as a case of nerves or tired eyes, but his wife would not buy it. She knew what she had seen, and it haunted her for many years to come.

Actually, she was not the first one to see the gentleman in the white ruffled shirt with the piercing black eyes. One of their waiters also had seen the ghost and promptly quit. The Village was lively enough without psychic phenomena, and how much does a ghost tip?

I looked over the stage and the area to the left near the old stairs to see whether any reflecting surface might be blamed for the ghostly apparition. There was nothing of the sort, nothing to reflect light. Besides, the lights had been off in the rear section, and those in the front were far too low to be seen anywhere but in the immediate vicinity of the door.

Under the circumstances I decided to arrange for a visit with psychic Ethel Johnson Meyers to probe further into this case. This expedition took place on January 8, 1962, and several observers from the press were also present.

The first thing Mrs. Meyers said, while in trance, was that

she saw three people in the place, psychically speaking. In particular she was impressed with an older man with penetrating dark eyes, who was the owner. The year, she felt, was 1804. In addition, she described a previous owner named Samuel Bottomslee, and spoke of some of the family troubles this man had allegedly had in his lifetime. She also mentioned that the house once stood back from the road, when the road passed farther away than it does today. This I found to be correct.

"I'm an Englishman and I have my rights here," the spirit speaking through Mrs. Meyers thundered, as we sat spellbound. Later I found out that the property had belonged to an Englishman before it passed into Burr's hands.

The drama that developed as the medium spoke haltingly did not concern Aaron Burr, but the earlier settlers. Family squabbles involving Samuel's son Alan, and a girl named Catherine, and a description of the building as a stable, where harness was kept, poured from Ethel's lips. From its looks, she could nor have known consciously that this was once a stable.

The period covered extended from 1775 to 1804, when another personality seemed to take over, identifying himself as one John Bottomsley. There was some talk about a deed, and I gathered that all was not as it should have been. It seemed that the place had been sold, but that the descendants of Samuel Bottomslee didn't acknowledge this too readily.

Through all this the initials A.B. were given as prominently connected with the spot.

I checked out the facts afterward; Aaron Burr's Richmond Hill estate had included these stables since 1797. Before that, the area belonged to various British colonials.

When I wrote the account of this séance in my book *Ghost Hunter*, I thought I had done with it. And I had, except for an occasional glance at the place whenever I passed it, wondering whether the man with the dark, piercing eyes was really Aaron Burr.

Burr's name came to my attention again in 1964 when I investigated the strange psychic phenomena at the Morris-Jumel Mansion in Washington Heights, where Burr had lived during the final years of his life as the second husband of Mme. Betsy Jumel. But the spectral manifestations at the Revolutionary house turned out to be the restless shades of Mme. Jumel herself and that of her late first husband, accusing his wife of having murdered him.

One day in January of 1967 I received a note from a young lady named Alice McDermott. It concerned some strange experiences of hers at the Cafe Bizarre—the kind one doesn't expect at even so oddly decorated a place. Ms. McDermott requested an interview, and on February 4 of the same year I talked to her in the presence of a friend.

She had gone down to the Village for several years as part of her social life—she was now twenty—and visited the Bizarre for the first time in 1964. She had felt strange, but could not quite pinpoint her apprehension.

"I had a feeling there was *something* there, but I let it pass, thinking it must be my imagination. But there was something on the balcony over the stage that seemed to stare down at me—I mean something besides the dummy suspended from the ceiling as part of the decor."

At the time, when Alice was sixteen, she had not yet heard of me or my books, but she had had some ESP experiences involving premonitions and flashes of a psychic nature.

Alice, an only child, was then working as a secretary in an office in Manhattan. Her father was a barge officer and her mother an accountant. She was a pretty blonde with a sharp mind and a will of her own. Persuaded to try to become a nun, she spent three months in a Long Island convent, only to discover that the religious life was not for her. She then returned to New York and took a job as a secretary in a large business firm.

After she left the convent she continued her studies also, especially French. She studied with a teacher in Washington Square, and often passed the Cafe Bizarre on her way. Whenever she did, the old feeling of something uncanny inside came back. She did not enter the place, but walked on hurriedly.

But on one occasion she stopped, and something within her made her say, "Whoever you are in there, you must be lonely!" She did not enter the place despite a strong feeling that "someone wanted to say hello to her" inside. But that same night, she had a vivid dream. A man was standing on the stage, and she could see him clearly. He was of medium height, and wore beige pants and black riding boots. His white shirt with a kind of Peter Pan collar fascinated her because it did not look like the shirts men wear today. It had puffy sleeves. The man also had a goatee that is, a short beard, and a mustache.

"He didn't took dressed in today's fashion, then?"

"Definitely not, unless he was a new rock'n'roll star."

But the most remarkable features of this man were his dark, piercing eyes, she explained. He just stood there with his hands on his hips, looking at Alice. She became frightened when the man kept looking at her, and walked outside.

That was the end of this dream experience, but the night before she spoke to me, he reappeared to her in a dream. This time she was speaking with him in French, and also to an old lady who was with him. The lady wore glasses, had a pointed nose, and had a shawl wrapped around her— "Oh, and a plain gold band on her finger."

The lady also wore a Dutch type white cap, Alice reported. I was fascinated, for she had described Betsy Jumel in her old age—yet how could she connect the ghostly owner of Jumel Mansion with her Cafe Bizarre experience? She could not have known the connection, and yet it fit perfectly. Both Burr and Betsy Jumel spoke French fluently, and often made use of that language.

"Would you be able to identify her if I showed you a picture?" I asked.

"If it were she," Alice replied, hesitatingly.

I took out a photograph of a painting hanging at Jumel Mansion, which shows Mme. Jumel in old age.

I did not identify her by name, merely explaining it was a painting of a group of people I wanted her to look at.

"This is the lady," Alice said firmly, "but she is younger looking in the picture than when I saw her."

What was the conversation all about? I wanted to know.

Apparently the spirit of Mme. Jumel was pleading with her on behalf of Burr, who was standing by and watching the scene, to get in touch with *me!* I asked Alice, who wanted to be a commercial artist, to draw a picture of what she saw. Later, I compared the portrait with known pictures of Aaron Burr. The eyes, eyebrows, and forehead did indeed resemble the Burr portraits. But the goatee was not known.

After my initial meeting with Alice McDermott, she contacted me again. The dreams in which Burr appeared to her were getting more and more lively, and she wanted to go on record with the information thus received. According to her, Aaron poured his heart out to the young girl, incredible though this seemed on the face of it.

The gist of it was a request to go to "the white house in the country" and find certain papers in a metal box. "This will prove my innocence. I am not guilty of treason. There is written proof. Written October 18, 1802 or 1803." The message was specific enough, but the papers of course were long since gone.

The white house in the country would be the Jumel Mansion.

I thanked Alice and decided to hold another investigation at the site of the Cafe Bizarre, since the restless spirit of the late Vice-President of the United States had evidently decided to be heard once more.

At the same time I was approached by Mel Bailey of Metromedia Television to produce a documentary about New York haunted houses, and I decided to combine these efforts and investigate the Burr stables in the full glare of television cameras.

On June 12, 1967 I brought Sybil Leek down to the Bizarre, having flown her in from California two days before. Mrs. Leek had no way of knowing what was expected of her, or where she would be taken. Nevertheless, as early as June 1, when I saw her in Hollywood, she had remarked to me spontaneously that she "knew" the place I would take her to on our next expedition—then only a possibility and she described it in detail. On June 9, after her arrival in New York, she telephoned and again gave me her impressions.

"I sense music and laughter and drumbeat," she began, and what better was there to describe the atmosphere at the Cafe Bizarre these nights? "It is a three-story place, not a house but selling something; two doors opening, go to the right-hand side of the room and something is raised up from the floor, where the drumbeat is."

Entirely correct; the two doors led into the elongated room, with the raised stage at the end.

"Three people ... one has a shaped beard, aquiline nose, he is on the raised part of the floor; very dark around the eyes, an elegant man, lean, and there are two other people near him, one of whom has a name starting with a Th."

In retrospect one must marvel at the accuracy of the description, for surely Sybil Leek had no knowledge of either the place, its connection with Burr, nor the description given by the other witnesses of the man they had seen there.

This was a brief description of her first impressions given to me on the telephone. The following day I received a written account of her nocturnal impressions from Mrs. Leek. This was still two days before she set foot onto the premises!

In her statement, Mrs. Leek mentioned that she could not go off to sleep late that night, and fell into a state of semi-consciousness, with a small light burning near her bed. Gradually she became aware of the smell of fire, or rather the peculiar smell when a gun had just been fired. At the same time she felt an acute pain, as if she had been wounded in the left side of the back.

Trying to shake off the impression, Mrs. Leek started to do some work at her typewriter, but the presence persisted. It seemed to her as if a voice was trying to reach her, a voice speaking a foreign language and calling out a name, Theo.

I questioned Mrs. Leek about the foreign language she heard spoken clairvoyantly.

"I had a feeling it was French," she said.

Finally she had drifted into deeper sleep. But by Saturday afternoon the feeling of urgency returned. This time she felt as if someone wanted her to go down to the river, not the area where I live (uptown), but "a long way the other way," which was precisely where the Burr stables were situated.

Finally the big moment had arrived. It was June 12, and the television crews had been at work all morning in and around the Cafe Bizarre to set up cameras and sound equipment so that the investigation could be recorded without either hitch or interruption. We had two cameras taking turns, to eliminate the need for reloading. The central area beneath the "haunted stage" was to be our setting, and the place was reasonably well lit, certainly brighter than it normally was when the customers were there at night.

Everything had been meticulously prepared. My wife Catherine was to drive our white Citroën down to the Bizarre with Sybil at her side. Promptly at 3:00 P.M. the car arrived, Sybil Leek jumped out and was greeted at the outer door by me, while our director, Art Forrest, gave the signal for the cameras to start. "Welcome to the Cafe Bizarre," I intoned, and led my psychic friend into the semi dark inside. Only the central section was brightly lit.

I asked her to walk about the place and gather impressions at will.

"I'm going to those drums over there," Sybil said firmly, and walked toward the rear stage as if she knew the way.

"Yes—this is the part. I feel cold. Even though I have not been here physically, *I know this place.*"

"What do we have to do here, do you think?" I asked.

"I think we have to relieve somebody, somebody who's waited a long time."

"Where is this feeling strongest?"

"In the rear, where this extra part seems to be put on."

Sybil could not know this, but an addition to the building was made years after the original had been constructed, and it was precisely in that part that we were now standing.

She explained that there was more than one person involved, but one in particular was dominant; that this was something from the past, going back into another century. I then asked her to take a chair, and Mrs. Renée Allmen and my wife Catherine joined us around a small table.

This was going to be a séance, and Sybil was in deep trance within a matter of perhaps five minutes, since she and I were well in tune with one another, and it required merely a signal on my part to allow her to "slip out."

At first, there was a tossing of the head, the way a person moves when sleep is fitful. Gradually, the face changed its expression to that of a man, a stern face, perhaps even a suspicious face. The hissing sound emanating from her tightly closed lips gradually changed into something almost audible, but I still could not make it out.

Patiently, as the cameras ground away precious color film,

I asked "whoever it might be" to speak louder and to communicate through the instrument of Mrs. Leek.

"Theo!" the voice said now. It wasn't at all like Sybil's own voice.

"Theo ... I'm lost ... where am I?" I explained that this was the body of another person and that we were in a house in New York City.

"Where's Theo?" the voice demanded with greater urgency. "Who are you?"

I explained my role as a friend, hoping to establish contact through the psychic services of Mrs. Leek, then in turn asked who the communicator was. Since he had called out for Theo, he was not Theo, as I had first thought.

"Bertram Delmar. I want Theo," came the reply.

"Why do you want Theo?"

"Lost."

Despite extensive search I was not able to prove that Bertram Delmar ever existed or that this was one of the cover names used by Aaron Burr; but it is possible that he did, for Burr was given to the use of code names during his political career and in sensitive correspondence.

What was far more important was the immediate call for Theo, and the statement that she was "lost." Theodosia Burr was Burr's only daughter and truly the apple of his eye. When she was lost at sea on her way to join him in 1813, he became a broken man. Nothing in the up-and-down life of the American Phoenix was as hard a blow of fate as the loss of his beloved Theo.

The form "Theo," incidentally, rather than the full name Theodosia, is attested to by the private correspondence between Theodosia and her husband, Joseph Alston, governor of South Carolina. In a rare moment of foreboding, she had hinted that she might soon die. This letter was written six months before her disappearance in a storm at sea and was signed, "Your wife, your fond wife, Theo."

After the séance, I asked Dr. Samuel Engle Burr whether the name Theo might apply to some other woman.

Dr. Burr pointed out that the Christian name Theodosia occurred in modern times only in the Burr family. It was derived from Theodosius Bartow, father of Aaron Burr's first wife and mother of the girl lost at sea. The mother had been Theodosia the elder, after her father, and the Burrs had given their only daughter the same unusual name.

After her mother's passing in 1794, the daughter became her father's official hostess and truly "the woman in the house." More than that, she was his confidante and shared his thoughts a great deal more than many other daughters might have. Even after her marriage to Alston and subsequent move to Carolina, they kept in touch, and her family was really all the family he had. Thus their relationship was a truly close one, and it was not surprising that the first thought, after his "return from the dead," so to speak, would be to cry out for his Theo!

I wasn't satisfied with his identification as "Bertram Delmar," and insisted on his real name. But the communicator brushed my request aside and instead spoke of another matter.

"Where's the gun?"

"What gun?"

I recalled Sybil's remark about the smell of a gun having just been fired. I had to know more.

"What are you doing here?"

"Hiding."

"What are you hiding from?"

"You."

Was he mistaking me for someone else?

"I'm a friend," I tried to explain, but the voice interrupted me harshly.

"You're a soldier."

In retrospect one cannot help feeling that the emotionally disturbed personality was reliving the agony of being hunted down by U.S. soldiers prior to his arrest, confusing it, perhaps, in his mind with still another unpleasant episode when he was being hunted, namely, after he had shot Hamilton!

I decided to pry farther into his personal life in order to establish identity more firmly.

"Who is Theo? What is she to you?"

"I have to find her, take her away ... it is dangerous, the French are looking for me."

"Why would the French be looking for you?" I asked in genuine astonishment. Neither I nor Mrs. Leek had any notion of this French connection at that time.

"Soldiers watch...."

Through later research I learned that Burr had indeed been in France for several years, from 1808 to 1812. At first, his desire to have the Spanish American colonies freed met with approval by the then still revolutionary Bonaparte government. But when Napoleon's brother Joseph Napoleon was installed as King of Spain, and thus also ruler of the overseas territories, the matter became a political horse of another color; now Burr was advocating the overthrow of a French-owned government, and that could no longer be permitted.

Under the circumstances, Burr saw no point in staying in France, and made arrangements to go back to New York. But he soon discovered that the French government wouldn't let him go so easily. "All sorts of technical difficulties were put in his way," writes Dr. Samuel Engle Burr, "both the French and the American officials were in agreement to the effect that the best place for the former Vice-President was within the Empire of France." Eventually, a friendly nobleman very close to Napoleon himself managed to gee Burr out. But it is clear that Burr was under surveillance all that time and probably well aware of it!

I continued my questioning of the entity speaking through an entranced Sybil Leek, the entity who had glibly claimed to be a certain Bertram Delmar, but who knew so many things only Aaron Burr would have known.

What year was this, I asked.

"Eighteen ten."

In 1810, Burr had just reached France. The date fit in well with the narrative of soldiers watching him.

"Why are you frightened?" I asked.

"The soldiers, the soldiers...."

"Have you done anything wrong?"

"Who are you?"

"I'm a friend, sent to help you!"

"Traitor! You ... you betrayed me...."

"Tell me what you are doing, what are you trying to establish here?"

"Traitor!"

Later, as I delved into Burr's history in detail, I thought that this exchange between an angry spirit and a cool interrogator might refer to Burr's anger at General James Wilkinson, who had indeed posed as a friend and then betrayed Burr. Not the "friend" ostensibly helping Burr set up his western colony, but the traitor who later caused soldiers to be sent to arrest him. It certainly fit the situation. One must understand that in the confused mental state a newly contacted spirit personality often finds himself, events in his life take on a jumbled and fragmentary quality, often flashing on the inner mental screen like so many disconnected images from the emotional reel of his life. It is then the job of the psychic researcher to sort it all out.

I asked the communicator to "tell me all about himself" in the hope of finding some other wedge to get him to admit he was Aaron Burr.

"I escaped ... from the French."

"Where are the French?"

"Here."

This particular "scene" was apparently being re-enacted in his mind, during the period he lived in France.

"Did you escape from any particular French person?" I asked.

"Jacques ... de la Beau...."

The spelling is mine. It might have been different, but it *sounded* like "de la Beau."

"Who is Jacques de la Beau?"

Clenched teeth, hissing voice—"I'm ... not ... telling you. Even ... if you ... kill me."

I explained I had come to free him, and what could I do for him?

"Take Theo away ... leave me ... I shall die... ."

Again I questioned him about his identity. Now he switched his account and insisted he was French, born at a place called Dasney, near Bordeaux. Even while this information was coming from the medium's lips, I felt sure it was a way to throw me off his real identity. This was not unusual in some cases. When I investigated the ghost of General Samuel Edward McGowan some years ago, it took several weeks of trance sessions until he abandoned an assumed name and admitted an identity that could later be proven. Even the discarnates have their pride and emotional "hang-ups," as we say today.

The name Jacques de la Beau puzzled me. After the séance, I looked into the matter and discovered that a certain Jacques Prevost (pronounced pre-voh) had been the first husband of Aaron Burr's first wife, Theodosia. Burr, in fact, raised their two sons as his own, and there was a close link between them and Burr in later years. But despite his French name, Prevost was in the British service.

When Burr lived in New York, he had opened his home to

the daughter of a French admiral, from whom she had become separated as a consequence of the French Revolution. This girl, Natalie, became the close companion of Burr's daughter Theodosia, and the two girls considered themselves sisters. Natalie's father was Admiral de Lage de Volade. This name, too, has sounds similar to the "de la Beau" I thought I had understood. It might have been "de la voh" or anything in between the two sounds. Could the confused mind of the communicator have drawn from both Prevost and de Lage de Volade? Both names were of importance in Burr's life.

"Tell me about your wife," I demanded now.

"No. I don't like her."

I insisted, and he, equally stubborn, refused.

"Is she with you?" I finally said.

"Got rid of her," he said, almost with joy in the voice.

"Why?"

No good to me ... deceived me ... married...."

There was real disdain and anger in the voice now.

Clearly, the communicator was speaking of the second Mrs. Burr. The first wife had passed away a long time before the major events in his life occurred. It is perfectly true that Burr "got rid of her" (through two separations and one divorce action), and that she "deceived him," or rather tricked him into marrying her: He thought she was wealthier than she actually was, and their main difficulties were about money. In those days people did not always marry for love, and it was considered less immoral to have married someone for money than to deceive someone into marrying by the prospects of large holdings when they were in fact small. Perhaps today we think differently and even more romantically about such matters; in the 1830s, a woman's financial standing was as negotiable as a bank account.

The more I probed, the more excited the communicator became; the more I insisted on identification, the more cries of

"Theo! Theo!" came from the lips of Sybil Leek.

When I had first broached the subject of Theo's relation-ship to him, he had quickly said she was his sister. I brought this up again, and in sobbing tones he admitted this was not true. But he was not yet ready to give me the full story.

"Let me go," he sobbed.

"Not until you can go in peace," I insisted. "Tell me about yourself. You are proud of yourself, are you not?"

"Yes," the voice came amid heavy sobbing, "the disgrace ... the disgrace...."

"I will tell the world what you want me to say. I'm here as your spokesman. Use this chance to tell the world your side of the facts!"

There was a moment of hesitation, and then the voice, gentler, started up again.

"I ... loved ... Theo.... I have to ... find her... ."

The most important thought, evidently, was the loss of his girl. Even his political ambitions took a back seat to his pater-nal love.

"Is this place we're in part of your property?"

Forlornly, the voice said,

"I had a lot ... from the river ... to here."

Later I checked this statement with Mrs. Leroy Campbell, curator of the Morris-Jumel Mansion, and a professional his-torian who knew the period well.

"Yes, this is true," Mrs. Campbell confirmed, "Burr's prop-erty extended from the river and Varick Street eastward."

"But the lot from the river to here does not belong to a Bertram Delmar," I said to the communicator. "Why do you wish to fool me with names that do not exist?"

I launched this as a trial balloon. It took off.

"She calls *me* Bertram," the communicator admitted now. "I'm not ashamed of my name."

I nodded. "I'm here to help you right old wrongs, but you

must help me do this. I can't do it alone."

"I didn't kill ... got rid of her... ." he added, apparently willing to talk.

"You mean, your wife?"

"Had to."

"Did you kill *anyone*?" I continued the line of discussion.

"Killed ... to protect ... not wrong!"

"How did you kill?"

"A rifle... ."

Was he perhaps referring to his service in the Revolutionary War? He certainly did some shooting then.

But I decided to return to the "Bertram Delmar" business once more. Constant pressure might yield results.

"Truthfully, will you tell us who you are?"

Deliberately, almost as if he were reading an official communique, the voice replied, "I am Bertram Delmar and I shall not say *that name*... ."

"You must say 'that name' if you wish to see Theo again." I had put it on the line. Either cooperate with me, or I won't help you. Sometimes this is the only way you can get a recalcitrant spirit to "come across"—when this cooperation is essential both to his welfare and liberation and to the kind of objective proof required in science.

There was a moment of ominous quiet. Then, almost inaudibly, the communicator spoke.

"An awful name ... *Arnot*."

After the investigation I played the sound tapes back to make sure of what I had heard so faintly. It was quite clear. "The communicator" had said "*Arnot*."

My first reaction was, perhaps she is trying to say Aaron Burr and pronounce Aaron with a broad ah. But on checking this out with both Mrs. Campbell and Dr. Burr I found that such a pronunciation was quite impossible. The night after the séance I telephoned Dr. Burr at his Washington home and read the salient points of the transcript to him.

When I came to the puzzling name given by the communicator I asked whether Arnot meant anything inasmuch as I could not find it in the published biographies of Burr. There was a moment of silence on the other end of the line before Dr. Burr spoke.

"Quite so," he began. "It is not really generally known, but Aaron Burr did use a French cover name while returning from France to the United States, in order to avoid publicity. That name was *Arnot.*"

But back to the Cafe Bizarre and our investigation.

Having not yet realized the importance of the word Arnot, I continued to insist on proper identification.

"You must cleanse yourself of ancient guilt," I prodded.

"It is awful ... awful... ."

"Is Theo related to you?"

"She's mine."

"Are you related to her?"

"Lovely ... little one ... *daughter.*"

Finally, the true relationship had come to light.

"If Theo is your daughter, then you are not 'Bertram.'"

"You tricked me ... go away ... or else I'll kill you!" The voice sounded full of anger again.

"If you're not ashamed of your name, then I want to hear it from your lips."

Again, hesitatingly, the voice said,

"*Arnot.*"

"Many years have gone by. Do you know what year we're in now?"

"Ten... ."

"It is not 1810. A hundred fifty years have gone by."

"You're mad."

"You're using the body of a psychic to speak to us...."

The communicator had no use for such outrageous claims.

"I'm not going to listen... ."

But I made him listen. I told him to touch the hair, face, and ears of the "body" he was using as a channel and to see if it didn't feel strange indeed.

Step by step, the figure of Sybil, very tensed and angry a moment before, relaxed. When the hand found its way to the chin, there was a moment of startled expression:

"No beard...."

I later found that not a single one of the contemporary portraits of Aaron Burr shows him with a chin beard. Nevertheless, Alice McDermott had seen and drawn him with a goatee, and now Sybil Leek, under the control of the alleged Burr, also felt for the beard that was not there any longer.

Was there ever a beard?

"Yes," Dr. Burr confirmed, "there was, although this, too, is almost unknown except of course to specialists like myself. On his return from France, in 1812, Burr sported a goatee in the French manner."

By now I had finally gotten through to the person speaking through Sybil Leek, that the year was 1967 and not 1810.

His resistance to me crumbled.

"You're a strange person," he said, "I'm tired."

"Why do you hide behind a fictitious name?"

"People ... ask ... too many ... questions."

"Will you help me clear your name, not Bertram, but your real name?"

"I was betrayed."

"Who is the President of the United States in 1810?" I asked and regretted it immediately. Obviously this could not be an evidential answer. But the communicator wouldn't mention the hated name of the rival.

"And who is Vice-President?" I asked.

"Politics ... are bad ... they kill you ... I would not betray anyone... I was wronged ... politics ... are bad... ."

How true!

"Did you ever kill anyone?" I demanded.

"Not wrong ... to kill to ... preserve.... . I'm alone."

He hesitated to continue.

"What did you preserve? Why did you have to kill another person?"

"*Another* ... critical ... I'm not talking!"

"You must talk. It is necessary for posterity."

"I tried ... to be ... *the best*.... . I'm not a traitor ... soldiers ... beat the drum ... then you die ... politics!!"

As I later listened to this statement again and again, I understood the significance of it, coming, as it did, from a person who had not yet admitted he was Aaron Burr and through a medium who didn't even know where she was at the time.

He killed to *preserve his honor*—the accusations made against him in the campaign of 1804 for the governorship of New York were such that they could not be left unchallenged. Another was indeed *critical* of him, Alexander Hamilton being that person, and the criticisms such that Burr could not let them pass.

He "tried to be the best" also—he tried to be President of the United States, got the required number of electoral votes in 1800, but deferred to Jefferson, who also had the same number.

No, he was not a traitor, despite continued inference in some history books that he was. The treason trial of 1807 not only exonerated the former Vice President of any wrongdoing, but heaped scorn and condemnation on those who had tried him. The soldiers beating the drum prior to an execution could have become reality if Burr's enemies had won; the treason incident under which he was seized by soldiers on his return from the West included the death penalty if found guilty. That was the intent of his political enemies, to have this ambitious man removed forever from the political scene.

"Will you tell the world that you are not guilty?" I asked.

"I told them … trial … I am not a traitor, a murderer…."

I felt it important for him to free himself of such thoughts if he were to be released from his earthbound status.

"I … want to die …" the voice said, breathing heavily.

"Come, I will help you find Theo," I said, as promised.

But there was still the matter of the name. I felt it would help "clear the atmosphere" if I could get him to admit he was Burr.

I had already gotten a great deal of material, and the séance would be over in a matter of moments. I decided to gamble on the last minute or two and try to shock this entity into either admitting he was Burr or reacting to the name in some telling fashion.

I had failed in having him speak those words even though he had given us many incidents from the life of Aaron Burr. There was only one more way and I took it. "Tell the truth," I said, "are you Aaron Burr?"

It was as if I had stuck a red-hot poker into his face. The medium reeled back, almost upsetting the chair in which she sat. With a roar like a wounded lion, the voice came back at me,

"Go away … GO AWAY!! … or I'll kill you!"

"You will not kill me," I replied calmly. "You will tell me the truth."

"I will kill you to preserve my honor!!"

"I'm here to preserve your honor. I'm your friend."

The voice was like cutting ice.

"You said that once before."

"You are Aaron Burr, and this is part of your place."

"I'M BERTRAM!"

I decided not to continue the shouting match.

"Very well," I said, "for the world, then, let it be Bertram, if you're not ready to face it that you're Burr."

"I'm Bertram ..." the entity whispered now.

"Then go from this place and join your Theo. Be Bertram for her."

"Bertram ... you won't tell?" The voice was pleading.

"Very well." He would soon slip across the veil, I felt, and there were a couple of points I wanted to clear up before. I explained that he would soon be together with his daughter, leaving here after all this time, and I told him again how much time had elapsed since his death.

"I tarried ... I tarried ..." he said, pensively.

"What sort of a place did you have?" I asked.

"It was a big place ... with a big desk ... famous house... ." But he could not recall its name.

Afterward, I checked the statement with Mrs. Campbell, the curator at the Morris-Jumel Mansion. "That desk in the big house," she explained, "is right here in our Burr room. I was originally in his law office."

But the restless one was no longer interested in talking to me.

"I'm talking to Theo ..." he said, quietly now, "in the garden... . I'm going for a walk with Theo ... go away."

Within a moment, the personality who had spoken through Sybil Leek for the past hour was gone. Instead, Mrs. Leek returned to her own self, remembering absolutely nothing that had come through her entranced lips.

"Lights are bright," was the first thing she said, and she quickly closed her eyes again.

But a moment later, she awoke fully and complained only that she felt a bit tired.

I wasn't at all surprised that she did.

Almost immediately after I had returned home, I started my corroboration. After discussing the most important points with Dr. Samuel Engle Burr over the telephone, I arranged to have a full transcript of the séance sent to him for his comments.

So many things matched the Burr personality that there could hardly be any doubt that it vas Burr we had contacted. "I'm not a traitor and a murderer," the ghostly communicator had shouted. "Traitor and murderer" were the epithets thrown at Burr in his own lifetime by his enemies, according to Professor Burr, as quoted by Larry Chamblin in the *Allentown Call-Chronicle*.

Although he was not a direct descendant of Aaron Burr, the Washington educator was related to Theodosia Barstow Burr, the Vice-President's first wife. A much-decorated officer in both world wars, Professor Burr was a recognized educator and the definitive authority on his famous namesake. In consulting him, I was getting the best possible information.

Aaron Burr's interest in Mexico, Professor Burr explained, was that of a liberator from Spanish rule, but there never was any conspiracy against the United States government. "That charge stemmed from a minor incident on an island in Ohio. A laborer among his colonists pointed a rifle at a government man who had come to investigate the expedition."

Suddenly, the words about the rifle and the concern the communicator had shown about it became clear to me: It had led to more serious trouble for Burr.

Even President Wilson concurred with those who felt Aaron Burr had been given a "raw deal" by historical tradition. Many years ago he stood at Burr's grave in Princeton and remarked, "How misunderstood ... how maligned!"

It was now 132 years since Burr's burial, and the falsehoods concerning Aaron Burr were still about the land, despite the two excellent books by Dr. Samuel Engle Burr and the discreet but valiant efforts of the Aaron Burr Association which the Washington professor heads.

In piecing together the many evidential bits and pieces of the trance session, it was clear to me that Aaron Burr had at last said his piece. Why had he not pronounced a name he had been justly proud of in his lifetime? He had not hesitated to call repeatedly for Theo, identify her as his daughter, speak of his troubles in France and of his political career—why this insistence to remain the fictitious Bertram Delmar in the face of so much proof that he was indeed Aaron Burr?

All the later years of his life, Burr had encountered hostility, and he had learned to be careful whom he chose as friends, whom he could trust. Gradually, this bitterness became so strong that in his declining years he felt himself to be a lonely, abandoned old man, his only daughter gone forever, and no one to help him carry the heavy burden of his life. Passing across into the nonphysical side of life in such a state of mind, and retaining it by that strange quirk of fate that makes some men into ghostly images of their former selves, he would not abandon that one remaining line of defense against his fellow men: his anonymity.

Why should he confide in me, a total stranger, whom he had never met before, a man, moreover, who spoke to him under highly unusual conditions, conditions he himself neither understood nor accepted? It seemed almost natural for Burr's surviving personality to be cautious in admitting his identity.

But his ardent desire to find Theo was stronger than his caution; we therefore were able to converse more or less freely about this part of his life. And so long as he needed not say he was Burr, he felt it safe to speak of his career also, especially when my questions drove him to anger, and thus lessened his critical judgment as to what he could say and what he should withhold from me.

Ghosts were people, too, and they were subject to the same emotional limitations and rules that govern us all.

Mrs. Leek had no way of obtaining the private, specific knowledge and information that had come from her entranced lips in this investigation; I myself had almost none of it until after the séance had ended, and thus could not have furnished her any of the material from my own unconscious mind. And the others present during the séance—my wife, Mrs. Allmen, and the television people knew even less about all this.

Neither Dr. Burr nor Mrs. Campbell were present at the Cafe Bizarre, and their minds, if they contained any of the Burr information, could not have been tapped by the medium either, if such were indeed possible.

Coincidence cannot be held to account for such rare pieces of information as Burr's cover name Arnot, the date, the goatee, and the very specific character of the one speaking through Mrs. Leek, and his concern for the clearing of his name from the charges of treason and murder.

That we had indeed contacted the restless and unfree spirit of Aaron Burr at what used to be his stables was now the only physical building still extant that was truly his own, I do not doubt in the least.

The defense rests, and hopefully, so does a happier Aaron Burr, now forever reunited with his beloved daughter Theodosia.

COME AND MEET MY GHOST!

*M*argaret Widdemer was a spirited lady in her sunny years, a famed author and prizewinner, who had for years made her home in the New York studio building on West Sixty-seventh Street called the Hotel des Artistes. It was the sort of place that cries out for a ghost, modeled on European studios and full of eerie, half-lit corridors and nooks. The tenants were painters, writers, and teachers.

Ms. Widdemer lived in a roomy duplex, with a pleasantly crammed living room downstairs, and a wooden staircase winding to the upper story, which was divided unevenly between her workroom and a small bedroom.

All her life, Margaret Widdemer, poet and novelist, had had psychic experiences of one kind or another. Pennsylvania-born, she had visions of the dead many times.

Ms. Widdemer bought her apartment in the mid-1940s, from a Mrs. Gertrude F., who had since passed on. Mrs. F. had another apartment a few doors away herself; she, her husband, and a daughter were among the original shareholders of the building, built around 1910.

Elizabeth Byrd, a mutual friend, had told me of her uncanny

feelings in Margaret Widdemer's apartment.

It intrigued me sufficiently to make an appointment for a visit, but I did not feel that the presence of a medium was required—the evidence was too slender. Thus I arrived at the Hotel des Artistes on a damp night in February, accompanied only by my tape recorder and immense good will toward whoever it was who was present in the place!

I asked Ms. Widdemer what her unusual experiences in the apartment had been.

"There have been unexplained noises, bangings of doors and such, and my cleaning woman would say, 'I thought you were in.' She would say 'I just saw someone walk up the stairs'—but, of course, I was not in. The same thing would happen to me. I was here alone, and I thought my maid had come in, because I heard footsteps going up and down the stairs, but on checking I found she hadn't come in at all."

Present were Elizabeth Byrd, Mrs. L. (a psychic neighbor from across the hall), and Barrie Gaunt, the young English designer and actor whose own haunted apartment we had visited not long before down on Charles Street.

For the past few minutes, Barrie had been restless and I saw him wandering about the place, up and down the stairs, as if searching for something or someone. The house was strange to him, of course, and I thought he was just exploring with the natural curiosity of the artist. But he seemed perplexed, and I began to wonder if he had sensed anything out of the ordinary.

"Someone came up these stairs," he finally said, "stopped about here and turned around—hate in the eyes. It's a woman."

His left hand felt strangely stiff, he added. And he had a feeling that someone was murdered here.

Elizabeth Byrd, too, had had an unusual experience in the apartment in April.

"I was having dinner with Margaret, and at one point

wanted to go to the powder room. I went up the stairs, and the minute I got to the top of the stairs, I was seized with fear. I blundered into the other rooms before I could get my bearings. I didn't want to yell for help, because Margaret walks with a cane and would have had to scramble up the stairs to help me. I couldn't get down again fast enough. I was really scared, and I don't scare easily."

I turned my attention once more to Barrie Gaunt.

"I feel a great tragedy here," he said, "especially on the staircase where the curve is. I feel an agonizing screaming. In the room directly above this, there is a complete turmoil. A very beautiful woman, I feel, also a man, and I feel there's been a death here, a death by violence. The woman is fighting for her life, but not physically. Rather, she is fighting for *her mentality*. The person who is dead in this apartment is the man."

Everybody stared at Barrie now, as it turned out that we had a medium among us, after all, even though I had not brought one.

"Go on," I said, but it was hardly necessary. Barrie was engrossed in his impressions.

"The tragedy involved both people in this apartment. I just know it." Still shaken with the eerie feelings that had beset him on the stairs, Barrie reiterated his conviction of a terrible struggle going on and the woman's agony stood vividly etched on his expressive face.

I decided it was time to break up our meeting, and thanked our hostess. A few days later, Margaret Widdemer was able to supply some of the answers to the questions raised by Barrie Gaunt.

"The F. girl, Christy, was a tall, very beautiful blonde with great blue eyes," she said. "When she was around seventeen, she suddenly went raving mad, and became so violent that she had to be removed. There was a history of disturbance on both sides of the family, it is alleged, and her hatred directed itself, for reasons unknown, against her own mother. She was placed in an insane asylum at Middletown, New York. Her mother could not even visit her, so violent was the poor girl's reaction."

"Then the girl lived here for a while, before they removed her?" I asked.

"Evidently so," Ms. Widdemer said; she explained that Mrs. L., her neighbor, had helped her gather this information.

Was it the father restraining his raving daughter that Barrie had sensed on the stairs? He was dead now, and no information on how he died was available.

The question now: Was the girl still living at the asylum? A few days later, that question, too, was answered. She had died some time ago, still raving mad.

Barrie Gaunt, of course, could not have known any of these facts. I took a series of photographs in the apartment, none of which showed anything unusual. Was it an etheric impression then that Barrie had sensed, a re-enactment of the emotional events of the past? Or was the ghost of the poor girl still holding on to her one-time home, struggling against the brute force that was to take her away from it forever?

THE SPY HOUSE GHOSTS
OF NEW JERSEY

*I*n June, 1696, one Daniel Seabrook, aged 26 and a planter by profession, took his inheritance of 80 pounds sterling and bought 202 acres of property from his stepfather, Thomas Whitlock. For 250 years this plantation was in the hands of the Seabrook family who worked the land and sailed their ships from the harbor. The "Spy House" is one of the finer pieces of Colonial architecture available for inspection in the eastern United States, having been restored meticulously over the years.

The house was built in the old manner, held together with wooden pegs. There were handmade bricks, filled with clay mortar. The house has two stories and is painted white. Every room had its own fireplace, as that was the only way in which Colonial houses could be heated.

The house, which was located near Middletown, New Jersey, could easily be reached from New York City. It was being kept by a group headed by curator Gertrude Neidlinger, helped by her historian-brother, Travis Neidlinger, and as a museum, it displays not only the furniture of the Colonial period but some of the implements of the whalers who were active in the area well into the nineteenth century. As an historical attraction, it is something that should not be missed by anyone, apart from any ghostly connections.

One of the rooms in the house was dedicated to the period of the Battle of Monmouth. This room, called the spy room by the British for good reasons, as we shall see, had copies of the documents kept among General Washington's private papers in the Library of Congress in Washington, D.C.

In 1778, the English were marching through Middletown, pillaging and burning the village. Along the shoreline the Monmouth militia and the men who were working the whale boats, got together to try to cut down the English shipping. General Washington asked for a patriot from Shoal Harbor, which was the name of the estate where the spy house was located, to help the American side fight the British. The volunteer was a certain Corporal John Stillwell, who was given a telescope and instructions to spy on the British from a hill called Garrett's Hill, not far away, the highest point in the immediate area.

The lines between British and Americans were intertwined and frequently intercut each other, and it was difficult for individuals to avoid crossing them at times. The assignment given Corporal Stillwell was not an easy one, especially as some of his own relatives favored the other side of the war. Still, he was able to send specific messages to the militia who were able to turn these messages into attacks on the British fleet.

At that point, Stillwell observed there were 1,037 vessels in the fleet lying off the New Jersey coastline, at a time when the American forces had no navy at all. But the fishermen and their helpers on shore did well in this phase of the Revolutionary War. John Stillwell's son, Obadiah Stillwell, seventeen years old, served as message carrier from his father's observation point to the patriots.

Twenty-three naval battles were fought in the harbor after the Battle of Monmouth. The success of the whaleboat operation was a stunning blow to the British fleet and a great embarrassment. Even daylight raids became so bold and successful that, in one day, two pilot boats were captured upsetting the harbor shipping.

Finally, the British gave the order to find the spy and end the rebel operation. The searching party declared the Seabrook homestead as a spy house, since they knew its owner, Major Seabrook, was a patriot. They did not realize that the real spy was John Stillwell, operating from Garrett's Hill. Nevertheless, they burned the spy house. It was later restored.

Gertrude Neidlinger turned to me for help with the several ghosts she felt in the house. Considering the history of the house, it was not surprising that there should be ghosts there. Miss Neidlinger, herself, had felt someone in the entrance room whenever she was alone in the house, especially at night. There was also a lady in white who comes down from the attic, walks along the hall and goes into what was called the blue and white room, and there tucks in the covers of a crib or bed. Then she turns and goes out of sight. Miss Neidlinger was not sure who she was, but thought she might have been the spirit of Mrs. Seabrook, who lived through the Revolutionary War in a particularly dangerous position, having relatives on both sides of the political fence.

I brought Ingrid Beckman, my psychic friend, to the spy house, which was located in Keansburg, New Jersey, near Middletown. The number on the house was 119, but of course everyone in the area calls it the Spy House. As Ingrid walked about the place, she immediately pointed out its ancient usage as an outpost. While we were investigating the house, we both clearly heard footsteps overhead where there was no one walking. Evidently, the ghosts knew of our arrival.

Without knowing anything about the history of the

house, Ingrid commented, "Down here around the fireplace I feel there are people planning strategy, worried about British ships." Then she continued, "This was to mobilize something like the minutemen, farming men who were to fight. This was a strategic point because it was the entry into New York."

I then asked Ingrid to tell me whether she felt any ghosts, any residues of the past still in the house.

When we went upstairs, Ingrid tuned into the past with a bang. "There's a woman here. She ties in with this house and something about spying, some kind of spying went on here." Then she added, "Somebody spied behind the American lines and brought back information."

Upstairs near the window on the first floor landing, Ingrid felt a man watching, waiting for someone to come his way. Ingrid felt there was a man present who had committed an act of treason, a man who gave information back to the British. His name was Samuels. She felt that this man was hanged publicly. The people call him an ex-patriot. This was the entity, Ingrid said, who couldn't leave this house out of remorse.

Ingrid also asserted that the house was formerly used as a public house, an inn, when meetings took place here. The curator, Miss Neidlinger, later confirmed this. Also, Ingrid felt that among the families living in the area, most of the members served in the patriot militia, but that there were occasional traitors, such as George Taylor. Colonel George Taylor might have been the man to whom Ingrid was referring. As for the man who was hanged, it would have been Captain Huddy, and he was hanged for having caused the death of a certain Philip White. Captain Joshua Huddy had been unjustly accused of having caused the death of the patriot Philip White and despite his innocence, was lynched by the patriots. Again, Ingrid had touched on something very real from history.

But ghostly lady and the man who was hanged and the man who stared out the window onto the bay were not the only ghosts at the spy house. On the Fourth of July, 1975, a group of local boys were in the house in the blue and white room upstairs. Suddenly, the sewing machine door opened by itself and the pedals worked themselves without benefit of human feet. One of the boys looked up, and in the mirror in the bureau across the room, he could see a face with a long beard.

Another boy looked down the hall and there he saw a figure with a tall black hat and a long beard and sort of very full trousers as they were worn in an earlier age. That was enough for them and they ran from the house and never went back again.

One of the ladies who assisted the curator, Agnes Lyons, refused to do any typing in the upstairs room because the papers simply will not stand still. A draft seemed to go by all the time and blow the papers to the floor, even though the windows were closed. A Mrs. Lillian Boyer also saw the man with the beard standing at the top of the stairs, wearing a black hat and dressed in the period of the later 1700s. He had very large eyes, and seemed to be a man in his forties. He just stood there looking at her and she of course wouldn't pass him. Then he seemed to flash some sort of light back and forth, a brilliant light like a flashlight. And there were footsteps all over the house at the same time. She could even hear the man breathe, yet he was a ghost!

If you want to visit the Spy House, it is now operated as a museum, and its address is in Port Monmouth, New Jersey.

THE STRANGE CASE OF
THE COLONIAL SOLDIER

*S*omerton, Pennsylvania, was a suburb of Philadelphia, albeit a pretty outlying one. It takes you all of an hour by car from downtown Philadelphia, but when you get there, it's worth it, especially Byberry Road. How the builders of modern chunks of concrete managed to overlook this delightful country lane in the backyard of the big city was beyond my knowledge, but the fact is that we have here a winding, bumpy road, good enough for one car at a time, that goes for several miles without a single high-rise building. Instead, old homes line it in respectable intervals, allowing even a bit of green and open spaces between the dwellings.

One of the most unusual sights along this winding road was a pretty, wooden Colonial house built in 1732, and untouched except for minor alterations, mainly inside the house. That in itself was a rarity, of course, but the owners who lived here since the Revolutionary period evidently were house-proud people who *cared*.

The tenants were David and Dolores Robinson, whose greatest pleasure was being in that house. They didn't advertise the fact they've got an authentic pre-Revolutionary home, but they're not exactly shy about it either; to them, it was a thrill to live as our ancestors did, without the constant urge to "improve" things with shiny new gadgets that frequently don't work, or to tear down some portion of their home just because it looked old or has been used for a long time.

The Robinsons were house-proud, and they had a keen sense of the antiquarian without any formal education in that area. Mr. Robinson worked for the telephone company and his wife worked for her brother, a photographer, as a retouch artist. Both were in early middle age and they had three children in the pre-teenage group.

Theirs was a happy family without problems or frustrations: They'd like to make a little more money, advance a little faster, get a better car—but that was the normal American's dream. With the Robinsons lived Mr. Robinson Senior, an elderly gentleman whose main occupation seemed to be watching TV.

I first heard of the Robinsons and their homestead when I appeared on a local radio show in the area, and I was contacted. I was fascinated by the prospect of an apparently untouched house with many layers of history clinging to it that a psychic might be able to sense. I put the house on my mental list of places to visit for possible psychometry experiments.

Finally, several years later, that opportunity arose, and a friend of ours, Tom Davis, drove us out to Byberry Road. There's something strange about Philadelphia distances; they grow on you somehow, especially at night. So it was with considerable delay that we finally showed up at the house, but we were made welcome just the same by the owners.

The house could not be missed even in the dark of night. It was the only one of its kind in the area, and sat back a bit from the road. With its graceful white pillars that supported the roof of the porch, it was totally different from anything built nowadays, or even in Victorian times. From the outside it looked smaller than it really was. There were three stories, and a storage room beneath the rear part of the house, the oldest portion. We entered through the front door and found ourselves in a delightfully appointed living room leading off to the left into the older portion of the house. The house had a mixture of Colonial and Victorian furniture in it; somehow not out of context with the over-all mood of the place, which was one of remoteness from the modern world. Across the narrow hall from the downstairs living room, a staircase led to the next floor, which contained bedrooms and one of the largest bathrooms I ever saw. Considering the Colonial reluctance to bathe to excess, it struck me as incongruous, until I realized later that the house had had some quasi-public usage at one period.

A few steps led from the living room to the rear section, which was the original portion of the house. A large fireplace dominated it. Next to it was a rear staircase also leading to the upper stories, and the low ceiling showed the original wooden beams just as they were in pre-Revolutionary days.

The Robinsons weren't particularly addicted to the psychic, but Mrs. Robinson admitted to having had ESP experiences all her life. When she was fourteen, she was reading in bed one night, and it was very, very late. This was against the rules, so she had made sure the door to her bedroom was shut. Suddenly, the door opened and her brother Paul stood there looking at her reproachfully. But, he had been dead for eight years. Dolores screamed and went under the covers. Her mother rushed upstairs to see what was the matter. When she arrived, the door was still wide open!

After that time, Mrs. Robinson often knew things before they really happened—such as who would be at the door before she answered it, or just before the telephone rang, who would be calling. Today, this was just a game to her, and neither her husband nor she takes it too seriously. Both of them were educated: Dolores had some college training, and her husband had electro-engineering skills that he used professionally.

Nevertheless, they didn't scoff at the possibility that an old house might contain some elements from its violent past.

When they first moved into the house in 1960, Mrs. Robinson felt right at home in it, as if she had always lived there. From the very first, she found it easy to move up and down the stairs even in the dark without the slightest accident or need to orient herself. It was almost as if the house, or someone in it, were guiding her steps.

But soon the Robinsons became acutely aware that the house was *alive:* There were strange noises and creaking boards, which they promptly ascribed to the settling of an old building. But there were also human footsteps that both husband and wife heard, and there were those doors. The doors, in particular, puzzled them. The first time Mrs. Robinson noticed anything unusual about the doors in their house was when she was working late over some photography assignments she had brought home with her. Her husband was out for the evening and the three children were fast asleep upstairs. The children have their bedrooms on the third floor, while the Robinsons sleep on the second floor. Suddenly Mrs. Robinson heard footsteps on the ceiling above her bedroom. Then the door of the stairwell opened, steps reverberated on the stairs, then the door to the second floor opened, and a blast of cold air hit her. Without taking her eyes from her work, Mrs. Robinson said, "Go back to bed!" assuming it was one of her children who had gotten up for some reason. There was no answer.

She looked up, and there was no one there. Annoyed, she rose and walked up the stairs to check her children's rooms. They were indeed fast asleep. Not satisfied and thinking that one of them must be playing tricks on her, she woke them one by one and questioned them. But they had trouble waking up, and it was evident to Mrs. Robinson that she was on a fool's errand; her children had not been down those stairs.

That was the beginning of a long succession of incidents

involving the doors in the house. Occasionally, she would watch with fascination when a door opened quite by itself, without any logical cause, such as wind or draft; or to see a door open for her just as she was about to reach for the doorknob. At least, whatever presence there was in the old house, was polite: It opened the door to a lady! But reassuring it was not, for to live with the unseen can be infuriating, too. Many times she would close a door, only to see it stand wide open again a moment later when she knew very well it could not do that *by itself.*

She began to wonder whether there wasn't perhaps a hidden tunnel beneath their back living room. Frequently they would hear a booming sound below the floor, coming from the direction of the cold storage room below. The doors would continually open for her now, even when she was alone in the house and the children could not very well be blamed for playing pranks on her. During the summer of 1966, there were nights when the activities in the house rose to frenzy comparable only with the coming and going of large crowds. On one occasion her daughter Leigh came down the stairs at night wondering who was in the living room. She could hear the noises up to the top floor! That night Mrs. Robinson was awakened six times by footsteps and closing doors.

Around that time also, her father-in-law reported a strange experience in his room on the second floor. He was watching television when his door opened late one night, and a woman came in. He was so startled by this unexpected visitor, and she disappeared again so quickly, he did not observe her too closely, but he thought she had either long black hair or a black veil. There was of course no one of that description in the house at the time.

Then there were those moments when an invisible rocking chair in the living room would rock by itself as if someone were in it.

Just prior to our visit, Mrs. Robinson's patience was being

sorely tried. It was the week of April 4, and we had already announced our coming about a week or so afterward. Mrs. Robinson was on the cellar stairs when she heard a clicking sound and looked up. A rotisserie rack was sailing down toward her! Because she had looked up, she was able to duck, and the missile landed on the stairs instead of on her head. But she thought this just too much. Opening doors, well, all right, but rotisserie racks? It was high time we went down to see her.

I carefully went all over the house, examining the walls, floors, and especially the doors. They were for the most part heavy hinged doors, the kind that do not slide easily but require a healthy push before they will move. We looked into the back room and admired the beams, and I must confess I felt very uneasy in that part of the house. Both my wife and I had an oppressive feeling, as if we were in the presence of something tragic, though unseen, and we could not get out of there fast enough.

I promised the Robinsons to return with a good psychometrist and perhaps have a go at trance, too, if I could get Mrs. Leek to come down with me on her next visit east. The prospect of finding out what it was that made their house so lively, and perhaps even learn more about its colorful past, made the mysterious noises more bearable for the Robinsons, and they promised to be patient and bear with me until I could make the required arrangements.

Finally Mrs. Leek and I were planning to appear on Murray Burnett's radio program together, and when I mentioned what else we intended doing in the area, Murray's eyes lit up and he offered to include himself in the expedition and drive us to and fro.

The offer was gladly accepted, and after a dinner at one of Murray's favorite places—during which not a word was exchanged about the Robinson house—we were off in search of adventure in his car. "It it's one thing I do well," he intoned, as we shot out onto the expressway, "it's driving an automobile." He did indeed. He drove with verve and so fast we missed the proper exit, and before long we found ourselves at a place called King of Prussia, where even a Prussian would have been lost.

We shrugged our combined shoulders and turned around, trying to retrace our steps. Murray assured me he knew the way and would have us at the Robinson house in no time at all. There was a time problem, for we all had to be back in the studio by eleven so that we could do the radio program that night. But the evening was still young and the Pennsylvania countryside lovely.

It was just as well that it was, for we got to see a good deal of it that evening. There was some confusion between Roosevelt Boulevard and Roosevelt Avenue, and the directions I had faithfully written down were being interpreted by us now the way two of Rommel's Afrika Korps officers must have studied the caravan routes.

"We should have turned off where we didn't," I finally remarked, and Murray nodded grimly. The time was about an hour after our appointed hour. No doubt the Robinsons must be thinking we're lost, I thought. At least I hoped that that's what they would think, not that we had abandoned *the project*.

The neighborhood seemed vaguely familiar now; no doubt it was. We had been through it several times already that same evening. Were the "forces" that kept opening and closing doors at the Robinson homestead preventing our coming so that they could continue to enjoy their anonymity?

When you're lost in Pennsylvania, you're really lost. But now Murray came to a decision. He turned north and we entered an entirely different part of town. It bore no similarity to the direction in which we wanted to go, but at least it was a well-lit section of town. I began to understand Murray's strategy: He was hoping we would run across someone—no, that's an unhappy word—*find* someone who just might know which way Somerton was. We met several motorists who didn't and several others who thought they did but really didn't, as we found out when we tried to follow their directions.

Ultimately, Murray did the smart thing: He hailed the first cop he saw and identified himself, not without pride. Everybody in Philadelphia knew his radio show.

"We're lost, officer," he announced, and explained our predicament.

"It's Mercury retrograding," Sybil mumbled from the back seat. All during our wild ghost chase she had insisted that astrologically speaking it was not at all surprising that we had gotten lost.

"Beg your pardon?" the officer said, and looked inside.

"Never mind Mercury," Murray said impatiently, "will you please show us the way?"

"I'll do better than that, sir," the policeman beamed back, "I'll personally escort you."

And so it came to pass that we followed a siren-tooting patrol car through the thick and thin of suburban Philadelphia.

Suddenly, the car in front of us halted. Murray proved how skillful a driver he really was. He did not hit anyone when he pulled up short. He merely jumbled *us*.

"Anything wrong, officer?" Murray asked, a bit nervously. It was half past nine now.

"My boundary," the officer explained. "I've already called for my colleague to take you on further."

We sat and waited another ten minutes, then another police car came up and whisked us in practically no time to our destination. When the Robinsons saw the police car escort us to their house, they began to wonder what on earth we had been up to. But they were glad to see us, and quickly we entered the house. Sybil was hysterical with laughter by now, and if we had had something to drink en route, the whole odyssey might have been a jolly good party. But now her face froze as she entered the downstairs portion of the house. I watched her expression change, but before I had a chance to question her, she went to the lady's room. On emerging from it she reported that the first word that had impressed itself upon her was a name—"Ross."

She explained that she felt the strongest influence of this person to the right of the fireplace in the oldest part of the house, so I decided we should go to that area and see what else she might pick up.

Although the house itself was started in 1732, the particular section we were in had definitely been dated to 1755 by local historians, all of whom admired the Robinson house as a showcase and example of early American houses.

"Seventeen forty-six is what I get," Sybil commented.

"Sybil's underbidding you," I remarked to Mrs. Robinson.

"This is some kind of a meeting place," Sybil continued her appraisal of the room, "many people come here ... 1744 ... and the name Ross. The whole house has an atmosphere which is not unpleasant, but rather *alive*."

Just as Mrs. Robinson had felt on first contact with the house, I thought. As for the meeting place, I later found out that the house was used as a Quaker meeting house in the 1740s and later, and even today the "Byberry Friends" meet down the road! John Worthington, the first owner of the house, was an overseer for the meeting house in 1752.

"There are many impressions here," Sybil explained as she psychometrized the room more closely, "many people meeting here, but this is superimposed on one dominant male person, this Ross."

After a moment of further walking about, she added, "The date 1774 seems to be very important."

She pointed at a "closet" to the right of the ancient fireplace, and explained that this personality seemed to be strongest there.

"It's a staircase," Mrs. Robinson volunteered, and opened the door of the "closet." Behind it a narrow, winding wooden staircase led to the upper floors.

I motioned to Sybil to sit down in a comfortable chair near the fireplace, and we grouped ourselves around her. We had perhaps thirty minutes left before we were to return to Philadelphia, but for the moment I did not worry about that. My main concern was the house: What would it tell us about its history? What tragedies took place here and what human emotions were spent in its old walls?

Soon we might know. Sybil was in deep trance within a matter of minutes.

"Ross," the voice speaking through Sybil said faintly now, "I'm Ross. John Ross.... Virtue in peace... ."

"Is this your house?"

"No."

"Then what are you doing here?"

"Praying. Hope for peace. Too much blood. People must pray for peace."

"Is there a war going on?"

"I say there's war ... the enemies are gone... ."

"Are you a soldier?"

"Captain—John—Ross," the voice said, stressing each word as if it were painful to pronounce it.

"What regiment?" I shot back, knowing full well that regimental lists exist and can be checked out for names.

"Twenty-first."

"Cavalry or Infantry?"

"I—am—for—peace."

"But what branch of the Army were you in?"

"Twenty-first of Horse."

This is an old English expression for cavalry.

"Who is your superior officer?" I asked.

"Colonel Moss is bad ... he must pray... ."

"Who commands?"

"Albright."

"Where did you serve?"

"Battle ... here... ."

He claimed to be thirty-eight years old, having been born in 1726. This would make him thirty-eight in the year 1764. His place of birth was a little place named Verruck, in Holstein, and when he said this I realized I had detected a very faint trace of a foreign accent in the entranced voice of the medium.

"Are you German then?" I asked.

"German?" he asked, not comprehending.

"Are you American?"

"American—is good," he said, with appreciation in his voice. Evidently we had before us a mercenary of the British Army.

"Are you British?" I tried.

"Never!" he hissed back.

"Whom do you serve?"

"The thirteen ... pray... ."

Was he referring to the thirteen colonies, the name by which the young republic was indeed known during the revolutionary war?

"This Albrecht... . What is his first name?"

"Dee-an-no ... I don't like him... . Peace for this country!!! It was meant for peace."

I could not make out what he meant by Dee-an-no, or what sounded like it. I then questioned the personality whether he was hurt.

"I wait for them to fetch me," he explained, haltingly, "sickness, make way for me!"

"Why are you in this house—what is there here?"

"Meeting place to pray."

"What religion are you?"

"Religion of peace and silence."

Suddenly, the medium broke into almost uncontrollable sighs and cries of pain. Tears flowed freely from Sybil's closed eyes. The memory of something dreadful must have returned to the communicator.

"I'm dying ... hands hurt.... Where is my hand?"

You could almost see the severed hand, and the broken tone of voice realizing the loss made it the more immediate and dramatic.

"I—am—for peace... ."

"What sort of people come here?"

"Silent people. To meditate."

What better way to describe a Quaker meeting house?

"Don't stop praying," he beseeched us.

We promised to pray for him. But would he describe his activities in this house?

"Send for the Friend ... dying."

He wanted spiritual guidance, now that he was at death's door. The term Friend is the name for what we call a Quaker.

Was there someone he wanted us to send for?

"William Proser ... my brother ... in England."

"Were you born in England?"

"No. William."

"He is your brother?"

"All—men—are—brothers."

He seemed to have trouble speaking. I started to explain what our mission was and that we wanted to help him find the elusive peace he so longed for.

"Name some of your fellow officers in the regiment," I then requested.

"Erich Gerhardt," the voice said. "Lieutenant Gerhardt."

"Was he in the cavalry? What regiment?"

"My—cavalry—Twenty-first—"

"What year did you serve together? What year are we in now?"

"Seventy-four."

"Where are you stationed?"

Sybil was completely immersed in the past now, with her face no longer hers; instead, we were watching a man in deep agony, struggling to speak again. Murray Burnett had his fingers at his lips, his eyes focused on the medium. It was clear he had never witnessed anything like it, and the extraordinary scene before him was bound to leave a deep and lasting impression, as indeed it did.

But the question went unanswered. Instead, Sybil was suddenly back again, or part of her, anyway. She seemed strangely distraught, however.

"Hands are asleep," she murmured, and I quickly placed her back into the hypnotic state so that the personality of Captain Ross might continue his testimony.

"Get me out, get me out," Sybil screamed now, "my hands … my hands are asleep… ."

I realized that the severed hand or hands of the Colonial soldier had left a strong imprint. Quickly I suggested that she go back into trance. I then recalled her to her own self, suggesting at the same time that no memory of the trance remain in her conscious mind.

Pearls of sweat stood on Sybil's forehead as she opened her eyes. But she was in the clear. Nothing of the preceding hour had remained in her memory. After a moment of heavy silence, we rose. It was time to return to the city, but Murray did not care. He knew that his producer, Ted Reinhart, would stall for time by playing a tape, if need be. The Robinsons offered us a quick cup of coffee, which tasted even more delicious than usual, under the circumstances. Everybody was very tense, and I thought how wise it had been of Mrs. Robinson to keep the children away from the séance.

Hurriedly, we picked up our gear and drove back to the station. It took us about one-fifth of the time it had taken us to come out. Murray Burnett showed his skill behind the wheel as he literally flew along the expressway. Traffic was light at this hour and we managed to get back just as the announcer said, "And now, ladies and gentlemen, Murray Burnett and his guests... ."

As if nothing had happened, we strode onto the platform and did a full hour of light banter. By the time we left Philadelphia to return to New York, though, Sybil was exhausted. When we staggered out of our coaches in New York, it was well past one in the morning. The silence of the night was a welcome relief from the turbulent atmosphere of the early evening.

The following day I started to research the material obtained in the Robinson homestead.

To begin with, the Robinsons were able to trace previous ownership back only to 1841, although the local historical society assured her that it was built in 1732. The early records are often sketchy or no longer in existence because so many wars—both of foreign origin and Native American—had been fought around the area, not counting fire and just plain carelessness.

The Robinsons were the ninth family to own the place since the Civil War period. Prior to that the only thing known for certain was that it had been a Quaker meeting house, and this fit in with the references Sybil had made in trance.

But what about Ross?

The gentleman had claimed that he was Captain John Ross, and the year, at the beginning of our conversation, was 1764.

In W. C. Ford's *British Officers Serving in America 1754-1774*, I found, on page 88, that there was a certain Captain John Ross, commissioned November 8, 1764. This man of course was a Tory, that is, he would have fought on the side of the British. Now the Revolutionary War started only in April 1775, and the man had expressed a dislike for the British and admiration for the "thirteen," the American colonies. Had he somehow switched sides during the intervening years? If he were a German mercenary, this would not have been at all surprising. Many of these men, often brought here against their desire, either left the British armies or even switched sides. Later on he referred to the date 1774, and Sybil had said it was important. At that time the war was already brewing even though no overt acts had happened. But the atmosphere in this area was tense. It was the seat of the Continental Congress, and skirmishes between Tories and Revolutionaries were not uncommon, although they were on a small or even individual level. What traumatic experience had happened to Captain Ross at that time? Did he lose his hands then?

I needed additional proof for his identity, of course. The name John Ross was fairly common. A John Ross was Betsy Ross's husband. He was guarding munitions on the Philadelphia waterfront one night in 1776 when the munitions and Ross blew up. Another John Ross was a purchasing agent for the Continental Army, and he used much of his own money in the process. Although Robert Morris later tried to help him get his money back, he never really did, and only recently his descendants petitioned Congress for payment of this ancient debt of honor. Neither of these was our man, I felt, especially so as I recalled his German accent and the claim that he was born in a little place called Verruck in Holstein. That place name really had me stumped, but with the help of a librarian at the New York Public Library I got hold of some German source books. There was a tiny hamlet near Oldesloe, Holstein, called Viertbruch. An English-speaking person would pronounce this more like "Vertbrook." Although it was not on any ordinary map, it was listed in Mueller's *Grosses Deutsches Wortbuch*, published in Wuppertal in 1958, on page 1008.

Proser, his brother's name, was a German name. Why had he adopted an English name? Perhaps he had spent many years in England and felt it more expedient. He also mentioned belonging to the 21st Cavalry Regiment. The Captain John Ross I found in the records served in the 31st, not the 21st. On the other hand, there is, curiously enough, another Ross, first name David, listed for the 21st Regiment for the period in question, 1774.

I could not trace the superior named Albright or Albrecht, not knowing whether this was someone German or English. Since the first name given us by the communicator was unclear, I can't even be sure if the Philip Albright, a captain in the Pennsylvania Rifles 1776-1777, according to F. B. Heitman, *Historical Register of the Continental Army during the War of the Revolution*, was this man. This Philip Albright was a rebel, and if he was only a captain in 1776 he could not have been John Ross's commanding officer in 1774, unless he had changed sides, of course.

I was more successful with the fellow officer Lieutenant "Gerhardt," who also served in "his" 21st Regiment, Ross had claimed. Spellings of names at that period were pretty free, of course, and as I only heard the names without any indication as to proper spelling, we must make allowances for differences in the letters of these names. I did trace a Brevet Lieutenant Gerard (first name not given) of the Dragoons, a cavalry regiment, who served in the Pulaski Legion from September 3, 1778 to 1782.

Is this our man? Did he change sides after the Revolutionary War started in earnest? He could have been a regimental comrade of John Ross in 1774 and prior. The source for this man's data was F. B. Heitman's *Historical Register of the Continental Army*, Volume 1775-1783, page 189. The Pulaski Legion was not restricted to Polish volunteers who fought for the new republic, but it accepted voluntary help from any quarters, even former Britishers or mercenaries so long as they wanted to fight for a free America. Many Germans also served in that legion.

The Colonel Moss who was "bad" might have been Colonel Moses Allen, a Tory, who was from this area and who died February 8, 1779. He was listed in Saffell's *Records of the Revolutionary War.*

It was a confusing period in our history, and men changed their minds and sides as the need of the times demanded. Had the unfortunate soldier whom we had found trapped here in this erstwhile Quaker meeting house been one of those who wanted to get out from under, first to join what he considered "the good boys," and then, repelled by the continuing bloodshed, could he not even accept *their* war? Had he become religiously aware through his Quaker contacts and had he become a pacifist by them? Very likely, if one was to judge the words of the colonial soldier from the year 1774 as an indication. His plea for peace sounds almost as if it could be spoken today.

Captain John Ross was not an important historical figure, nor was he embroiled in an event of great significance in the overall development of the United States of America. But this very anonymity made him a good subject for our psychometric experiment. Sybil Leek surely could not have known of Captain Ross, his comrades, and the Quaker connections of the old house on Byberry Road. It was her psychic sense that probed into the impressions left behind by history as it passed through and onward relentlessly, coating the house on Byberry Road with an indelible layer of human emotions and conflict.

I sincerely hope we managed to "decommission" Captain Ross in the process of our contact, to give him that much-desired "peace and silence" at last.

OLD LANDLADIES DON'T DIE: NOR DO THEY FADE AWAY

*M*rs. G. threw a hasty look toward the third floor window of the modest wooden house on Mountview Place, set back a few paces from the street. Then she shuddered and quickly hurried past, without looking back. Mrs. G. knew that was the best way to pass *that* house.

Everyone in the neighborhood knew the house was haunted and there was no point in seeing things one wasn't supposed to. Still—if the figure at the window were there, perhaps a glance would not hurt. It was a question of curiosity versus fear of the unknown, and fear won out.

The house itself looked like a typical middle-class dwelling built around the turn of the twentieth century. White sides were trimmed in green, and a couple of steps led up to the entrance door. Its three stories—you could call the third floor an attic, if you prefer—looked no different than the floors in any of the smaller houses in suburban Pittsburgh. There was an appropriately sized backyard to the rear of the house, with some bushes and flowers. And there were houses on both sides of this one. The block was quiet with very little traffic running through it. By car, it was about forty minutes from downtown Pittsburgh, and most local people don't go there more than maybe once in a while to shop. Life on Mountview Place might be unexciting and drab, and if it weren't for people like Mrs. G. worrying about the third floor window, nobody would even notice the house. But things were a little different when the house was new and the neighborhood was a lot more rustic than it was now.

The early history of the house was somewhat shrouded, except that it was already in existence exactly as it looks today at the turn of the century. At that time Mr. Allshouse, the local plumber—he had his own shop and was then in his late sixties—was only a mere child. So he did not know the strange man who came to live in the house until many years later. But in 1908, a Hollander named Vander bought the house, and he and his family lived in it until his wife died. In 1953 he left the house, and thereby hangs the first part of this strange tale. Although there were three children in the Vander family, he evidently had decided not to remain where his wife had died, but we can't be altogether sure as to why he left. In later years Mr. Allshouse and Vander had become friends, and even after his wife's passing Vander maintained contact with the plumber.

One day Allshouse was walking toward the house when he met Vander's niece en route. They stopped to chat and he mentioned where he was going. "Then you don't know?" the niece intoned. "My uncle has been dead for a month."

This came as a surprise to the plumber and he wondered how the otherwise hale and hearty Hollander had died so suddenly. He remembered well their initial meeting. This was several years earlier, when Vander had needed some repairs done in the house. The work completed, the plumber presented his bill. Mr. Vander asked him to wait.

"Don't believe much in banks," he explained. "You don't mind taking cash, do you?"

"Not at all," the plumber assured him. The Dutchman then walked up the already shakey stairs to the attic. Allshouse could clearly hear him walking about up there as if he were moving some heavy object around, looking for something. Then the sound of a drawer closing was heard, and soon after, the Dutchman's heavy footsteps came down the stairs again.

"Here's your money," he said and smiled. He was a friendly man who didn't mind a chat with strangers. After a minute or two of discussing the state of the world and the weather in Pittsburgh in particular, the two men parted.

And now the Hollander was dead. It seemed very strange to the plumber. Why had Vander left the comfortable house just before his death and what was to happen to the house now?

Two weeks went by, and other matters occupied the plumber's mind. He was walking down Trenton Avenue one afternoon, when he looked up and who should be trotting towards him but Mr. Vander!

Without thinking, the plumber called out a friendly "Hello!" The man did not react, so Allshouse shouted, "Mr. Vander! Mr. Vander!"

At this the man, who had meanwhile passed him, turned, smiled rather wanly, and said, "Hello."

But he did not stop to chat as he had always done before, and it seemed strange that this time Vander was cool and distant when normally he had been so friendly.

Long after the Dutchman had disappeared in the opposite direction, the plumber wondered why his friend had behaved so strangely. Then it suddenly hit him that the man had been dead and buried for six weeks.

Prior to his death Vander had sold the house to a couple named McBride. Apparently it was a private transaction for no one knows exactly how it happened, or even why, but the

McBrides were installed in the house by the time Mr. Vander passed on, or at least part of the way on.

The McBrides had no children, and Mrs. McBride was crippled, having once fallen in an alley. Consequently she dragged one leg in a rather pronounced manner when walking.

Around 1964, Mrs. McBride died, leaving the house to her husband Franklin. Soon after, Mr. McBride's usual calm behavior changed rapidly. Where he had hardly been known for any eccentricities in the neighborhood, he seemed now a subject for discussion up and down the street. For one thing, he soon refused to go upstairs under any circumstances, and made his bed in an old Morris chair in the front parlor downstairs.

On more than one occasion, neighbors saw the man run out into the street in a state of abject fear. Not understanding his reasons, gossip blamed it on alcohol, but the fact is Mr. McBride never drank anything at all.

Ultimately, the widow's sister, a Mrs. Naugle, had him placed in the state mental institution at Torrence, where he was still living.

The power of attorney then passed into her hands, and it was she who rented the house to the Kennedy family. The house had stood empty for about a year after Mr. McBride's forced departure. In that time, dust had gathered and the house looked eerie even in the daytime. But at night people absolutely refused to walk close by it, and even sensible people would rather cross the street to the other side then face walking close to its windows.

But, Mrs. Evelyn Kennedy had not heard anything special about the house one way or the other.

It seemed like the kind of house she wanted for her brood, and so she and her husband rented it in 1965. For almost a year, the Kennedys lived quietly in the house on Mountview Place and kept busy with the ordinary routines of daily living.

In the family there was, first of all, Mrs. Evelyn Kennedy

herself, a portly lady of mixed Irish-German ancestry, aged forty-five, and a lively and articulate housewife. At one time she had operated a beauty parlor downtown but now she was much too busy for that. Some of her equipment was still in the attic and on occasion she would perform her erstwhile duties for friends or members of the family there.

Mr. Wilbert Kennedy managed a nearby gas station. Five years her senior, he was a wiry, quiet-spoken man who was rarely around the house, the nature of his business being one of long hours.

Of their four children, two were married and lived away from home. The other two daughters, Claudia and Penny, live with their parents. Claudia was married, but her husband had disappeared, and at twenty-four, she was kept busy with her two children, Debra, then seven, and Maria, then one year old. Penny, unmarried, was eighteen at the time they moved into the house. Except for an occasional friend, this was the entire cast of characters in the strange tale that was about to unfold.

On July 7, 1966, the landlady, Mrs. Naugle, decided she wanted to sell the house. Actually, it belonged to her brother-in-law in the institution, but as she had power of attorney, there was really nothing to stop her. Why she suddenly decided to sell, no one but she knows and she wasn't likely to tell us. But the very same real estate dealer, a man named McKnight, who had gotten the Kennedys into the house, was now entrusted with the disposal of the house to a new owner. Where this would leave the tenants no one knew or cared.

Actually, selling the house should not have proved too difficult. It was reasonably well kept, had an attractive exterior and a nice, large backyard, and the block was quiet and tree-lined. The downstairs parlor was separated from the dining room by a heavy oaken double door that could be pulled back entirely to make the downstairs into one large room, if one had many guests. To the right was the staircase that led straight up two flights. The second story contained the bedrooms and the third floor, actually the attic, was occupied by an additional bedroom in front and a large "rear room" which Mrs. Kennedy had filled with the remnants of her beauty parlor days and sundry suitcases, boxes, and the sort of things people have placed into attics ever since houses were built with them. The house was eminently suitable for any family with children.

Although the For Sale sign was up outside their home, the Kennedys continued with their daily business. Somehow they felt it would be some time before the house would be sold and then, perhaps, to an owner who did not wish to live in it. Why worry?

Penny, a determined young lady, had decided she preferred the privacy of the attic to the family presence on the second floor and moved her bed to the empty bedroom in the attic. The day after the For Sale sign had been installed outside, she came down to use the bathroom. When she went back up to the attic, she found her way barred by a woman standing at the window. Since it was broad daylight, Penny had ample opportunity to look her over. She was an elderly woman with gray hair, wearing a somewhat unusual amount of rouge on her face. Her blue dress was like a long robe. In her hands she held some beads, and when Penny noticed her, the woman held out her arms toward her, all the while smiling at her. But Penny did not feel friendly at all. She knew there couldn't possibly be anyone of flesh-and-blood standing there. She let out a scream and rushed down the stairs, almost falling in the process.

Within hours, she was back in her old room on the second floor, and ten horses couldn't get her up into the attic again.

But her troubles were far from over, even on the second floor. The water kept turning itself on day and night. Her alarm clock was unplugged. Jewelry disappeared and could not be found, despite careful and exhaustive search. The next day it would be back at the same spot it had disappeared from.

Soon, the phenomena spread to other members of the

family. Mrs. Evelyn Kennedy, suffering from arthritis and a bad heart, would sometimes be unable to bend down because of swollen legs. One day she found herself all alone in the house. Her shoes were always kept under a chest of drawers in the bedroom. That day the shoes had somehow been pushed too far back under the chest and she could not reach them.

"Oh my," she said out loud. "I wish I could get at my shoes. What shall I do?"

With that she entered her bathroom for a shower. Afterwards, as she opened the bathroom door, the door hit something solid. She looked down. Someone had placed her shoes, which a few minutes before had been under the chest of drawers in her room, in front of the bathroom door. Yet, she was alone in the house.

Mrs. Kennedy put two and two together. Who was the woman in the blue robe that had frightened her daughter Penny?

Cautiously, she called the landlady, Mrs. Naugle and explained what had happened.

"Oh my God," the lady sighed, "that sounds just like my sister. She was laid out in a blue robe."

But she would not discuss this any further. It upset her, and she wanted no part of it.

Shortly after, Mrs. Kennedy was ironing downstairs in the parlor. All of a sudden, a heavy object shot out of the door jamb and narrowly missed her. She stopped working and examined the object. It was a homemade pin of some sort. When she showed it to the landlady, the latter turned away, advising her to destroy the object. It was even harder to talk about the house after that incident.

Sobbing sounds were soon heard in the dining room when it was completely empty. Up in the attic the family would hear the sound of someone dragging legs, someone crippled, and they remembered in terror how the late Mrs. McBride had been thus afflicted. Was this her ghost, they wondered?

They had scarcely enough time to worry about what to do about all this that had suddenly burst upon them, when Mrs. Kennedy got to talking to the mailman, a Mr. Packen, who lived nearby. Somehow the talk turned to psychic phenomena and the mailman nodded gravely.

"I seen her, too," he confided, "back in '63, I seen her sweeping the pavement. Right in front of the house. I seen her."

"Who have you seen?" asked Mrs. Kennedy, as if she didn't know.

"Who but that lady, Mrs. McBride?" the mailman answered. "Big as life she was."

He in turn had been no stranger to this sort of thing. In his own house down the street he once saw a little old lady who seemed strangely familiar. As a mailman, he knows most of his "customers" well enough and the little old lady in his house rang a bell.

"What are you doing in my house?" he demanded. "You're supposed to be dead!"

Reproachfully, he glanced at her and she nodded sadly and dissolved into the evening mist. So, it wasn't particularly shocking for him to hear about the goings-on at the Kennedy house.

The little old lady who had visited the mailman apparently had some business of her own, and as it was unfinished business that keeps these denizens of the netherworld from going off into the Great Beyond. He wondered what it was she had wanted.

One afternoon, ten-year-old Debra was playing in the downstairs parlor, when she felt herself not alone. In looking up she saw a little old lady standing in the room. Wearing black clothes, she seemed strangely old-fashioned and unreal to her, but there was no doubt in Debra's mind that she had a visitor. When she rose to meet the stranger, the woman disappeared. Having heard of her Aunt Penny's encounter with the lady on the stairs, she knew at once that this was not the same person.

Whereas the lady on the stairs had been tall and smiling, this woman was short and bent and quizzical in her expression.

The excitement of this vision had hardly died down when Mrs. Kennedy found her work in the kitchen, washing dishes, interrupted by the feeling that she was about to have a visitor. Since she was alone in the house at the moment, she immediately proceeded to the front door to open it. Without thinking anything special, she opened the front door and standing there and waiting was a lady. She was short of stature, her dress had big, puffed sleeves, she wore gloves and carried a big black umbrella. Mrs. Kennedy also noticed a golden pin and the bustle of her dress. In particular, she was astonished to see her hat, which was large and had a big bill on it—something no up-to-date woman would wear.

As she still wondered who this strange woman might be, she motioned to her to come in, and the woman did, brushing past her. Only then did it occur to Mrs. Kennedy that she had not heard the doorbell ring! Turning around and going after her visitor, she found that no one had come in.

Now she, too, realized that someone other than the late Mrs. McBride, if indeed it was she, who kept coming to the house. It was the mailman's friend, strange as it might seem, but from the description she was sure it was the same person.

The mystery deepened even further when Debra reported seeing a man in the kitchen at a time when no man was in the house. The man had worn a blue shirt and brown pants, but they were not the sort of clothes worn by modern people. He stood in a corner of the kitchen as if he belonged there and though Debra was frightened, she managed to see enough of the wraith, before he faded away again.

It was a Monday night, some weeks after this experience that Claudia and Penny were on the stairs alone. Mr. Kennedy and the two grandchildren were already in bed in their rooms. All the lights were out and only the street lights cast a reflection of sorts into the house through the windows. Suddenly the two girls heard the sound of someone running from the kitchen toward the living room. They looked up and what they saw made their blood turn to ice: there in the dim light of the kitchen stood the outline of a very large man. *With a huge leap, he came after them.* Faster than lightning, they ran up the stairs, with the shadowy man in hot pursuit. As they looked back in sheer terror, they saw him coming, but he stopped at the landing. Then he was gone, just disappeared like a puff of smoke.

From that moment on, the two young women refused to stay downstairs at night.

The downstairs parlor was as "unsafe" from the incursions of the ghosts as was the attic, and before long even the backyard was no longer free from whatever it was that wanted attention. It was almost as if the unseen forces were engaged in a campaign of mounting terror to drive home the feeling that the Kennedy's were not in possession of the house: the ghosts were.

Lights would go on and off by themselves. Water would gush in the bathroom, and when they investigated, they found someone unseen had turned the tap on. Late at night, they often heard someone crying softly in their backyard. Enough light from the windows illuminated that plot of land to assure them that it was no human agent. They huddled together, frightened, desolate, and yet unwilling to give up the house that they truly loved. The attic was particularly active during those weeks immediately following the landlady's decision to sell their house. Someone was moving heavy furniture around up there at night—or so it sounded. Nothing ever was changed in the morning. Mrs. Kennedy sought the advice of a good friend, Mrs. Lucille Hags, who had been to the house often.

One evening, when things had been particularly active, Evelyn Kennedy dialed her friend. The soothing voice at the other end of the phone momentarily calmed her. But then she clearly heard someone else dialing her phone.

"Are you dialing?" she asked her friend, but Mrs. Hags had not touched her telephone. Perhaps there had been some kind of cross-connection. Mrs. Kennedy decided to ignore it and bravely started to tell her friend what had happened that evening at the house.

"I wonder if it has something to do with Mrs. McBride," she ventured. No sooner had she said this, when heavy breathing, the breath of someone very close by, struck her ear.

"Do you hear that?" she asked, somewhat out of breath now herself.

"Yes, I did," said Mrs. Hags. Six times the heavy breathing interfered with their telephone conversation during the following weeks. Each time it started the moment either of them mentioned the phenomena in the house. Was one of their ghostly tenants listening in? So it would seem. The telephone people assured Mrs. Kennedy there was nothing wrong with her line.

Nothing wrong? she asked herself. Everything was wrong; the house was all wrong and what were they to do?

One sunny morning she decided to fight back. After all, this had been their happy home for a while now and no phantoms were going to drive them out of it. She tried to reason it out, but no matter how many of the noises she could explain by ordinary causes, so many things remained that simply could not be explained away. There were, as far as she could make out, three ghosts in the house. The two women and the heavy-set man. She wasn't quite sure who the man was, and yet it seemed to her it must be the Hollander, Vander, whose money had always been hidden up there in the attic. Had he returned for it, or was he simply staying on because he didn't like the way he left? Those were the questions racing through Mrs. Kennedy's mind often now.

To be sure, at least one of the *stay-behinds* was friendly.

There was the time Mrs. Kennedy slipped on the stairs

and was about to fall headlong down the whole flight of stairs. It was a warm summer day and she was alone at home, so that she would have lain there helpless had she injured herself. But something kept her from falling! Some force stronger than gravity held on to her skirts and pulled her back onto her feet. It wasn't her imagination and it wasn't a supreme effort of her own that did it. She was already half into the air, falling, when she was yanked back, upright.

Shortly after, she managed to repair to the attic, where her hair-drying equipment was stored. As she sat there, resting, she suddenly felt something wet and cold across her legs. She reached down only to feel a soft, moist mass that dissolved rapidly at her touch! This was enough to give her the willies, and she began to fear for her life, bad heart and all.

And yet, when the prospective buyers came more fre-quently to look at the house, and it seemed that the house might be sold after all, she found herself turning to her ghostly protector.

"Please, Mrs. McBride," she prayed silently, "don't let her sell the house!"

As if by a miracle, the most interested buyer who had been close to a decision in favor of taking the house, went away and was never seen again. The house remained unsold. Coincidence? If there be such things, perhaps. But not to Mrs. Kennedy.

She did not particularly care to have word of their predica-ment get around. It was bad enough to have ghosts, but to be known, as a haunted family was even worse. And yet how could it be avoided? It wasn't just she and her two daughters who experienced these strange things.

Even her husband, who wasn't exactly given to belief in ghosts, was impressed when he saw a chair move from under a desk by its own force. He tried it several times afterwards, hoping he could duplicate the phenomena by merely stomping his feet or gently touching the chair, but it required full force to move it.

The insurance man who had been servicing them for years was just as doubtful about the whole thing, when he heard about it.

"No such thing as a ghost," he commented as he stood in the hallway. At this moment the banister started to vibrate to such an extent they thought it would explode. He grabbed his hat and took his doubts to the nearest bar.

Sandra, a friend, had been sitting with Mrs. Kennedy downstairs not long ago, when suddenly she clearly heard someone in the bedroom overhead, the footsteps of someone running across the floor.

"I didn't know you had other company," she remarked to Mrs. Kennedy.

"I don't," Mrs. Kennedy answered dryly, and the friend left, somewhat faster than she had planned to.

Penny, then 21 years old and single, turned out to be more psychic than the rest of them. Hardly had she recovered from her terrible experience on the stairs, when something even more unspeakable occurred.

One evening, as she was retiring for the night, and had the lights turned off in her room, she felt something cold lie down in bed beside her. With a scream she jumped out and switched the lights back on. There was nothing, but a chill still pervaded the entire area!

In the summer of 1967, Penny found herself alone on the stairs on one occasion, when she suddenly heard a voice speak to her.

"It's all right... she can come out now," some woman said somewhere in back of her. There was no one visible who could have spoken these words and no one nearby. Besides, it was not a voice she recognized. It sounded strangely hollow and yet imperious at the same time. Someone was giving an order, but who, and to whom? Clearly, this someone still considered herself mistress of this house.

Although Penny had no interest in psychic matters, she wondered about these phenomena. Who was the man she had seen on the stairs? Who was the woman whose voice she had heard?

Somewhere she read an advertisement for a pendulum as an aide to psychic perception. As soon as it had come in the mail, she retired to her room, and tried it out.

Holding the pendulum over a piece of board, she intoned, more in jest than for serious research reasons, "Mr. Vander, are you here?"

With a swift move, the pendulum was ripped from her hands and landed clear across the room. She didn't use it again, nor does she really care if Mr. Vander was the ghost she saw. She just wanted to be left alone.

Somehow, the summer passed, and it was in September 1967, that Mrs. Kennedy realized there was more to this triangle of ghosts than just their presence. She was standing outside the house, chatting with a neighbor.

"Are the children having a party?" the neighbor asked.

"Why, no," she replied, knowing full well the children were all out of the house at the moment.

She was wondering why her neighbor had asked such a peculiar question, and was about to say so, when she heard a loud noise coming from the empty house: it sounded indeed as if a group of children were having a party upstairs, running up and down in the house. All she could do was shrug and turn away.

Maria, the three-year-old, was a precocious youngster who speaks better than her years would call for. One day she accompanied her grandmother to the attic. While Mrs. Kennedy was busy with her chores in the front room, the little girl played in the rear of the attic. Suddenly she came running out of the back room and beckoned her grandmother to follow her.

"There is a nice lady back there and she likes me," she explained.

Immediately, Mrs. Kennedy went back but she saw nothing this time.

Whether this visit to the attic had stirred up some sort of psychic contact, or whether her growing years now allowed her to express herself more clearly, the little girl had something more to say about the ghosts before long. Naturally, no one discussed such matters with her. Why frighten the child?

"There is a little boy in the attic," Maria explained earnestly, "and his name is Yackie. He died up there. He plays snowball out the window because he isn't allowed out of the attic."

At first these stories were dismissed as the fantasies of a child. Mrs. Kennedy was even a bit amused about the way Maria said "Yackie" instead of Jackie. They did not wish to stop her from telling this story over and over, out of fear that repressing her might make it more interesting. But as the weeks went on the little girl developed a strange affinity for the attic, especially the rear portion.

"Why are you always running up there, Maria?" her grandmother finally asked.

"Because." the little girl said, and became agitated, "because there is a man up there. Yackie told me about him."

"What about this man?"

"He died. He was shot in the head and all of his blood came out and he's buried in the back yard under the bushes."

"Why was he shot in the head, child?" the grandmother asked, almost as if she believed the story.

"Because he was crazy and he cried, that's why," the child replied. He grandmother was silent for a moment, trying to sort things out.

Could a three-year-old make up such a yarn? she wondered.

"Come," the little girl said, and took her by the hand, "I'll show you." She led Mrs. Kennedy to the dining room window and pointed at the bushes in their backyard.

"It's under the bushes there," Maria repeated and stared out the window.

Mrs. Kennedy shuddered. It was a spot she had wondered about many times. No matter how she tried, no matter what she planted, *nothing would grow on that spot!*

But as the weather turned colder, the house seemed to settle down and the disturbances faded away. True, no one came to inquire about buying it either. The Kennedys half-believed their troubles might just have faded away, both their worldly and their unworldly difficulties.

They thought less and less about them, and a spark of hope returned to Mrs. Kennedy about staying on at the house. She tried to make some discreet inquiries about the former owners of the house and even attempted to find the official records and deeds of sale. But her efforts were thwarted on all sides. Neighbors suddenly turned pale and would not discuss the matter. Nobody admitted knowing anything at all about Mr. Vander. Why, for instance, had she been told he left no children when he died? Only accidentally did she discover that there were three children. Was one of them named Jackie perhaps? She could not be sure.

The winter came, and a bitterly cold winter it was. Late in January, her composure was rudely shattered when a representative of the real estate agent paid them a visit. The house was being offered for sale once again.

That day one of her married daughters was visiting Mrs. Kennedy. She had brought her baby along and needed some toys for it to play with. "Go up into the attic. There's plenty of stuff there," Mrs. Kennedy suggested.

The woman, accompanied by her sister Claudia, went up into the attic. She was barefoot and casually dressed. Suddenly, Claudia pushed her to one side. "Watch out," she said and pointed to the floor boards. There, stuck between two boards, with the cutting edge pointing up, was a single-edged razor blade.

Somewhat shaken by their experience, the two women went back downstairs, after having pulled the blade out of the floor with some difficulty. It had been shoved into the crack between the boards with considerable strength. Nobody in the house used single-edged razor blades. In fact, few people did in these days. The only man in the house used an electric shaver.

Suddenly, the activities started all over. The front door would continually open by itself and shut by itself, and there was never anyone there when someone went to check. This happened mainly at night and in each case Mrs. Kennedy found the door securely locked. The door she and the others heard open was not a physical door, apparently, but an echo from the past!

The Kennedys were patient for several days. Then they decided that something had to be done. It was a nice house all right, but sooner or later someone would buy it, and they couldn't afford to buy it themselves, unfortunately. Since they could neither stop the landlady from trying to sell it, nor the ghostly inhabitants from playing in it, it was perhaps the wisest thing to look for another home.

By April they had finally found a nice house in nearby Penn Hills, and the moment they set foot in it, they knew it would do fine.

With her deeply developed physic sense Mrs. Kennedy also knew at once that she would have no problems with unseen visitors in *that* house.

It gave them a degree of pleasure to be moving out on their landlady rather than waiting to be evicted by the new owner. Gradually their belongings were moved to their new home.

On the last day, when almost everything had already been removed, Mrs. Kennedy, her husband, and their son, who had come to help them move, stood in the now almost empty house once more. There were still a few boxes left in the cellar. The two men went back into the cellar to get them out, while Mrs. Kennedy waited for them upstairs.

"Come," Mr. Kennedy said, and shivered in the spring air, "it's late. Let's finish up."

The clock of a nearby church started to strike twelve midnight.

They loaded the boxes into the car, carefully locked the front door of the house and then the garden gate.

At this precise moment, all three clearly heard the front door open and close again, and loud steps reverberate inside the empty house.

"There must be someone in there," Mrs. Kennedy's son murmured. He did not believe in ghosts and had always poopooed the tales told by his mother and sisters.

Quickly he unlocked the gate and front door once more and re-entered the dark house.

After a few moments, he returned, relocked the door and gate and, somewhat sheepishly, shook his head.

"Nothing. It's all empty."

Not at all, Mrs. Kennedy thought, as the car pulled out into the night, not at all.

That was only the reception committee for the next tenant.

PREMONITIONS IN GEORGIA

$\mathcal{M}$rs. W. was a housewife living in Athens, Georgia. She was also a certified nursery school teacher, the mother of six children, and she had had ESP experiences for many years past. She was living proof that ESP messages can be very precise at times in giving the recipient an indication of what the message was all about and to prepare the recipient for any shock that might come his or her way. In 1946 Mrs. W. was living in another city in Georgia. At that time she had one son age two and a half years and another six months old. She was also pregnant with another child. During that period she had many vivid dreams of a psychic nature. But after the third child was born she was particularly disturbed one night by a dream that became so powerful that it awoke her. She found herself crying uncontrollably, so much so that her husband was genuinely concerned. When she became calmer she told her husband she had dreamed she saw her brothers and sisters and her mother looking at her through the glass of their front door, saying, "Call an ambulance." The dream had no meaning for her, so after a while she went back to sleep and didn't think about it again.

Three months later the dream became a reality. Her brother appeared at her front door and standing outside the glass said, "Call an ambulance." He then explained that their father, who lived on the next street and who had no telephone, had suffered a heart attack while preparing for bed. The father died three days later. It was only after her grief ceased that Mrs. W. realized that in her dream she had seen all members of her family except one—her father was not in it. Had she understood this properly perhaps she would have been more prepared for the shock that was to come her way shortly.

The relationship with her father had been a close one, so she was not surprised that after his passing there were times when she felt him standing near her. She did not see him, yet she knew of his presence. She hesitated to discuss this with her husband out of fear of being ridiculed or worse. During that time she awakened her husband five or six separate times and asked him to get up and shut the door since Daddy had come in. Her husband didn't like it, but when she insisted, he did get up in order to please his wife. They never discussed it until many years later when her husband admitted that each time she had asked him to close the door it was indeed open and there had been no reason for it to be open.

Mrs. W's husband was the editor of a county newspaper and a very logical man. He learned to accept his wife's special talent as the years rolled by, but there were times when he wished that she weren't as psychic as she was. One night she dreamed that a plane crash had taken place somewhere in back of their house and she saw some Army men drive up in a jeep and take away the bodies of those killed. In the morning she told her husband of this dream. He didn't say anything. Two weeks later, however, he told his wife to quit having "those crazy dreams." It appeared that Mr. W had been traveling away from home in the direction one might properly call "back of the house," when he saw that an Army plane had crashed and Army personnel in a jeep had driven up to the site and removed some bodies, just as his wife had told him. Mrs. W. realized that she had a very special talent and perhaps had been chosen by some superior intelligence as a communicator.

A month after her daughter Karen was born, Mrs. W. happened to be lying down for an afternoon nap. She was facing the wall when she felt compelled to turn over in the opposite direction. There she saw the figure of a man in a white robe standing by her bed. Her first thought was that she still had in her system some of the drug that had been given her during the birth and that she was indeed hallucinating. She thought it best to turn back to the wall. Immediately, however, she felt a strong compulsion to turn back, and this time she saw the man pointing his finger at her with a stern look on his face. She got the impression she was to get up immediately and follow him. She did just that and walked straight into the next room. As if acting in a daze she saw herself dial her husband at his office. As soon as her husband came to the phone she told him not to ask questions but if he ever intended to do something that she had asked him for, this was the time to do it. She told him to go at once to a place called Curry's Creek to see if their son Joe was there. Her husband objected. He knew, he said, that the five-year-old was not there. Nevertheless Mrs. W. insisted. Her plea was so urgent she impressed her husband sufficiently that he did indeed go down to the creek.

Ten minutes later he telephoned her asking her how she knew that the boy was indeed at the creek. It appeared that he had found the little boy at the edge of the water looking down into it. The creek furnished the town's water supply and was next to a busy highway a mile outside of town. The child had never been there before. Had Mr. W. not arrived in time the child might very well have drowned. Mrs. W then realized that the man in the white robe had come to save their child.

THE GIRL GHOST OF KENTUCKY

*M*rs. D. and her son Bucky lived in a comfortable house on a hilltop in suburban Kentucky, not far from Cincinnati, Ohio. It was a pleasant white house, not much different from other houses in the area. The surroundings were lovely and peaceful, and there was a little man-made pond right in front of the house. Nothing about the house or the area looked in the least bit ghostly or unusual. Nevertheless, Mrs. D. needed my help in a very vexing situation.

Six months after Mrs. D. had moved into the house, she began to hear footsteps upstairs, when there was no one about, and the sound of marble being rolled a across the hall. But, anything supernatural was totally alien to Mrs. D.

Nevertheleass, she had a questioning and alert mind, and was not about to accept these phenomena without finding out what caused them. When the manifestations persisted, she walked up to the foot of the stairs and yelled, "Why don't you just come out and show yourself or say something instead of making all those noises?"

As if in answer, an upstairs door slammed shut and then there was utter silence. After a moment's hesitation, Mrs. D.

dashed upstairs and made a complete search. There was no one about and the marble, which seemingly had rolled across the floor, was nowhere to be seen.

When the second Christmas in the new house rolled around, the D.'s were expecting Bucky home from the Army. He was going to bring his sergeant and the sergeant's wife with him, since they had become very friendly. They celebrated New Year's Eve in style and high spirits (not the ethereal kind, but the bottled type).

Nevertheless, they were far from inebriated when the sergeant suggested that New Year's Eve was a particularly suitable night for a séance. Mrs. D. would have no part of it at first. She had read all about phony séances and remembered what her Bible said about such matters.

But later, after her husband had gone to bed, the remaining celebrants decided to have a go at it.

They joined hands and sat quietly in front of the fireplace. Nothing much happened for a while. Then Bucky, who had read some books on psychic phenomena, suggested that they needed a guide or control from the other side of life to help them, but no one had any suggestions concerning to whom they might turn.

More in jest than as a serious proposal, Mrs. D. heard herself say, "Why don't you call your Indian ancestor, Little White Flower!" Mr. D. was part Cherokee, and Bucky, the son, would, of course, consider this part of his inheritance too. Mrs. D. protested that all this was nonsense, and they should go to bed. She assured them that nothing was likely to happen. But the other three were too busy to reply, staring behind her into the fireplace. When she followed the direction of their eyes she saw what appeared to be some kind of light similar to that made by a flashlight. It stayed on for a short time and then disappeared altogether.

From that day on, Mrs. D. started to find strange objects

around the house that had not been there a moment before. They were little stones in the shape of Indian arrows. She threw them out as fast as she found them. Several weeks later, when she was changing the sheets on her bed, she noticed a huge red arrow had been painted on the bottom sheet—by unseen hands.

One afternoon she was lying down on the couch with a book trying to rest. Before long she was asleep. Suddenly she awoke with a feeling of horror that seemed to start at her feet and gradually work its way up throughout her entire body and mind. The room seemed to be permeated with something terribly evil. She could neither see nor hear anything, but she had the feeling that there was a presence there and that it was very strong and about to overcome her.

For a few weeks she felt quite alone in the house, but then things started up again. The little stone arrowheads appeared out of nowhere again, all over the house. Hysterical with fear, Mrs. D. called upon a friend who had dabbled in metaphysics and asked for advice. The friend advised a séance in order to ask Little White Flower to leave.

Although Little White Flower was not in evidence continually and seemed to come and go, Mrs. D. felt the Indian woman's influence upon her at all times. Later the same week, Little White Flower put in another appearance, this time visual. It was toward four o'clock in the morning, when Mrs. D. woke up with the firm impression that her tormentor was in the room. As she looked out into the hall, she saw on the wall a little red object resembling a human eye, and directly below it what seemed like half a mouth. Looking closer, she discerned two red eyes and a white mouth below. It reminded her of some clowns she had seen in the circus. The vision remained on the wall for two or three minutes and then vanished completely.

After several postponements, I was finally able to come to

Kentucky and meet with Mrs. D. in person. On June 20, I sat opposite the slightly portly, middle-aged lady who had corresponded with me so voluminously for several months.

As I intoned my solemn exorcism and demanded Little White Flower's withdrawal from the spot, I could hear Mrs. D. crying hysterically. It was almost as if some part of her was being torn out and for a while it seemed that *she* was being sent away, not Little White Flower.

The house had been quiet ever since; Little White Flower had presumably gone back to her own people and Mrs. D. continued to live in the house without further disturbances.

THE OLD HOUSE IN ARKANSAS

*H*ollygrove was only a small town in eastern Arkansas, but to Sharon H. it was the center of her world. She lived there with her farmer husband in quiet rural Arkansas, far from metropolitan centers. Little Rock was a long way off, and not a place one was likely to visit often. Her mother lived in Helena. Traveling east on Highway 86 and then on 49 Sharon had gone back and forth a few times in her young life. She knew the area well. It was not an area of particular merit but it had one advantage: it's very quiet. About halfway between Hollygrove and Helena stood an old house that attracted Sharon every time she passed it. There was no reason for the attraction, and yet whenever she passed the old house something within her wondered what the house's secret was.

Sharon was then in her early twenties. She had lived with an extraordinary gift of ESP since infancy. That was a subject one didn't discuss freely in her part of the world. People either ridiculed you or, worse, think you're in league with the devil. So Sharon managed to keep her powers to herself even though at times she couldn't help surprising people. She would often hear voices of people who weren't even within sight. If she

186

wanted someone to call her, all she had to do was visualize the person and, presto, the person would call her up. Whenever the telephone rings she knew exactly who was calling. Frequently she had heard her neighbors talking 500 yards from her house; she was so sensitive she couldn't stand the television when it was turned on too loud.

Her husband, a farmer of Swiss extraction, was somewhat skeptical of her powers. He was less skeptical now than he was when he first met her. Back in the summer of 1963, when she and her then boyfriend, later-to-be her husband, first kept company she was already somewhat of a puzzle to him. One day, the fifteen-year-old girl insisted they drive into Helena, which was about five miles from where they were then. Her boyfriend wanted to know why. She insisted that there was a baseball game going on and that a private swimming party was in progress at the municipal pool. She had no reason to make this statement, however, nor any proof that it was correct, but they were both very much interested in baseball games, so her boyfriend humored her and decided to drive on to Helena.

When they arrived at Helena they found that a baseball game was indeed going on and that a private swimming party was in progress at the municipal pool, just as Sharon had said. Helena has a population of over 10,000 people. Sharon lived 25 miles away. How could she have known this?

In March of 1964 her maternal grandmother passed away. Sharon had been close to her but for some reason was unable to see her in her last moments. Thus the death hit her hard, and she felt great remorse at not having seen her grandmother prior to her passing. On the day of the funeral she was compelled to look up, and there before her appeared her late grandmother. Smiling at her, she nodded and then vanished. But in the brief moment when she had become visible to Sharon, the woman understood what her grandmother wanted her to know. The message was brief. Her grandmother understood why she had not been able to see her in her last hours and wanted to forgive her.

In April of 1964, when she was just sixteen years old, she married her present husband. They went to Memphis, Tennessee, for four days. All during their honeymoon Sharon insisted on returning home. She felt something was wrong at home, even though she couldn't pinpoint it. Though it wasn't a hot period of the year she felt extremely warm and very uncomfortable. Eventually her husband gave in to her urgings and returned home with her. Assuming that her psychic feelings concerned an accident they might have had on the road, she insisted that they drive very carefully and slowly. There was no accident. However, when they entered the driveway of her home she found out what it was she felt all that distance away. A large fertilizer truck had hit a gasoline truck in front of her mother's house. A tremendous fire had ensued, almost setting her mother's house on fire. The blaze could be seen clearly in towns over 5 miles away. Both trucks burned up completely. It was the heat from the fire she had felt all the way to Memphis, Tennessee.

The house outside of Hollygrove, however, kept on calling her and somehow she didn't forget. Whenever she had a chance to drive by it she took it, looking at the house and wondering what its secret was. On one such occasion it seemed to her that she heard *someone play a piano inside the vacant house.* But that couldn't very well be; she knew that there was no one living inside. Perhaps there were mice jumping up and down the keyboard, if indeed there was a piano inside the house. She shook her head, dismissing the matter. Perhaps she had only imagined it. But somehow the sound of songs being played on an old piano kept on reverberating in her mind. She decided to do some research on the house.

Tom Kameron ran an antique shop in Hollygrove, and

since the old house was likely to be filled with antiques he would be the man to question about it. That at least was Sharon's opinion. She entered the shop pretending to browse around for antiques. A lady clerk came over and pointed at an old lamp. "I want to show you something that you'll be interested in," she said. "This came from the old Mulls house here." Sharon was thunderstruck. The Mulls house was the house she was interested in. She began to question the clerk about the antiques in the Mulls house. Apparently a lot of them had been stolen or had disappeared during the last few years. Since then a caretaker had been appointed who guarded the house. At this point the owner of the shop, Tom Kameron, joined the conversation. From him Sharon learned that the house had belonged to Tom Mulls, who had passed away, but Mrs. Mulls, although very aged, was still alive and living in a sanitarium in Little Rock. Kameron himself had been a friend of the late owners for many years.

The house had been built by a Captain Mulls who had passed away around 1935. It was originally built in St. Augustine, Florida, and was later moved all the way to Hollygrove.

The captain wasn't married, yet there was a woman with him in the house when it stood in Hollygrove. This was a young Native American woman he had befriended and who lived with him until her death. The man who later inherited the house, Tom Mulls, was an adopted son. Apparently Captain Mulls was very much in love with his Native American lady. After her death he had her body embalmed and placed in a glass casket that he kept in a room in the house. It stayed there until he died, and when Tom took over the house he buried the casket in the cemetery not far away. Her grave still exists in that cemetery.

There were many relics and papers dealing with Native American folklore in the house during her lifetime, but they had all disappeared since. The Native American woman played the piano very well indeed, and it was for her that the captain had bought a very fine piano. Many times he would sit listening to her as she played song after song for his entertainment.

The house had been vacant for many years but people couldn't help visiting it, even though it was locked. They would go up to the front steps and peer in the windows. Sharon was relieved to hear that she was not the only one strangely attracted to the old house. Others had also been "called" by the house as if someone inside were beckoning to them. Over the years strangers who had passed by the house had come to Mr. Kameron with strange tales of music emanating from the empty house. What people had heard wasn't the rustling of mice scurrying over a ruined piano keyboard but definite tunes, song after song played by skilled hands. Eventually the house would pass into the hands of the state since Mrs. Mulls had no heirs. But Sharon doubted that the ghost would move out just because the house changed hands again. She felt her presence, very much alive and wholly content to live on in the old house. True, she was playing to a different kind of audience than she did when Captain Mulls was still alive, but then it was just possible that the captain has decided to stay behind also if only to listen to the songs his Native American lady continued to play for his entertainment.

THE MAN IN GRAY

$\mathcal{B}$elleville, Illinois was a sleepy town about an hour's drive from St. Louis and had nothing in particular to offer in the way of commerce or beauty except for a few charming old houses. The people who lived in Belleville were seldom troubled by the controversies of the day and the industrial strife of nearby East St. Louis.

On Main Street near 17th there was an old brick house which had stood the test of time well: built 125 years earlier by a coal miner named Meyer, it had since been remodeled and also been added to, but the original structure was still sound and no one thought of tearing it down or replacing it with something more up to date.

The house consisted of two stories, with the front parlor well lit by large windows looking onto Main Street. There were four rooms downstairs, a kitchen, and a hallway leading to second section of the house that in turn led to a small back yard. The house stood near the corner and was accessible from downtown in a matter of minutes. Eventually, it had passed out of the Meyer family into other hands, and its history was obscure until it became the property of a certain Mr. and Mrs. Joseph Stricken. Little else was known about them but their names. After they passed on, the house was acquired by two young sisters, Dollie and Judy Walta, who bought it not as living quarters, but in order to turn the place into studios for their music business. The Walta girls were music teachers. Dollie, born in 1929 and Judy, born in 1939, were two of ten children of Fred and Julia Walta, who had come to America from Czechoslovakia while still young. The Waltas gave their family a good education, but Judy rebelled against the strict discipline of school and quit after two years of high school. This, despite a very high IQ.

At sixteen, Judy was already an accomplished musician, and she decided to devote her life to the teaching of music. She was a teacher of piano. Dollie, the elder sister, taught guitar and jointly they operated a music studio in the house for many years. They came here every day except on weekends, and generally left by 9 P.M., or earlier, depending on how many pupils they had that day. Once in a while, they also came in on Saturday mornings.

At other times, and at night, the house was deserted and well locked up, but the chance of burglars breaking in was small due to its solid construction and the fact that it was on Main Street, usually well guarded by the local police department.

For the first six years of their tenancy, the sisters noticed nothing out of the ordinary in the old house. True, there were the usual squeaking floorboards and the aching sounds of an old house settling on its foundations. But that was to be expected and no one paid any heed to such things. In 1962 they decided to make some alterations in the house to make the layout more suitable to their needs. Shortly after, Judy Walta came in late one night, because she had forgotten to leave one of the inner doors unlocked so the cleaning woman could get in there in the morning.

She entered from the rear door, which led to 17th Street, and did not bother to turn on any lights since the door she wanted to unlock was only a few steps beyond the back door.

Swiftly, she unlocked it and then turned around to leave again. As she did so, she passed a white, misty figure in the hall. There was no mistaking it for anything else, and as the whole incident took her so by surprise, she just backed away from it and out the rear door.

The next morning, she discussed the matter with her sister and, as nothing further happened out of the ordinary, they dropped the subject.

One of their students, a young man by the name of Jim Bawling, had been unhappy at his home and gotten into the habit of spending a great amount of time in their studio. In fact, it had gotten to be a kind of "home away from home" to him and he became genuinely attached to the place and the sisters. Almost every afternoon he would come in and chat with them, whenever they were free to do so.

Eventually, he joined the Navy, and on his first leave, he returned to Belleville for a visit. But, on August 26, 1962, the young man drowned in an accident. On August 30, the day after his funeral, the sisters were in the room used for lessons, when a pencil, which had been his, and which he had left on his desk on his very last visit, started to roll off the desk, bounced on the eraser and dropped—pointing to the chair which had been his last seat!

There was no one close to the desk at the time, nor was there any movement or vibration outside the house. Moreover, the room was built on a slant and the pencil rolled *against* the slant.

Shortly after this incident, the sisters and many of their students began hearing the back door open by itself and close again. This was immediately followed by footsteps of someone walking through the hall. At first, they would get up to see who it was, but there was never anyone to be seen.

Gradually, they realized that these were not the footsteps of a living person. The visitor would come at various times of the day or evening, and then stay away for several months. Then it would all resume. The sisters became used to these sounds, and hardly looked up when they became audible. One day the steps continued and then they could clearly hear someone sit down in the sailor's old chair!

It was clear to them that Jim was trying to make himself felt and wanted to continue his old friendship with them from where he now was. This did not bother them, but it bothered some of their pupils who held less broadminded views of ghosts.

The sisters were sure it was Jim, for this was his chair, and he always came in through the rear door rather than the front entrance.

The footsteps continued and the door would still open and close by itself, and Judy would just nod, and Dollie would say "Hello, Jim" and go on with her work.

But it soon became apparent to Dollie that the footsteps were not always the same: sometimes they were soft and light, as if made by a young person, while at other times they were the heavy, almost clumsy steps of a big man.

On March 25, 1966 the two women were in different parts of the studio busy with their chores. Judy was in the middle room, while Dollie was in the bathroom, with the door open. The time was 1:20 in the afternoon. Independently of each other, the two women saw the same figure of a man suddenly appear out of nowhere. At first, Judy saw him. He was a big man, about 5 feet, 11 inches tall, and heavy-set, dressed in gray, and where his face should have been there was just a gray mass. But unmistakably this was a human figure. Thirty seconds later, he appeared to Dollie. She looked at him, and could see right through him into the other room!

The women both had the impression that the man was looking *at them*. As he disappeared toward the rear of the house, they realized they had not heard a single sound.

Naturally, they knew this was not Jim, their erstwhile pupil. But who was it?

Since the appearance of the man in gray, the footsteps were not heard again, but the door kept opening and closing as before. Word of their strange house got around and though they did not exactly cherish the notion, their pupils began to discuss the phenomena with them.

One young man, whose work in the police had trained him to be a particularly competent observer of details, came forward to tell of a strange encounter on May 26 of that year. He was in the downstairs studio room at about 8 P.M. when he suddenly came face to face with a man in gray. He took him to be about thirty years of age and, just like the sisters, he could not make out any facial characteristics. It was almost as if the man did not want his face to be recognized and was hiding it in a blur.

One Saturday, Judy had come to make sure the building was properly locked. This was August 27, 1966 and between 3 and 3:30 P.M. she observed in the empty building the snapping of door locks, and a footstep—just one footstep—near the door leading from the hall into the basement of the house. This was immediately followed by the sound of several objects falling to the floor, although nothing was moving. One sound in particular reminded her of the noise made by dropping a small package to the floor, *or the muffled sound of a silencer on a gun,* she thought, with a shudder. What was she thinking? This seemed like a bad melodrama by now.

All this activity began to get on her nerves. The following Tuesday, August 30, the two women had their friends Rita and Mike in the house. It was after teaching hours and the four-some was just sitting around relaxing. Rita had been taking piano lesson for the past year and was familiar with the "problems" of the house, but Mike laughed at it all, especially the man in gray. "You and your ghosts," he chortled; "It's all in your minds."

At that moment, the toilet was being flushed violently. They looked at each other. Everybody was accounted for and the toilet could not flush by itself. Mike tried and tried to see whether it might accidentally have done so. But it couldn't have. His face took on a more thoughtful mien as he sat down again.

A drum teacher named Dick P., working out of the studio, often told of the same noises—the back door opening and closing and the footsteps of an unseen visitor coming up and stopping inside the house. One night in early 1966, he was driving by the house. He knew from the sisters that there had never been anything unusual observed upstairs. He also knew the house was locked up tight and empty. But to his surprise, the upper story was lit up as if someone were up there. No reflection from passing cars could account for this. He drove on.

Jack McCormick was a clerk for the Internal Revenue Service, an outfit with little use for ghosts, since they don't pay taxes. His son had been studying with the Walta sisters for the past year and a half, and it was and was his custom to wait for his son in the downstairs waiting room. He, too, had been constantly unnerved by the sound of the door opening and closing and footsteps of someone not appearing.

Joe Bauer, a freight handler for the railroad, had heard the heavy footfalls of a man coming in the rear door, only to find no one there. Mrs. Bauer took two lessons a week, and he often stayed with her until about eight or nine in the evening. Everyone got hungry by that time, so one of them would run out for hamburgers. One night while they—the two sisters and the Bauers—were eating and watching TV, Mrs. Bauer felt an icy hand on her back. She felt each and every finger, but when she shook herself and turned around, she saw that no one was near her. Needless to say, it did not help her appetite.

A little while after, all four saw the umbrella, which had been standing idly and quietly in its stand, move by its own volition. One of the sisters got up and stopped it. But the umbrella would not obey. A few moments later, it started swinging again. At the same time, the back door opened and closed with a bang. Everyone was out of the house faster than you could say "ghost" that evening.

The sisters decided something had to be done about the power frightening them in the house. First, the house itself needed to be carefully scrutinized. It was then they discovered that it actually consisted of three separate units, with the front section, where today's main entrance is, constructed at a later date than the rear. The original entrance had been to the rear, and what was the entrance at the time the house had been built, back in the 1840s, was now situated *inside* the house, in the middle of the hallway. It so happened this was the exact *spot* where the ghostly footsteps had always stopped dead.

The soft footsteps they took to be the sailor's were never heard again nor was anything happening that they could consciously connect with him. They assumed the phenomena he might have caused were merely his way of saying goodbye and that he had long since found a better place to hang around.

But the heavy footsteps and the man in gray remained. So did the mystery of who he was and why he was disturbing the peace of the house. Judy started to talk to various neighbors and take frequent trips to the local library. Under the guise of doing research into the background of their house for reasons of historical curiosity, she managed to dredge up quite a bit of information, not necessarily all of it reliable or even true.

The trouble was that in the 19th century, Main Street had not yet been named and the town was quite different. It was difficult to trace individual addresses. There was, for instance, the rumor that eighty years ago a grocer named Jack Meyer had been murdered in their house. She tried to get proof of this and found that a certain George Meyer, occupation unknown, had indeed been murdered in 1888 in Belleville, Illinois. But there was nothing to show that he had resided at this address.

She continued to search and finally hit paydirt. The local paper of Tuesday, June 26, 1923, carried a one-column notice that immediately excited her.

"Jacob Meyer, aged 77, shot himself today. Aged west side coal miner was despondent because of ill health. Was found dead in chair by wife, bullet through his brain."

Apparently Meyer had been brooding over his bad health the night before. At 10:15 he had lunch—miners rise early for breakfast—and then took a rest in his usual chair. When his wife called out to him and got no reply, she checked to see what was the matter and found blood trickling down his face. Horrified, she called on her brother Alex White to come and help. The brother, who resided next door, came and found life ebbing from the aged man. An instant later, Meyer was dead. At his feet was the .32 caliber revolver he had used to blow his brains out. The bullet had passed through his head and lay nearby on the floor. What was strange that *nobody had heard the shot*, even though several members of the family had been within a few feet of the man all that time. How as it possible? Evidently he had held the gun to his temple and fired at close range and the sound had somehow been muffled.

There had been no threat of suicide beforehand, but Meyer had told his wife on arising, "Mary, I am feeling very bad today."

Meyer had retired six months before due to failing health. Prior to that he had still worked at a nearby mine, despite his advanced age. A native of Germany, where he had been born in 1845, Meyer had come to America to seek his fortune.

Judy Walta put the clipping down and suddenly many things began to fall in place for her.

Why hadn't the ghost shown his face? Was he ashamed of having committed suicide, considered an act of cowardice in those days? Or was it because the bullet had literally torn his face to shreds.

The footsteps were those of a heavy man. Meyer was a heavy man. But the man in gray did not look 77 years of age. This at first threw the sisters for a loop until they understood, from psychic literature, that the dead usually return in their mental imagines to that which they consider the prime of life—usually around age thirty, or thereabouts.

They had noticed that the phenomena occurred towards the end of the month, usually after the twentieth and at no other times.

Meyer had killed himself on June 26, 1923. The suicide, according to the newspaper, took place at their address, in their house, which was Meyer's at the time.

The sound, heard by Judy, of a package dropping sharply to the floor could very well have been a re-enactment of the fatal shot that killed him.

In Jacob Meyer's day, the entrance was to the rear of the house and he would have come home that way, every day, from the mine. Was he simply continuing to go through his daily routine, refusing to accept the reality of his suicide?

Somehow the understanding of the problem changed the atmosphere in the house. Not that the phenomena ceased, far from it, but it appeared that the ghostly resident had finally found a kind of relationship with the flesh-and-blood inhabitants of what was once his home.

Cigar smoke now could be smelled on several occasions, although there was no cigar smoker in the house and all doors and windows wore shut airtight. The smoke did not originate outside the house. This smell was soon followed, or rather augmented by, the smell of freshly brewed coffee at times when no one was brewing any coffee. The sound of papers rattling, someone sitting down in the chair as if to read his newspaper over his morning coffee and perhaps smoke a cigar, and scraping noises of a chair being half-dragged across the floor in plain view of the sisters contributed to their conviction that their ghostly visitor, far from being ready to leave upon being recognized, was getting ready for a long—to him—comfortable stay.

If the sisters had any doubts as to the identity of the unbidden guest, these were soon dispelled. On the night of April 27, 1967, Dollie and Judy were about to leave the studio for the night, when they both distinctly heard the sound of a shot coming from inside the building. They had just locked the back door and knew the house was quite empty. They debated whether to run or go back in and check. Curiosity won out, and they unlocked the door again and went back inside. They checked the studio and nothing was out of place. They had just gotten ready to leave again, when they heard another shot. The second shot sounded quite *muffled*, whereas the first one had been loud and clear. It came from the area of the furnace room in the middle of the house.

In November, Dollie was walking under the doorway between the front and back rooms, an area hitherto free from psychic phenomena. She was stopped cold by something that resisted her advance although she could not see anything unusual. She felt that she was walking through heavy water, halfway up to her knees. This was a physical thing, she realized, and in sudden horror it occurred to her that she was trying to penetrate the etheric body of Mr. Meyer. Hastily retreating, she left the house in a hurry.

That same month a hat disappeared without a trace. Judy had bought it for a friend for Christmas and had kept it in a box along with other Christmas gifts. None of the other items were disturbed, but the hat was gone. The puzzle was made worse by her discovery, several days later, of three dollar bills in the receipt book. Since neither of the sisters, nor anyone else, had placed the money there, this was strange indeed. On checking their receipts and figures they found they were exactly three dollars over. It so happened that the hat, which was never seen again, had cost three dollars.

The reputation of the house as a haunted abode seeped out despite the sisters' reluctance to discuss it except with their friends and pupils, when necessary. One day a woman walked by the house to see if she could have a look at the "ghost." As she looked at the front windows, she found herself tripped by an unseen force. Neighbors picked her up, but word got back to Judy, and she interviewed the lady afterwards. Shaking her head, the woman insisted nothing had happened, she had not fallen. Judy was happy to let it go at that. Who wants to admit being tripped by the ghost of a man dead for forty years?

About that time Judy discovered that the ghostly miner's wedding to Mary White had taken place on September 9, 1867. When a man celebrates his one hundredth wedding anniversary he should not have time for such foolishness as tripping people outside haunted houses.

Quite possibly, Mrs. Meyer has since taken Mr. Meyer in hand and made a better home for him beyond the veil. At any rate, the door in the rear no longer opened and closed as it used to, and perhaps Jacob Meyer was now retired for good.

THE GHOSTLY MAID

I received a curious letter from a Mrs. Stewart of Chicago, Illinois, explaining that she was living with a ghost and didn't mind, except that she had lost two children at birth and this ghost was following not only her but also her little girl. This she didn't like, so could I please come and look into the situation?

I could and did. On July 4, I celebrated Independence Day by trying to free a hung-up lady ghost on Chicago's South Side. The house itself was an old one, built around the late 1800s, and not exactly a monument of architectural beauty. But its functional sturdiness suited its present purpose—to house a number of young couples and their children, people who found the house both convenient and economical.

In its heyday, it had been a wealthy home, complete with servants and backstairs for them to go up and down on. The three stories were even then connected by an elaborate buzzer system, which, however, hadn't worked for years.

I did not wish to discuss the phenomena at the house with Mrs. Stewart until after Sybil Leek, who was with me, had had a chance to explore the situation. My good friend Carl Subak, a stamp dealer, had come along to see how I worked. He and I had known each other thirty years ago when we were both students, and because of that he had overcome his own skepticism and come along. Immediately on arrival, Sybil ascended the stairs to the second floor as if she knew where to go. Of course she didn't?I had not discussed the matter with her at all. But despite this promising beginning, she drew a complete blank when we arrived in the apartment upstairs.

"I feel absolutely nothing," she confided and looked at me doubtfully. Had I made a mistake? On a hot July day, had we come all the way to the South Side of Chicago on a wild ghost chase?

We gathered in a bedroom where there was a comfortable chair and windows on both sides that gave onto an old-fashioned garden; there was a porch on one side and a parkway on the other. The furniture, in keeping with the modest economic circumstances of the owners, was old and worn, but it was functional and they did not seem to mind.

In a moment, Sybil Leek had slipped into trance. But instead of a ghost's personality, the next voice we heard was Sybil's own, although it sounded strange. Sybil was "out" of her own body, but able to observe the place and report back to us while still in trance.

The first thing she saw were maps, in a large round building somehow connected with the house we were in.

"Is there anyone around?" I asked.

"Yes," Sybil intoned, "James Dugan."

"What does he do here?"

"Come back to live."

"When was that?"

"1912."

"Is there anyone with him?"

"There is another man. McCloud."

"Anyone else?"

"Lots of people."

"Do they live in this house?"

"Three, four people ... McCloud ... maps ..."

"All men?"

"No … girl … Judith … maidservant …"

"Is there an unhappy presence here?"

"Judith … she had no one here, no family…that man went away … Dugan went away …"

"How is she connected with this Dugan?"

"Loved him."

"Were they married?"

"No. Lovers."

"Did they have any children?"

There was a momentary silence, then Sybil continued in a drab, monotonous voice.

"The baby's dead."

"Does she know the baby's dead?"

"*She cries … baby cries* … neglected … by Judith … guilty …"

"Does Judith know this?"

"Yes."

"How old was the baby when it died?"

"A few weeks old."

Strange, I thought, that Mrs. Stewart had fears for her own child from this source. She, too, had lost children at a tender age.

"What happened to the baby?"

"She put it down the steps."

"What happened to the body then?"

"I don't know."

"Is Judith still here?"

"She's here."

"Where?"

"This room … and up and down the steps. She's sorry for her baby."

"Can you talk to her?"

"No. She cannot leave here until she finds—You see if she could get Dugan …"

"Where is Dugan?"

"With the maps."

"What is Dugan's work?"

"Has to do with roads."

"Is he dead?"

"Yes. She wants him here, but he is not here."

"How did she die?"

"She ran away to the water ... died by the water ... but is here where she lived ... baby died on the steps ... downstairs ..."

"What is she doing here, I mean how does she let people know she is around?"

"She pulls things ... *she cries* ..."

"And her Christian name?"

"Judith Vincent, I think. Twenty-one. Not white. From an island."

"And the man? Is he white?"

"Yes."

"Can you see her?"

"Yes."

"Speak to her?"

"She doesn't want to, but perhaps ..."

"What year does she think this is?"

"1913."

"Tell her this is the year 1965."

Sybil informed the spirit in a low voice that this was 1965 and she need not stay here any longer. Dugan was dead, too.

"She has to find him," Sybil explained and I directed her to explain that she need only call out for her lover in order to be reunited with him "Over There."

"She's gone ..." Sybil finally said, and breathed deeply.

A moment later she woke up and looked with astonishment at the strange room, having completely forgotten how we got here, or where we were.

There was no time for explanations now, as I still wanted

to check out some of this material. The first one to sit down with me was the owner of the flat, Mrs. Alexandra Stewart. A graduate of the University of Iowa, twenty-five years old, Alexandra Stewart worked as a personnel director. She had witnessed the trance session and seemed visibly shaken. There was a good reason for this. Mrs. Stewart, you see, had met the ghost Sybil had described.

The Stewarts had moved into the second floor apartment in the winter of 1964. The room we were now sitting in had been hers. Shortly after they moved in, Mrs. Stewart happened to be glancing up toward the French doors, when she saw a woman looking at her. The figure was about five feet three or four, and wore a blue-gray dress with a shawl, and a hood over her head, for which reason Mrs. Stewart could not make out the woman's features. The head seemed strangely bowed to her, almost as if the woman were doing penance.

I questioned Mrs. Stewart on the woman's color in view of Sybil's description of Judith. But Mrs. Stewart could not be sure; the woman could have been white or black. At the time, Mrs. Stewart had assumed it to be a reflection from the mirror, but when she glanced at the mirror, she did not see the figure in it. When she turned her attention back to the figure, it had disappeared. It was toward evening and Mrs. Stewart was a little tired, yet the figure was very real to her. Her doubts were completely dispelled when the ghost returned about a month later. In the meantime she had had the dresser that formerly stood in the line of sight moved farther down, so that any reflection as explanation would simply not hold water. Again the figure appeared at the French doors. She looked very unhappy to Mrs. Stewart, who felt herself strangely drawn to the woman, almost as if she should help her in some way as yet unknown.

But the visual visitations were not all that disturbed the Stewarts. Soon they were hearing strange noises, too. Above all there was the crying of a baby, which seemed to come from the second-floor rear bedroom. It could also be heard in the kitchen, though less loud, and it seemed to come from the walls. Several people had heard it and there was no natural cause to account for it. Then there were the footsteps. It sounded like someone walking down the backstairs, the servants' stairs, step by step, hesitatingly, and not returning, but just fading away!

They dubbed their ghostly guest "Elizabeth," for want of a better name. Mrs. Stewart did not consider herself psychic, nor did she have any interest in such matters. But occasionally things had happened to her that defied natural explanations, such as the time just after she had lost a baby. She awoke from a heavy sleep with the intangible feeling of a presence in her room. She looked up and there, in the rocking chair across the room, she saw a woman, now dead, who had taken care of her when she herself was a child. Rocking gently in the chair, as if to reassure her, the Nanny held Mrs. Stewart's baby in her arms. In a moment the vision was gone, but it had left Alexandra Stewart with a sense of peace. She knew her little one was well looked after.

The phenomena continued, however, and soon they were no longer restricted to the upstairs. On the first floor in the living room, Mrs. Stewart heard the noise of someone breathing close to her. This had happened only recently, again in the presence of her husband and a friend. She asked them to hold their breath for a moment, and still she heard the strange breathing continue as before. Neither of the men could hear it, or so they said. But the following day the guest came back with another man. He wanted to be sure of his observation before admitting that he too had heard the invisible person breathing close to him.

The corner of the living room where the breathing had been heard was also the focal point for strange knockings that faulty pipes could not explain. On one occasion they heard the breaking of glass, and yet there was no evidence that any glass had been broken. There was a feeling that someone other than the visible people was present at times in their living room, and it made them a little nervous even though they did not fear their "Elizabeth."

Alexandra's young husband grew up in the building trade, and then worked as a photographer. He too had heard the footsteps on many occasions, and he knew the difference between them and a house settling or timbers creaking—these were definitely human noises.

Mrs. Martha Vaughn was a bookkeeper who had been living in the building for two years. Hers was the apartment in the rear portion of the second floor, and it included the back porch. Around Christmas of 1964, she heard a baby crying on the porch. It was a particularly cold night, so she went to investigate immediately. It was a weird, unearthly sound—to her it seemed right near the porch, but there was nobody around. The yard was deserted. The sound to her was the crying of a small child, not a baby, but perhaps a child of from one to three years of age. The various families shared the downstairs living room "like a kibbutz," as Mrs. Stewart put it, so it was not out of the ordinary for several people to be in the downstairs area. On one such occasion Mrs. Vaughn also heard the breaking of the *invisible* glass.

Richard Vaughn was a laboratory technician. He too had heard the baby cry and the invisible glass break; he had heard pounding on the wall, as had the others. A skeptic at first, he tried to blame these noises on the steam pipes that heat the house. But when he listened to the pipes when they were acting up, he realized at once that the noises he had heard before were completely different.

"What about a man named Dugan? Or someone having to do with maps?" I asked.

"Well," Vaughn said, and thought back, "I used to get mail

here for people who once lived here, and of course I sent it all back to the post office. But I don't recall the name Dugan. What I do recall was some mail from a Washington Bureau. You see, this house belongs to the University of Chicago and a lot of professors used to live here."

"Professors?" I said with renewed interest.

Was Dugan one of them?

Several other people who lived in the house experienced strange phenomena. Barbara Madonna used to live there too. But in May of that year she moved out. She worked three days a week as a secretary and moved into the house in November of the previous year. She and her husband much admired the back porch when they first moved in, and had visions of sitting out there drinking a beer on warm evenings. But soon their hopes were dashed by the uncanny feeling that they were not alone, that another presence was in their apartment, especially around the porch. Soon, instead of using the porch, they studiously avoided it, even if it meant walking downstairs to shake out a mop. Theirs was the third-floor apartment, directly above the Stewart apartment.

A woman by the name of Lolita Krol also had heard the baby crying. She lived in the building for a time and bitterly complained about the strange noises on the porch.

Douglas McConnor was a magazine editor, and he and his wife moved into the building in November of the year Barbara Madonna moved out, first to the second floor and later to the third. From the very first, when McConnor was still alone— his wife joined him in the flat after their marriage a little later—he felt extremely uncomfortable in the place. Doors and windows would fly open by themselves when there wasn't any strong wind.

When he moved upstairs to the next floor, things were much quieter, except for one thing: always on Sunday nights, noisy activities would greatly increase toward midnight.

Footsteps, the sounds of people rushing about, and of doors opening and closing would disturb Mr. McConnor's rest. The stairs were particularly noisy. But when he checked, he found that everybody was accounted for, and that no living person had caused the commotion.

It got to be so bad he started to hate Sunday nights.

I recounted Sybil's trance to Mr. McConnor and the fact that a woman named Judith had been the central figure of it.

"Strange," he observed, "but the story also fits my ex-wife, who deserted her children. She is still very much alive. Her name was Judith."

Had Sybil intermingled the impression of a dead maidservant with the imprint left behind by an unfit mother? Or were there two Judiths? At any rate the Stewarts did not complain further about uncanny noises, and the woman in the blue-gray dress never came back.

On the way to the airport, Carl Subak seemed unusually silent as he drove us out to the field. What he had witnessed seemed to have left an impression on him and his philosophy of life.

"What I find so particularly upsetting," he finally said, "is Sybil's talking about a woman and a dead baby—all of it borne out afterwards by the people in the house. But Sybil did not know this. She couldn't have."

No, she couldn't.

In September, three years later, a group consisting of a local television reporter, a would-be psychic student, and an assortment of clairvoyants descended on the building in search of psychic excitement. All they got out of it were more mechanical difficulties with their cameras. The ghosts were long gone.

THE GHOST HUSBAND

*P*eople all over the world have moved into houses that seemed ordinary and pleasant, and spent years without ever encountering anything out of the ordinary. Then, one day, something happens to disturb their tranquility: a ghost appears, strange noises were heard, and a psychic presence makes itself known.

Why is it that phenomena sometimes occur at times long after someone moves into an affected house? Of course, there are just as many cases where the ominous presence is felt the very moment one steps across the threshold. But in cases where ghosts make their presence manifest long after the new tenants have moved in, certain conditions have not been right for such manifestations to take place at the beginning. For instance, it may involve the presence of youngsters in the household who furnish the energy for ghosts to appear. Or it may be that the shadowy entities remaining behind in the house are dimly aware of the new tenants, but wish to find out more about them before manifesting to them. Either way, once manifestations begin, the owner of the house has the choice of either ignoring them, fighting them—or coming to terms with them.

In the majority of cases, unfortunately, people simply think that by ignoring the phenomena or trying hard to explain them by so-called natural causes, the matter can be solved. Ignoring problems never helps, in any area of life. When it comes to psychic phenomena, the phenomena may become worse, because even the most benighted ghost, barely aware of its predicament, will become more powerful, more restless, by being ignored.

Take Mrs. A.M.B., for instance. She lived in central Illinois and was by training and profession a practical nurse, engaged in psychiatric work. If anything, she can distinguish psychosis from psychic activity. She has also had ESP abilities ever since she can remember. When she was twelve years old, she was playing in front of her house when she met what to her was an old man, inquiring about a certain widow living in the next block of the village. Mrs. B. knew very well that the lady had become a widow when her husband was killed while working as a crossing guard during a blizzard the previous winter. She remembered the man well, but the stranger did not resemble the deceased at all, so she assumed he was a relative inquiring about the dead man.

The stranger wanted to know where the widow had moved to. Mrs. B. explained that the lady had gone to visit a sister somewhere in Missouri, due to the fact, of course, that her husband had been killed in an accident. At that, the stranger nodded; he knew of the accident, he said. "Come," Mrs. B. said to the stranger, "I'll show you where another sister of the widow lives, not more than two blocks away from here. Perhaps they can tell you what town in Missouri she was visiting." The stranger obliged her, and the two were walking along the front porch, toward the steps leading down into the street, still in conversation. At that moment, her mother appeared at the front door in back of her and demanded to know what she was talking about. The woman was surprised, and explained that the gentleman was merely asking where Mrs. C. had gone, and added, "I told him she went to

Missouri." But the mother replied, in a surprised tone of voice, "What are you talking about? I don't see anyone." The little girl immediately pointed at the visitor, who by that time had had enough time to get to the steps, for the front porch was rather large.

But—to her shock—she saw no one there! Immediately the girl and her mother walked into the yard, looking about everywhere without finding any trace of the strange visitor. He had simply vanished the moment the little girl had turned around to answer her mother.

LIZZY'S GHOST

*M*rs. Carolyn K. lived in Chicago, Illinois, with her husband and four children. She had for years been interested in ESP experiences, unlike her husband, who held no belief of this kind. The family moved into its present home some years earlier. Mrs. K. did not recall any unusual experiences for the first six years, but toward the end of April, six years after they moved in, something odd happened. She and her husband had just gone to bed and her husband fell asleep almost immediately. Mrs. K., however, felt ill at ease and was unable to fall asleep, since she felt a presence in the bedroom.

Within a few minutes she saw, in great detail, a female figure standing beside the bed. The woman seemed about thirty years old, had fair skin and hair, a trim figure, and was rather attractive. Her dress indicated good taste and a degree of wealth, and belonged to the 1870s or 1880s. The young woman just stood there and looked at Mrs. K., and vice versa. She seemed animated enough, but made no sound. Despite this, Mrs. K. had the distinct impression that the ghost wanted her to know something specific. The encounter lasted for ten or fifteen minutes, then the figure slowly disintegrated.

The experience left Mrs. K. frightened and worried. Immediately she reported it to her husband, but he brushed the incident aside with a good deal of skepticism. In the following two weeks, Mrs. K. felt an unseen presence all about the house, without, however, seeing her mysterious visitor again. It seemed that the woman was watching her as she did her daily chores. Mrs. K. had no idea who the ghost might be, but she knew that their house was no more than fifty years old and that there had been swamp land on the spot before that. Could the ghost have some connection with the land itself, or perhaps with some of the antiques Mrs. K. treasured?

About two weeks after the initial experience, Mr. K. was studying in the kitchen, which was located at the far eastern end of the house, while Mrs. K. was watching television in the living room at the other end of the house. Twice she felt the need to go into the kitchen and warn her husband that she felt the ghost moving about the living room, but he insisted it was merely her imagination. So she returned to the living room and curled up in an easy chair to continue watching television. Fifteen minutes later, she heard a loud noise reverberating throughout the house. It made her freeze with fright in the chair, when her husband ran into the living room to ask what the noise had been.

Upon investigation, he noticed a broken string on an antique zither hanging on the dining room wall. It was unlikely that the string could have broken by itself, and if it had, how could it have reverberated so strongly? To test such a possibility, they broke several other strings of the same zither in an effort to duplicate the sound, but without success. A few weeks went by, and the ghost's presence persisted. By now Mrs. K. had the distinct impression that the ghost was annoyed at being ignored. Suddenly, a hurricane lamp hanging from a nail on the wall fell to the floor and shattered. It could not have moved of its own volition.

Again some time passed, and the ghost was almost forgotten. Mrs. K's older daughter, then six years old, asked her mother early one morning who the company was the previous evening. Informed that there had been no guests at the house, she insisted that a lady had entered her bedroom, sat on her bed and looked at her, and then departed. In order to calm the child, Mrs. K. told her she had probably dreamt the whole thing. But the little girl insisted that she had not, and furthermore, she described the visitor in every detail including the "funny" clothes she had worn. Appalled, Mrs. K. realized that her daughter had seen the same ghostly woman. Apparently, the ghost felt greater urgency to communicate now, for a few days later, after going to bed, the apparition returned to Mrs. K.'s bedroom. This time she wore a different dress than on the first meeting, but it was still from the 1880s. She was wiping her hands on an apron, stayed only for a little while, and then slowly disintegrated again.

During the following year, her presence was felt only occasionally, but gradually Mrs. K. managed to snatch a few fleeting impressions about her. From this she put together the story of her ghost. She was quite unhappy about a child, and one evening the following winter, when Mrs. K. felt the ghost wandering about in their basement, she actually heard her crying pitifully for two hours. Obviously, the distraught ghost wanted attention, and was determined to get it at all costs.

One day the following summer, when Mrs. K. was alone with the children after her husband had left for work, one of the children complained that the door to the bathroom was locked. Since the door can be locked only from the inside, and since all four children were accounted for, Mrs. K. assumed that her ghost lady was at it again. When the bathroom door remained locked for half an hour and the children's needs became more urgent, Mrs. K. went to the door and demanded in a loud tone of voice that the ghost open the door. There was anger in her voice and it brought quick results. Clearly the click of a lock being turned was heard inside the bathroom and, after a moment, Mrs. K. opened the bathroom door easily. There was no one inside the bathroom, of course. Who, then, had turned the lock—the only way the door could be opened?

For a while things went smoothly. A few weeks later, Mrs. K. again felt the ghost near her. One of her daughters was sitting at the kitchen table with her while she was cutting out a dress pattern on the counter. Mrs. K. stepped back to search for something in the refrigerator a few feet away, when all of a sudden she and her daughter saw her box of dressmaking pins rise slightly off the counter and fall to the floor. Neither one of them had been near it, and it took them almost an hour to retrieve all the pins scattered on the floor.

A little later, they clearly heard the basement door connecting the dining room and kitchen fly open and slam shut by itself, as if someone in great anger was trying to call attention to her presence. Immediately they closed the door, and made sure there was no draft from any windows.

An instant later, it flew open again by itself. Now they attached the chain to the latch—but that didn't seem to stop the ghost from fooling around with the door. With enormous force, it flew open again as far as the chain allowed, as if someone were straining at it. Quickly Mrs. K. called a neighbor to come over and watch the strange behavior of the door but the minute the neighbor arrived, the door behaved normally, just as before. The ghost was not about to perform for strangers.

One evening in the summer some years later, Mr. K. was driving some dinner guests home and Mrs. K. was alone in the house with the children. All of a sudden, she felt her ghost following her as she went through her chores of emptying ashtrays and taking empty glasses into the kitchen. Mrs. K. tried bravely to ignore her, although she was frightened and she knew that her ghost knew it, which made it all the more difficult to carry on.

Not much later, the K. family had guests again. One of the arriving guests pointed out to Mrs. K. that their basement light was on. Mrs. K. explained that it was unlikely, since the bulb had burned out the day before. She even recalled being slightly annoyed with her husband for having neglected to replace the bulb. But the guest insisted, and so the K's opened the basement door only to find the light off. A moment later another guest arrived. He wanted to know who was working in the basement at such a late hour, since he had seen the basement light on. Moreover, he saw a figure standing at the basement window looking out. Once more, the entire party went downstairs with a flashlight, only to find the light off and no one about.

That was the last the K's saw or heard of their ghost. Why had she so suddenly left them? Perhaps it had to do with a Chicago newspaperwoman's call. Having heard of the disturbances, she had telephoned the K's to offer her services and that of celebrated psychic Irene Hughes to investigate the house. Although the K's did not want any attention because of the children, Mrs. K. told the reporter what had transpired at the house. To her surprise, the reporter informed her that parallel experiences had been reported at another house not more than seven miles away. In the other case, the mother and one of her children had observed a ghostly figure, and an investigation had taken place with the help of Irene Hughes and various equipment, the result of which was that a presence named Lizzy was ascertained.

From this Mrs. K. concluded that they were sharing a ghost with a neighbor seven miles away, and she, too, began to call the ghostly visitor Lizzy. Now if Lizzy had two homes and was shuttling back and forth between them, it might account for the long stretches of no activity at the K. home. On the other hand, if the ghost at the K's was not named Lizzy, she would naturally not want to be confused with some other unknown ghost seven miles away. Be this as it may, Mrs. K. wished her well, wherever she was.

LITTLE GIRL LOST

$\mathcal{M}$rs. J. P. lived in Central Illinois, in an old three-story house with a basement. Prior to her acquiring it, it had stood empty for six months. As soon as she had moved in, she heard some neighborhood gossip that the house was presumed haunted. Although Mrs. P. was not a skeptic, she was level-headed enough not to take rumors at face value.

She looked the house over carefully. It seemed about eighty years old, and was badly in need of repair. Since they had bought it at a bargain price, they did not mind, but as time went on, they wondered how cheap the house had really been. It became obvious to her and her husband that the price had been low for other reasons. Nevertheless, the house was theirs, and together they set out to repaint and remodel it as best they could. For the first two weeks, they were too busy to notice anything out of the ordinary. About three weeks after moving in, however, Mr. and Mrs. P. began hearing things such as doors shutting by themselves, cupboards opening, and particularly, a little girl persistently calling, "Mama, Mama" with a great deal of alarm. But, Mr. and Mrs. P. tried to ignore the phenomena.

One evening, however, they were having a family spat over something of little consequence. All of a sudden a frying pan standing on the stove lifted off by itself, hung suspended in midair for a moment, and then was flung back on the stove with full force. Their twelve-year-old son flew into hysterics, Mr. P. turned white, and Mrs. P. was just plain angry. How dare someone invade their privacy? The following week, the ten-year-old daughter was watching television downstairs in what had been turned into Mrs. P.'s office, while Mr. P. and their son were upstairs also watching television. Suddenly, a glass of milk standing on the desk in the office rose up by itself and dashed itself to the floor with full force. The child ran screaming from the room, and it took a long time for her father to calm her down.

As a result of these happenings, the children implored their mother to move from the house, but Mrs. P. would have none of it. She liked the house fine, and was not about to let some unknown ghost displace her. The more she thought about it, the angrier she got. She decided to go from floor to floor, cursing the ghost and telling him or her to get out of the house, even if he or she used to own it.

But that is how it is with Stay-Behinds: they don't care if you paid for the house. After all, they can't use the money where they are, and would rather stay on in a place they are familiar with.

THE SUICIDE GHOST

$\mathcal{I}$n Springfield, Illinois, lived a couple named Gertrude and Russell Meyers. He worked as a stereotypist on the local newspaper, and she was a high-school teacher. Both of them were in their late twenties and couldn't care less about such things as ghosts.

At the time of their marriage, they had rented a five-room cottage that had stood empty for some time. It had no particular distinction but a modest price, and was located in Bloomington, where the Meyerses then lived.

Gertrude Meyers came from a farm background and had studied at Illinois Wesleyan as well as the University of Chicago. For a while she worked as a newspaperwoman in Detroit, later taught school, and as a sideline wrote a number of children's books. Her husband Russell, also of farm background, attended Illinois State Normal University at Normal, Illinois, and later took his apprenticeship at the *Bloomington Pantograph*.

The house they had rented in Bloomington was exactly like the house next to it, and the current owners had converted what was formerly one large house into two separate units, laying a driveway between them.

In the summer, after they had moved into their house, they went about the business of settling down to a routine. Since

221

her husband worked the night shift on the newspaper, Mrs. Meyers was often left alone in the house. At first it did not bother her at all. Sounds from the street penetrated into the house and gave her a feeling of people nearby. But when the chills of autumn set in and the windows had to be closed to keep it out, she became gradually aware that she was not really alone on those lonely nights.

One particular night early in their occupancy of the house, she had gone to bed leaving her bedroom door ajar. It was ten-thirty and she was just about ready to go to sleep when she heard rapid, firm footsteps starting at the front door, inside the house, and coming through the living room, the dining room, and finally approaching her bedroom door down the hall leading to it.

She leapt out of bed and locked the bedroom door. Then she went back into bed and sat there, wondering with sheer terror what the intruder would do. But nobody came.

More to calm herself than because she really believed it, Mrs. Meyers convinced herself that she must have been mistaken about those footsteps. It was probably someone in the street. With this reassuring thought on her mind, she managed to fall asleep.

The next morning, she did not tell her new husband about the nocturnal event. After all, she did not want him to think he had married a strange woman! But the footsteps returned, night after night, always at the same time and always stopping abruptly at her bedroom door, which, needless to say, she kept locked.

Rather than facing her husband with the allegation that they had rented a haunted house, she bravely decided to face the intruder and find out what this was all about. One night she deliberately waited for the now familiar brisk footfalls. The clock struck ten, then ten-thirty. In the quiet of the night, she could hear her heart pound in her chest.

Then the footsteps came, closer and closer, until they got to her bedroom door. At this moment, Mrs. Meyers jumped out of bed, snapped on the light, and tore the door wide open.

There was nobody there, and no retreating footsteps could be heard.

She tried it again and again, but the invisible intruder never showed himself once the door was opened.

The winter was bitterly cold, and it was Russell's habit of building up a fire in the furnace in the basement when he came home from work at three-thirty A.M. Mrs. Meyers always heard him come in, but did not get up. One night he left the basement, came into the bedroom and said, "Why are you walking around this freezing house in the middle of the night?"

Of course she had not been out of bed all night, and told him as much. Then they discovered that he, too, had heard footsteps, but had thought it was his wife walking restlessly about the house. Meyers had heard the steps whenever he was fixing the furnace in the basement, and by the time he got upstairs they had ceased.

When Mrs. Meyers had to get up early to go to her classes, her husband would stay in the house sleeping late. On many days he would hear someone walking about the house and investigate, only to find himself quite alone. He would wake up in the middle of the night thinking his wife had gotten up, but immediately reassured himself that she was sleeping peacefully next to him. Yet there was *someone* out there in the empty house!

Since everything was securely locked, and countless attempts to trap the ghost had failed, the Meyerses shrugged and learned to live with their peculiar boarder. Gradually the steps became part of the atmosphere of the old house, and the terror began to fade into the darkness of night.

In May of the following year, they decided to work in the garden and, as they did so, they met their next-door neighbors for the first time. Since they lived in identical houses, they had something in common, and conversation between them and the neighbors—a young man of twenty-five and his grandmother—sprang up.

Eventually the discussion got around to the footsteps. It seemed that they, too, kept hearing them. After they had compared notes on their experiences, the Meyerses asked more questions. They were told that before the house was divided, it belonged to a single owner who had committed suicide in the house. No wonder he liked to walk in both halves of what was once his home!

THE PHANTOM DOG

*T*here were reports of wild animals appearing after their deaths, but the majority of animal-related psychic incidents concern domestic animals, especially dogs and cats. Perhaps it was because our pets take on part of our human personality and thus rise above the status of "dumb animals," or perhaps because the bond of love was so strong between master and pet.

Mrs. Elwood Kruse was a housewife in Burlington, Iowa. Her husband was an electrical engineer; neither of them was a student of occult matters, although Mrs. Kruse had a history of premonitions and similar ESP experiences. She had learned to live with it and, if anything, it made her even more cautious in accepting unorthodox happenings than if she had no such abilities. She had always loved animals and, having been raised in the country, had always been surrounded by dogs, cats, birds, or fish. Her husband at first had some reservations about having animals in a home, but eventually he gave in and allowed her to get a puppy for their daughters.

It was Christmas, 1964 when she bought an Irish setter puppy and named him Fiaca. The children were elated, and even Mr. Kruse, not overly fond of dogs, came to like the animal.

On December 18, 1965, her husband had to telephone

Mrs. Kruse to tell her the sad news. Their dog had been run over by a car and killed instantly. Mrs. Kruse was terribly upset. The Christmas season was at hand and memories of Fiaca's arrival a year before would sadden the holidays. But they tried to bear up under their loss.

On the day before Christmas, exactly one year to the day after the dog's arrival at the Kruse home, Mrs. Kruse was in the kitchen when suddenly she heard a strange noise at the front door. It sounded like a dog scratching to be let in. At once she thought, oh, Fiaca wants to get into the house—then the chilling thought came to her that this could not very well be since he was dead. So she went to the front door and peeked through the glass, but there was nothing outside that could have made the noise. She returned to her kitchen explaining her experience as due to her missing the dog at this time of year.

The incident slipped her mind until a few days after the holiday. She heard the sound very clearly again and knew it was not her imagination playing tricks. Again she looked out the door and saw nothing special. The house was new; the storm door was made of aluminum, and the noise was that of animal claws raking up and down on the metal, just as Fiaca used to do. There was no tree close enough to have caused the noise with branches scraping against the door. She told her husband about the second experience but he would not believe her.

The sounds kept coming back, usually in the afternoon. Then one night in the second week of January 1966, it happened again. This time she was not alone but was playing bridge in the living room with her husband and their friends Mr. and Mrs. Marvin Turl. Mr. Turl was a psychology student with an interest in parapsychology.

Mr. Kruse and Susan Turl kept playing, evidently not hearing anything. But Marvin Turl looked up. He too had heard the scratching. He knew nothing at that time of Mrs. Kruse's earlier experiences. But he confirmed that the noise sounded to him like a dog scratching on the door to be let in. Mrs. Kruse and Mr. Turl went to the door and flipped the porch light on. There was no dog outside. Nothing.

The next day Mrs. Kruse confided the strange happenings to her mother and found her receptive to the idea of a psychic phenomenon involving their dog. She suggested that Mrs. Kruse acknowledge her dog's presence verbally the next time the scratching occurred, and open the door as if the dog were actually present.

Two days went by with Mrs. Kruse hoping the ghostly scratching would return. On the third day, in the afternoon, she heard the familiar scratching again. Quickly she went to the door, opened it wide, and said, "Come on in, Fiaca." She felt terribly silly doing this, but after she had done it, the depression over the dog's untimely death seemed somehow to have left her and she felt better about the whole matter. She returned to the kitchen and continued her work.

A little later she found herself in the living room. Imagine her surprise when she found the carpet near the front door covered by a whitish substance, similar to fine dust. The substance trailed into the dining room, where it disappeared for a stretch, only to reappear near the door leading from the kitchen to the living room. She found more of the white substance in the hall, most of it at the end where Fiaca used to curl up on the carpet and sleep. From that spot he could observe all three bedrooms, and it was his favorite spot.

Although Mrs. Kruse had no knowledge of the nature of ectoplasm or materializations, it struck her at once that the white substance marked exactly the way Fiaca used to go about the house: from the front door into the dining room, then a mad dash through the kitchen, and then down the hall to check the bedrooms.

She looked at the white stuff but did not touch it. A little later, her father passed by it and also observed it. But by nightfall it had somehow dissolved. The scratching at the front door was never heard again after that day.

Perhaps, Mrs. Kruse thinks, the dog wanted to come home one more time to make sure everything was all right. The Kruses were glad he took the trouble, for they know that Fiaca was all right too, in his new place.

CONVERSATION WITH A GHOST

$\mathcal{D}$avid H. lived in Michigan. When he was eight he had his first encounter with a ghost. The house his parents lived in was more than a hundred years old, and rather on the large side. David slept in one of two main rooms on the upper floor of the house; the room next to it was unfurnished. One night he was lying in bed when he had a sudden urge to sit up, and as he did so he looked down the hall. All of a sudden he noticed a small, shadowlike man jump down from the attic and run toward him. But instead of coming into his room, he turned down the stairs. David could see that he wore a small derby hat but what was even more fascinating was the fact that the figure walked about two inches above the floor! After the figure had disappeared, David thought it was all his imagination. A particularly bright eight-year-old, he was not easily taken in by fantasies or daydreams.

But the strange figure reappeared several times more, and eventually David came to the conclusion that it was real. He asked his parents whether he could swap rooms with them, and they agreed to let him sleep downstairs. It was about that time that his mother told him that she had heard the old piano playing at night downstairs. She had thought that it was the cat climbing up on the keys, but one night the piano played in plain view of herself and one of her daughters, without even a trace of the cat in the room. There was also the sound of pages in a book being turned in the same area, although nobody had a book or turned any pages.

David settled down in his room on the lower floor, and he forgot all about his ghostly experiences. Shortly after, he heard a crunching noise on the stairs, as if someone were walking on them. He assumed it was his mother coming down the stairs to tell him to turn off his radio, but no one came.

As he grew older, he moved back upstairs, since the room on the ground floor had become too small for him. This proved to be somewhat of a strain for him: many times he would be lying in bed when someone would call his name. But there was never anyone there. Exasperated, the youngster spoke up, challenging the ghost to give some sign of his presence so that there could be communication between them. "If you can hear me, make a noise," David said to his ghost. At that very moment, the door to his room began to rattle without apparent cause. Still unconvinced, since the door had rattled had before because of natural causes, David continued his monologue with, "If you are there, show yourself," and at that moment he heard a strange noise behind him. The door to his closet, which had been closed, was slowly opening. This wasn't very reassuring, even though it might represent some kind of dialogue with the ghost.

Shortly thereafter, and in broad daylight, just as he had gotten home from school, David heard a very loud noise in the upper portion of the house: it sounded as if all their cats were tearing each other to pieces, and the sound of a lot of coat hangers falling down augmented the bedlam. Quickly, David ran up the stairs—only to find neither cats nor fallen coat hangers. And to this day, David doesn't know who the strange visitor was.

THE ELECTROCUTED
GHOST

$\mathcal{M}$rs. Jane Eidson was a housewife in suburban Minneapolis. At the time that I was in touch with her, she was middle-aged and had five children, ranging in age from nine to twenty. Her husband, Bill, traveled four days each week. For eight years they had lived in a cottage-type brick house that was twenty-eight years old.

The first time the Eidsons noticed that there was something odd about their otherwise ordinary-looking home was when they had been in the house for a short time. Mrs. Eidson was in the basement sewing, when all of a sudden she felt that she was not alone—she wanted to run upstairs. She suppressed this strong urge but felt very uncomfortable. Another evening shortly after, her husband was down there practicing a speech when he had the same feeling of another presence. His self-control was not as strong as hers, and he came upstairs immediately.

In discussing their strange feelings with their next-door neighbor, they discovered that the previous tenant also had complained about the basement. Their daughter Rita had never wanted to go to the basement by herself and, when pressed for a reason, finally admitted that there was a man down there. She described him as dark-haired and wearing a plaid shirt. Sometimes he would stand by her bed at night and she would become frightened, but the moment she thought of calling her mother, the image disappeared. Another spot where she felt his presence was the little playhouse at the other end of their yard.

The following spring, Mrs. Eidson noticed a bouncing light at the top of the stairs as she was about to go to bed in an upstairs room that she occupied while convalescing from surgery. The light followed her to her room as if it had a mind of its own. When she entered her room the light left, but the room felt icy. She was disturbed by this, but nevertheless went to bed and soon had forgotten all about it as sleep came to her. Suddenly, in the middle of the night, she woke and sat up in bed.

Something had awakened her. At the head of her bed she saw a man who was "beige-colored," as she put it. As she stared at the apparition it went away, again leaving the room very chilly.

About that same time, the Eidsons noticed that their electric appliances were playing tricks on them. There was the time at five A.M. when their washing machine went on by itself, as did the television set in the basement, which could only be turned on by plugging it into the wall socket. When they had gone to bed, the set was off and there was no one around to plug it in.

Who was so fond of electrical gadgets as to turn them on in the small hours of the morning?

Finally Mrs. Eidson found out. In May 1949, a young man who was just out of the service had occupied the house. His hobby was electrical wiring, it seems, for he had put in a strand of heavy wires from the basement underground through the yard to the other end of the property. When he attempted to hook them up with the utility pole belonging to the electric company, he was killed instantly. It happened near the place where Mrs. Eidson's girl had seen the apparition. Since the wires were still in her garden, Mrs. Eidson was not at all surprised that the dead man liked to hang around.

And what better way for an electronics buff to manifest as a ghost than by appearing as a bright, bouncy light? The dead electrician was playing tricks in the Eidson home, so Mrs. Eidson decided that the family would move. They found a new home—one a little less unusual than their former one.

THE GHOST OF THE
HENPECKED HUSBAND

Mike l. lived in Tennessee, where his family had been in residence for several generations. Ever since he could remember, he had had psychic ability. At the time when a favorite uncle was in the hospital, he was awakened in the middle of the night to see his uncle standing by his bed.

"Goodbye, Michael," the uncle said, and then the image faded away. At that instant, Mike knew that his uncle had passed away, so he went back to sleep. The following morning, his mother awoke him to tell him that his uncle had passed away during the night.

In April, he and his wife moved to a residential section in one of the large cities of Tennessee. They bought a house from a lady well in her seventies who had the reputation of being somewhat cranky. She was not too well liked in the neighborhood.

Shortly after they had settled down in the house, they noticed footsteps in the rafters over their bedroom. Regardless of the hour, these footsteps would come across the ceiling from one side of the room to the other. Whenever they checked, there was no one there who could have caused the footsteps.

While they were still puzzled about the matter, though not shocked?since they had had psychic presences in other houses, something still more remarkable occurred. There were two floor lamps in the living room, on opposite sides of the room. One night, Mr. L. awoke and noticed one of the floor lamps lit. Since he clearly remembered having turned it off on going to bed, he was puzzled, but he got out of bed and switched it off again. As if to complement this incident, the other floor lamp came on by itself a few nights later, even though it had been turned off by hand a short time before.

This was the beginning of an entire series of lights being turned on in various parts of the house, seemingly by unseen hands. Since it was their practice not to leave any lights on except for a small night light in their daughter's room, there was no way in which this could be explained by negligence or on rational grounds. The house had a basement, including a small space below the wooden front porch. As a result of this hollow space, if anyone were walking on the porch, the steps would reverberate that much more audibly. The L.'s frequently heard someone come up the porch, approach the door, and stop there. Whenever they looked out, they saw no one about. Not much later, they were awakened by the noise of a large number of dishes crashing to the floor of the kitchen, at least so they thought. When they checked, everything was in order; no dish had been disturbed.

They were still wondering about this when they caught the movement of something—or someone—out of the corner of their eye in the living room. When they looked closer, there was no one there. Then the dresser in the bedroom *seemed* to be moving across the floor, or so it sounded. By the time they got to the room, nothing had been changed.

One night, just after retiring, Mr. L. was shocked by a great deal of noise in the basement. It sounded as if someone were wrecking his shop. He jumped out of bed, grabbed a gun, opened the basement door, and turned on the light. There was an audible scurrying sound, as if someone were moving about, followed by silence.

Immediately Mr. L. thought he had a burglar, but realized he would be unable to go downstairs undetected. Under the circumstances, he called for his wife to telephone the police while he stood at the head of the stairs guarding the basement exit. As soon as he heard the police arrive, he locked the only door to the basement and joined them on the outside of the house. Together they investigated, only to find no one about, no evidence of foul play. Even more inexplicable, nothing in the shop had been touched. About that time, Mr. L. noticed a tendency of the basement door to unlock itself, seemingly of its own volition, even though it was Mr. L.'s custom to lock it both at night and when leaving the house. During the daytime, Mrs. L. frequently heard footsteps overhead when she was in the basement, even though she was fully aware of the fact that there was no one in the house but her.

By now, Mr. and Mrs. L. realized that someone was trying to get their attention. They became aware of an unseen presence staring at them in the dining room, or bothering Mrs. L. in one of the other rooms of the house. Finally, Mike L. remembered that a Rosicrucian friend had given them a so-called Hermetic Cross when they had encountered ghostly troubles in another house. He brought the cross to the dining room and nailed it to the wall. This seemed to relieve the pressure somewhat, until they found a calendar hung in front of the cross, as if to downgrade its power.

Mr. L. made some further inquiries in the neighborhood to find out who the unseen intruder might be. Eventually he managed to piece the story together. The woman from whom they had bought the house had been a widow of about nine years when they had met her. The husband had been extremely unhappy in the house; he was not permitted to smoke, for instance, and had to hide his cigarettes in a neighbor's basement. Nothing he did in his own house met with his wife's approval, it appeared, and he died a very unhappy man. Could it not be that his restless spirit, once freed from the shackles of the body, finally enjoyed his unobstructed power to roam the house and do whatever he pleased? Or perhaps he could now even enjoy the vicarious thrill of frightening the later owners, and for the first time in his long life, become the stronger party in the house.

RETURN TO CLINTON COURT

When I investigated Clinton Court, in New York City, back in 1960, and wrote about it in *The Ghost Hunter*, I never dreamed I'd have to come back and talk to a ghost again. But sometimes, the dead won't stay still. Our first visit had been somewhat impaired by a nervous real estate firm who wanted us out of the house as quickly as possible. Ethel Johnson Meyers went into trance in the lower portion of what was once the stables and carriage house of Governor Clinton. Now located in the heart of Hell's Kitchen, it was then a rural neighborhood in which the Clinton Mansion, now gone, was surrounded by fields and woodlands close to the North River.

Ethel Meyers' trance was fully described in the chapter called "The Clinton Court Ghosts" in *The Ghost Hunter.* When we left the downstairs apartment where Ethel and I had spent a quiet hour, I was pretty sure there would be no further need for our services. The apartment was then in a state of disrepair, there was no tenant as yet, and all we had to sit on were a bench and a completely worn-out chair someone had left behind.

I thought no more of charming Clinton Court, so neatly

tucked away behind an iron gate and probably unknown to most New Yorkers, until 1964, when a Ms. Alyce Montreuil wrote to me of her experiences in the house at 422H West Forty-sixth Street, New York.

As a friend of the tenants who had taken one of the two apartments making up the former carriage house, she had had her brush with the uncanny. I reported this in detail in *Ghosts I've Met;* how the upstairs door near the porch atop the stairs would not stay closed, how the door seemingly unlocked itself, and how her dogs would freeze when approaching the staircase leading to the upper apartment.

Again I thought I had done my duty to restless Clinton Court by reporting these later developments during the tenancy of Danny Brown and Frank Benner, between 1959 and 1963. Meanwhile, the tower apartment had also acquired new tenants, Mr. and Mrs. Dan Neary, who had lived there since 1963.

Somehow Clinton Court would not leave me alone. A young student of the occult named Bob Nelson wrote to me of doors opening by themselves. But he had read my book, and I was afraid it might have inspired him to look for these things. Then in February of 1965, Mrs. Leo Herbert contacted me after seeing Sybil Leek and myself "de-ghosting" (or trying to "de-ghost") June Havoc's house, situated behind theirs, on Miss Havoc's television program.

Her husband, a direct descendant of Victor Herbert, was property master for all David Merrick shows, and Mrs. Herbert was a dancer. They had lived in the two top floors composing the upper apartment since 1964. There were some odd things going on in the place, and would Sybil Leek and I please come and have a talk with whoever it was who was causing them?

No sooner said than done. On March 28, about a dozen people assembled in the upstairs living room of the Herberts. They included the downstairs neighbors, the Nearys; some people living in the front, or un-haunted section of Clinton Court; Bob Nelson, Carl Gewritz, the Herbert children, and Mr. and Mrs. Biff Liff; Gail Benedict, public relations director, Bill Hazlett, and Peter Hahn of North American Newspaper Alliance; Catherine and me; and, of course, Sybil Leek, resplendent in purple dress, stockings, and cape.

Promptly at nine, we dimmed the lights and grouped ourselves around the room roughly in a circle, with Sybil stretching out on a chair in the upper center.

After the usual few moments of hypnosis, I had Sybil safely entranced, and I waited for the ghost to make himself or herself known. I knew there were several layers of consciousness in the place, and I could not be sure about the ones who would break through the barrier and use Sybil's vocal cords to communicate with us.

Her lips moved silently for a few moments while I strained not to miss the first words. Gradually the sounds became intelligible and I moved closer.

"What is your name?" I asked.

"Walker."

I asked the ghost to speak up.

"George ... Walker," the voice said, plainly now.

"Is this your house?"

"No. George ... I have blood in my mouth ... hurt."

"Who hurt you?"

"Don't know ... dying ... I'm dying ... too late ..."

"Do you live here?"

"No ... Brice."

"What street?"

"No street. Brice. South."

"What year is this?"

"Ninety-two."

"What can we do to help you?"

"I want to live ... doctor."

"Which doctor do you want us to call?"

"Warren. East ... Easton."

It sounded like East Hampton to me, but I wasn't sure. The voice had difficulty maintaining an even tone.

"How did you get to this house?" I inquired.

"Went to the river ... everybody ... friends, soldiers ... Alfred ... came to rest ..."

"Why did you come to this house?"

"I like it ... remembered ... coming here to see George ... two Georgies."

"What is this other George's name?"

"Clinton. George Clinton ... I dic ..."

"Are you a soldier?"

"Yes... Colonel ... George ... Walker."

"What regiment?"

"Two-four."

"Who is the commanding general?"

"Wilson."

"First name?"

"Amos ... nobody bothers ..."

"Yes, I do. I will help you. Who attacked you?"

"I don't know."

I asked what he wanted in this house.

"I want to stay ... no house, field! Can't get to the house."

"Where were you born?" I changed the subject before the ghost could get too upset to give us information.

"Brice ... Carolina ..."

"When did you come up here?"

The voice hesitated.

"Eight-three ... no, ninety-three ... eighty-eight."

"How did you get hurt?"

"Blood in my chest ... knife ..." He added that it was a man, a soldier, but he did not recognize him.

Suddenly, the jaws of the medium started to quiver and the

voice began to give out.

"Can't talk ..." I calmed him, and his tone became once more steadier.

"What other regiments were here?" I resumed.

"Queens ... Nine ... "

"Were you in any campaign?"

"Brice ..."

"What town is Brice near?"

"Pike's Hill."

"What colony?"

"North Carolina."

"Any other town it is near to?"

"Pike's Hill, Three Hills ..."

I asked him whether he knew anyone else here, but the ghost replied he couldn't see things in the "field," only smoke.

"The house is too far. I can't get there," he repeated.

"What is your wife's name?"

"Martha ... Brice."

"Children?"

"Three."

"Your father's name?"

"Stephen ... Brice ... Burnt Oak."

"Is that the name of a house?"

"Yes ..."

"Is he alive or dead?"

"Dead."

"When did he die?"

"Fifty-nine."

"Where is he buried?"

"Burnt Oak."

"Cemetery?"

"In the garden."

"What denomination was he?"

"Catholic."

"Were you Catholic?"

"Yes ... French Catholic."

"Were you baptized?"

"St. Teresa."

"Where is this?"

"Pike Hill."

"What year were you born?"

"Thirty-four."

"Any brothers who were officers?"

"Clifford ... Colonel ... fourteenth regiment, stationed Pike Hill."

"Cavalry or infantry?"

"Infantry."

"Any other brothers who were officers?"

"Aaron ... Captain ..."

"Where stationed?"

"Don't know."

I felt it was time to release this unhappy one. Gently, I suggested his pain was no more, and asked him to join his loved ones.

A moment later he slipped away. I then asked that Sybil Leek, still deeply entranced, answer my questions, without awakening. This was actually switching from deep trance to clairvoyant trance in the middle of the séance, but Sybil had extraordinary powers of the mind and was a disciplined medium. Sybil's own voice responded to me now. She sounded somewhat sleepy and wasn't her usual crisp self, but nevertheless she was clearly audible.

I asked her to look around and report what she saw. Sybil's etheric body was now "on the other side" for the time being, and she was able to see the same things a permanent resident of that other world would be seeing.

She described a house with three windows, with a "sort of office" inside.

243

"There are people here who should not be here ... girls!" she said.

"What happens here?" I asked.

"Something to do with the staircase ... something happened ... trying to see ... I don't like it ... someone hanging ... don't like it ... a man ..."

"What does he look like?"

"Six ... young men ... gray clothes ... someone hung *him* ... I don't want to look ..."

"Is there anyone else on the staircase?" I inquired.

"Yes," Sybil said in halting tones. "That girl."

"How old is she?"

"Twenty-five, twenty-six."

"What is she doing on the staircase?"

"She has seen *him*. Doesn't care. She wants someone to take him away, but then she forgets about it. She was wrong about the man ... liking him ... I see her living in this house and she is very happy, until she gets frightened by the man. She doesn't like the staircase. Someone takes the staircase and *puts it somewhere else* ... I don't want to stay here ... bad house."

"What about the staircase?" I pressed Sybil.

"She moved the staircase and then got to go back to the old staircase and then they caught up with her."

"Who caught up with her?"

"The man's friends. The man who was hung. She was very ill. He had her move the staircase. They knew it was there. And so she kept going back. And then she died ... *somebody pushed her*. And she hurt her back, she couldn't walk, bad house."

"The girl—because she's frightened. She throws things onto the ground. She runs up the stairs—the other stairs trying to get away—she doesn't like music—reminds her of sad song—the music starts things off here."

"How long ago did she die?"

"Eighteen-four-o—about …"

"Is she causing all the disturbances in this house?" I asked.

"No … a man, and she, and others … lot of people pass through … to the river."

"Anyone else on the staircase?"

"No."

"Look at the door. Is anybody at the door?"

"Animal … dog … scratching … nobody there to let it in … she's inside."

"Is this her house?"

"Sort of. Lives here … Goes to the door because of the scratching noise."

"Is it her dog?"

"Dog lives in the house … strange, she wants to go, and she can't."

"Why?"

"Because she would have no money. She is wanting to open the door, let the dog in."

"Is the woman on the other side?"

Sybil's voice was somewhat puzzled.

"*I'm* on the other side."

Of course she was … temporarily.

"Is she the same girl you saw on the stairs?"

"Yes."

"Is there anyone else here?"

"No."

"Do you see any children here?"

"Four children. Not here now. Not very strong."

"Look at the staircase once more. Was there any kind of tragedy on the staircase?"

"I see someone who falls. Older man. The girl … is used to the staircase now. She keeps *staying* on this staircase."

"You mean like the man who was hanged?"

"Yes. It is very confusing. She is on the staircase waiting

for something else, I think. Someone and something else to happen. Someone to come, she is very confused."

I felt that Sybil had been "under" long enough and decided to bring her out of her trance. This was accomplished quickly. When Sybil awoke, she remembered very little, as usual.

The group was animated now as everyone sought to sum up reactions and feelings. Our bearded host, Leo Herbert, who was next to Sybil with the entrance door at his back, was the first to speak.

"It is very strange, but just before Hans put Sybil under, I felt that there was a draft. I got up, and shut the door, but I could still feel this coldness, right here, on me. It just never left, and feels pretty much like that this moment, though not with the intensity it had when you were hypnotizing Sybil. I had the feeling if I moved out of this spot, Sybil would talk louder."

Sybil's entranced voice was not loud on this occasion, and some of the group farther back in the room had difficulty hearing her.

"Did you have any psychic experiences in this house prior to our session tonight?" I asked Leo Herbert.

"I have heard noises from upstairs, where I sleep, and I came down here to investigate and found no one here," Herbert said, "but I had the feeling of a *presence* here. As if somebody had just been here. This was only two and a half weeks ago. The first time when I awakened, I thought that I heard footsteps down here, and I waited a long time and heard nothing, and after fifteen minutes, I went back to bed. An hour later I was awakened again, went directly down, checked the windows and door and found them all locked. Yet I felt someone had been present here."

I then turned to Mrs. Herbert, who was sitting on the comfortable couch next to Catherine.

"What about you—have you had any uncanny experiences here?"

"About a year ago, I was alone in the apartment," the slender brunette answered, "when I was sure someone was throwing pebbles against the skylight of the roof above our bedrooms. I also heard footsteps on the roof."

"Did you look to see who it was?"

"No, I was terrified."

"Did you find any pebbles on the roof?"

"No, nothing. I went up the next morning, but there was nothing on the roof. No pebbles."

I thanked Mrs. Herbert and approached the Nearys, who lived below the Herberts. Mrs. Neary was quite willing to talk to me, although she had originally been a skeptic about ghosts.

"The sounds in the house are so much more varied than ever before," she volunteered. "I have heard a bell ringing, yet there was no bell. On at least six occasions lately, I have felt someone brush past me, yet nobody could be seen. I have had a sense of shadow. There are all sorts of strange noises. Primarily in the area of the wall between the living room and kitchen. Sometimes there is ticking in the wall."

I asked for quiet, and read aloud Ms. Montreuil's letter to me, relating the experiences she had had at the house while a guest of previous tenants. I stressed that Sybil Leek did not know where we would be going that evening. She had no advance information, because we never discuss cases beforehand. I had directed the driver to take us to 420 West Forty-sixth Street, carefully avoiding the use of "Clinton Court." On arrival, I had hustled her upstairs, so that she had no chance to study the house or familiarize herself with it.

And yet much of what came through Sybil Leek's entranced lips matched the earlier testimony of Ethel Johnson Meyers. Much was new, too, and could be checked without too much difficulty. I felt Ethel had "sensed" a girl on the staircase, and so had Sybil.

That the stairs had been moved was unknown to both Ethel and Sybil at the time, yet both said they had been. Sybil spoke of a man hanged on the stairs, which might very well refer to Old Moor, the sailor hanged for mutiny on the Battery, but buried here in Potter's Field. Clinton Court was built above the old Potter's Field.

The girl, waiting for someone and for something to happen, was felt by both mediums. And the story of the pebbles and footsteps on the roof meshes with Mrs. Meyer's tale of a girl pushed off the roof to her death.

The officer named Walker was a new character in the ever-expanding ghostly cast of Clinton Court. Could he be traced?

Sometimes it was even difficult to trace a living officer, and tracing a dead one isn't easy. I did not expect to be completely successful, but I had hoped that at least one or two names could be traced or proved correct.

Sybil, in trance speaking with the voice and mind of Col. George Walker, had referred to a commanding officer by the name of Amos Wilson. He also said his doctor was one Dr. Warren, and that he had come to New York in 1788. We don't know, at least from the psychic end, whether he was still on active duty in 1792, when presumably his death occurred. He might have been retired and his visit to New York might not have been connected with his military career at all.

It was therefore with considerable interest that I found in Heitman's *Historical Register of Officers of the Continental Army* that a George Walker had been a Second Lieutenant, serving in that capacity to 1783, and that one Amos Wilson, First Lieutenant, had served at least in 1776; also, one John Warren, Surgeon, was recorded for the period from 1777 to 1783. These officers served with Northern regiments, while Walker claimed North Carolina as his home. However, it was not unusual for officers, or men, for that matter, to serve in regiments based in other regions of the country than their own colony. Many Southerners did indeed come north during the revolutionary and post-revolutionary period to serve with established "Yankee" regiments.

In trance, Walker claimed to have had a brother named Aaron Walker, with the rank of Captain. I found a Lt. Aaron Walker, attached to a Connecticut regiment in 1776. George Walker—the one I found listed—served in New Jersey, incidentally, which could have brought him into nearby New York.

I did not locate Walker's other brothers, nor did I come across his father or wife, but we must keep in mind that the records of the period were not complete. Certainly the claimed friendship with George Clinton fits in chronologically. The ghost also spoke several times of a place called Brice, North Carolina, and described it as being near Pike's Hill. There was a Pikes*ville*, North Carolina.

As for Brice, North Carolina—or perhaps Bryce, as the spelling was never given—this took a bit more searching. Finally, the reference librarian of the North Carolina State Library in Raleigh, Mrs. Helen Harrison, was able to supply me with some information.

The *Colonial Records*, which was a list of incorporated towns, early maps, postal guides, etc., revealed nothing about such a place. The State Department of Archives and History also checked their files without success. But in *Colonial Records*, vol. IV, page 16, there was *mention* of a sawmill being erected at Brice's Creek, Newbern, in 1735, and of Samuel Pike receiving a land grant at Newbern in 1748.

"Brice started to acquire land grants as early as 1707," Mrs. Harrison pointed out, "and it is known that Brice built a fort on his plantation and that patents were granted for land on Brice's Creek as late as 1758. It seems possible that this settlement may be the Brice to which you refer."

What about Pike's Hill and Three Hills, which the ghost said were close to each other and to Brice?

"In 1755," Mrs. Harrison stated, "there was a movement to build the capital at Tower Hill, Craven County, N.C. It interested me to find that *all three* of these places are located in Craven County, though Tower Hill may have no connection with Three Hills."

On re-hearing the tapes, I find I cannot be absolutely sure whether the ghost said Tower Hill or Three Hills. It could have been either.

So there you have it. How could Sybil Leek (or I, for that matter) know these minute details that were so obscure even a local historian had difficulty tracing them?

Not a ghost of a chance, I think.

GHOSTLY GOINGS-ON IN OKLAHOMA

J am indebted to a young lady by the name of Lori Buzza for the verified account of a friend who had been psychic from her early years onward. The friend's name was Penny McDaniel. She had come to terms with her ESP faculty and was no longer frightened by it. She was able to foretell when a telephone might ring and had, on occasion, done trance work in which personalities of the deceased had come through her. But in 1965 when she was in her early teens something happened that really frightened her, when she visited her grandmother in an area of Oklahoma that was Indian territory. Part of the present-day house was built over a spot where there was once an old log cabin. One of the rooms of the house was in fact built on the exact foundations of that nonexistent cabin.

There were other guests there besides her parents and Penny, so the question of where each was to sleep came up and caused some problems. The grandmother tried to fix the young girl a cot in the living room, but Penny insisted that that was perfectly ridiculous since there seemed to be a very nice bedroom not being used by anyone. After an embarrassing silence her grandmother explained that the bedroom Penny was referring to would not be available to her either. Why not, Penny wanted to know. Because, explained her grandmother, somewhat uneasily, people had been hearing strange noises and seeing inexplicable things in that room and it had been finally closed off and no one had entered it for years. Nonsense, Penny decided. She was not afraid of such things as haunted rooms. There was no such thing as ghosts and if the others were too scared to sleep in the closed-off room, she certainly wasn't. Finally her grandmother shrugged and gave her the key to the room.

No one wanted to come along with her to help her make up the bed, so Penny went on her own. When she stuck the key into the lock and opened the door she was greeted by musty air. Evidently the room had not been aired out or entered for many years. Everything was covered with thick dust, but the hour was late and Penny was not in the mood to clean up. All she did was make up the bed and go to sleep, not touching anything else.

It must have been the middle of the night when she awoke with a jolt. She had a feeling of a presence in the room. She looked around and at the foot of her bed stood a woman dressed in pioneer clothes. Her figure was completely white and as Penny looked at her she seemed to fade away slowly. Penny decided she was dreaming and started to turn over and go back to sleep. A moment later when she was still not fully asleep she heard sounds by the side of her bed. It sounded as if some animal were passing by. She turned and to her horror saw the perfect imprints of a dog's forepaws on the side of the bed. At this point she screamed. Her mother came rushing in and turned on the lights. At the side of the bed there were paw prints in the dust on the floor and not far away from the paw prints, at the foot of the bed, were a set of woman's footprints.

After this, Penny did not sleep for the rest of the night. She sat up in the living room waiting for daybreak. Her mother had, in the meantime, gone back to sleep, assuming that Penny would be all right away from the haunted room. It was around six o'clock in the morning when Penny had a strong impulse to get up and walk out of the house. As if driven by an unseen force she found herself walking in the yard, turning around the back of the house and directing her steps to a spot directly under the windows of the very bedroom she had slept in earlier that night. As she looked down on the ground she discovered the skeleton of a hand and a foot and scraps of scalp placed there in a perfect triangle. Looking at what she instantly knew were human remains, she screamed for her mother and then passed out.

It was three days later that she came to in a local hospital. As soon as she had recovered her wits, Penny, her brother Tom, and Mrs. McDaniel, the mother, joined forces to investigate the occurrence. Digging into local historical records, they discovered that there had been ample reason for the frightening event to take place.

Back during pioneer days a log cabin had stood on the spot where the haunted room was later built. In it lived a family consisting of a husband, a wife, and a sheepdog. There were no neighbors directly nearby so no one was sure exactly when the tragedy happened. One day the nearest neighbors, some distance away, saw smoke rising from the homestead and decided to investigate. On approaching the house they discovered that Indians had burned the cabin and all the family killed, including the dog. The bodies were all burned except the woman's. It was already late in the day and the neighbors decided not to brave the Indians they assumed were still lurking around the area and returned to their own homes. The next morning they returned to bury the family. It was then that they discovered that the Indians had apparently returned during the night and had cut off the woman's right hand and foot and had also scalped her. As they were searching through the rubble of the cabin they discovered the missing hand and foot and scalp placed in a triangle beneath where two windows of the log cabin had been in back of the house. They had been placed there in some sort of ritual.

THE GHOST WHO WOULD
NOT LEAVE

*H*ardly had I finished investigating the rather colorful haunting in the New York State home of *Newsday* columnist Jack Altschul, which resulted in my name appearing in his column as a man who goes around chasing ghosts, than I heard from a gentleman, now deceased, who was the public relations director of the Sperry Company and a man not ordinarily connected with specters.

Ken Brigham wanted me to know that he had a resident ghost at his summer home in Maine, and what was I to do about it. He assured me that while the lady ghost he was reporting was not at all frightening to him and his family, he would, nevertheless, prefer she went elsewhere. This is a sentiment I have found pervasive with most owners of haunted property, and while it shows a certain lack of sentimentality, it is a sound point of view even from the ghost's perspective because being an earthbound spirit really has no future, so to speak.

All this happened in January of 1967. I was keenly interested. At the time, I was working closely with the late Ethel Johnson Meyers, one of the finest trance mediums ever, and it occurred to me immediately that, if the case warranted it, I would get her involved in it.

I asked Mr. Brigham, as was my custom, to put his report in writing, so I could get a better idea as to the nature of the haunting. He did this with the precision expected from a public relations man representing a major instrument manufacturer. Here then is his initial report:

"As a member of the public relation/advertising profession, I've always been considered a cynical, phlegmatic individual and so considered myself. I'm not superstitious, I walk under ladders, have never thought about the "spirit world," am not a deeply religious person, etc., but ...

Eight years ago, my wife and I purchased, for a summer home, a nonworking farm in South Waterford, Maine. The ten-room farmhouse had been unoccupied for two years prior to our acquisition. Its former owners were an elderly couple who left no direct heirs and who had been virtually recluses in their latter years. The house apparently was built in two stages; the front part about 1840, and the ell sometime around 1800. The ell contains the original kitchen and family bedroom; a loft overhead was used during the nineteenth century for farm help and children. The former owners for many years occupied only a sitting room, the kitchen, and a dining room; all other rooms being closed and shuttered. The so-called sitting room was the daily and nightly abode. We never met the Bells, both of whom died of old age in nursing homes in the area, several years before we purchased the farm. They left it to relatives; all the furniture was auctioned off.

"The first summer my wife and I set about restoring the farmhouse. The old kitchen became our living room; the Bell's sitting room became another bedroom; the old dining room, our kitchen. One bright noontime, I was painting in the new living room. All the doors were open in the house. Aware that someone was looking at me, I turned toward the bedroom door and there, standing in bright sunlight, was an elderly woman; she was staring at me. Dressed in a matronly house-dress, her arms were folded in the stance common to many housewives. I was startled, thinking she must have entered the house via the open front door and had walked through the front sitting room to the now-bedroom. Behind her eyeglasses, she maintained a passive, inquisitive expression. For a moment or two, we stared at each other. I thought, What do you say to a native who has walked through your house, without sounding unneighborly? And was about to say something like what can I do for you? when she disappeared. She was there and then she wasn't. I hurried through the bedrooms and, of course, there was no one.

"Once or twice that summer I was awakened by a sudden, chill draft passing through the second-floor room we used as a master bedroom. One early evening, while I was taking a shower, my wife called me from the living room with near-panic in her voice. I hurried downstairs as quickly as possible only to have her ask if I intended to remain downstairs.

"Before closing the house up for the winter, I casually described the apparition to local friends without disclosing my reasons, excusing the inquiry from a standpoint I was inter-ested in the previous owners. Apparently my description was accurate, for our friends wanted to know where I'd seen Mrs. Bell; I had difficulty passing it off.

"My wife wasn't put off, however, and later that evening we compared notes for the first time. The night she called me, she explained, she had felt a cold draft pass behind her and had looked up toward the door of the former sitting room (which was well lighted). There, in the door, was the clear and full shadow of a small woman. My wife then cried out to me. The chill breeze went through the room and the shadow disap-peared. My wife reported, however, that surprisingly enough she felt a sense of calm. No feeling of vindictiveness.

"Over the years, we've both awakened spontaneously to the chill draft and on more than one occasion have watched a pinpoint light dance across the room. The house is isolated and on a private road, discounting any possible headlights, etc. After a moment or so, the chill vanishes.

A couple of times, guests have queried us on hearing the house creak or on hearing footsteps, but we pass these off.

"The summer before last, however, our guests' reaction was different.

A couple with two small children stayed with us. The couple occupied the former sitting room, which now is furnished as a Victorian-style bedroom with a tremendous brass bed. Their daughter occupied another first-floor bedroom, and their son shared our son's bedroom on the second floor. A night light was left on in the latter bedroom and in the bathroom, thereby illuminating the upper hallway, and, dimly, the lower hallway. My wife and I occupied another bedroom on the second floor that is our custom.

"During the early hours of the morning, we were awakened by footsteps coming down the upper hallway.

"They passed our door, went into the master bedroom, paused, continued into our room and after a few minutes, passed on and down the staircase. My wife called out, thinking it was one of the boys, possibly ill. No answer. The chill breeze was present, and my wife again saw the woman's shadow against the bedroom wall. The children were sound asleep.

"In the morning, our adult guests were quiet during breakfast, and it wasn't until later that the woman asked if we'd been up during the night and had come downstairs. She'd been awakened by the footsteps and by someone touching her arm and her hair. Thinking it was her husband, she found him soundly sleeping. In the moonlight, she glanced toward a rocking chair in the bedroom and said she was certain someone had moved it and the clothes left on it. She tried to return to sleep, but again was awakened, certain someone was in the room, and felt someone move the blanket and touch her arm.

"My wife and I finally acknowledged our ghost, but our woman guest assured us that she felt no fright, to her own surprise, and ordinarily wouldn't have believed such nonsense, except that I, her host, was too worldly to be a spiritualist.

"At least one other guest volunteered a similar experience.

Finally I admitted my story to our local friends, asking them not to divulge the story in case people thought we were kooks. But I asked them if they would locate a photograph of the Bell family. Needless to say, the photograph they located was identical with my apparition. An enlargement now was given a prominent place in our living room.

"Although this experience hasn't frightened us with the house, it has left us puzzled. My wife and I both share the feeling that "whatever [it is] is more curious than unpleasant; more interested than destructive."

I was impressed and replied we would indeed venture Down East. It so happened that Catherine, to whom I was married to at the time, and I were doing some traveling in upper New Hampshire that August, and Ethel Johnson Meyers was vacationing at Lake Sebago. All that needed to be done was coordinate our travel plans and set the date.

Mr. Brigham, who then lived in Great Neck, New York, was delighted and gave us explicit instructions on how to traverse New Hampshire from Pike, New Hampshire, where I was lecturing at the Lake Tarleton Club, to our intended rendezvous with Ethel in Bridgton, Maine, at the Cumberland Hotel. The date we picked was August 14, 1967. Ken and Doris Brigham then suggested we could stay over at the haunted house, if necessary, and I assured them that I doubted the need for it, being a bit cocksure of getting through to, and rid of, the ghost all in the same day.

Crossing the almost untouched forests from New

Hampshire to Maine on a road called the Kancamagus Highway was quite an experience for us: we rode for a very, very long time without ever seeing a human habitation, or, for that matter, a gas station. But then the Native Americans whose land this was never worried about such amenities.

Before we left, we had received a brief note from Ken Brigham about the existence of this road cutting through the White Mountains. He also informed me that some of the witnesses to the phenomena at the house would be there for our visit, and I would have a chance to meet them, including Mrs. Mildred Haynes Noyes, a neighbor who was able to identify the ghostly apparition for the Brighams. Most of the phenomena had occurred in the living room, downstairs in the house, as well as in the long central hall, and in one upper-story front bedroom as well, Mr. Brigham added.

At the time I had thought of bringing a television documentary crew along to record the investigations, but it didn't work out, and in the end I did some filming myself and sound recorded the interviews, and, of course, Ethel Meyers's trance.

When we finally arrived at the house in question in Waterford, Maine, Ethel had no idea where she was exactly or why. She never asked questions when I called on her skills. Directly on arrival she began pacing up and down in the grounds adjacent to the house as if to gather up her bearings. She often did that, and I followed her around with my tape recorder like a dog follows its master.

"I see a woman at the window, crying," she suddenly said and pointed to an upstairs window. "She wears a yellow hat and dress. There is a dog with her. Not from this period. Looking out, staring at something."

We then proceeded to enter the house and found ourselves in a very well appointed living room downstairs; a fire in the fireplace gave it warmth, even though this was the middle of August. The house and all its furnishings were kept as much as possible in the Federal period style, and one had the feeling of having suddenly stepped back into a living past.

When we entered the adjacent dining room, Ethel pointed at one of the tall windows and informed us that the lady was still standing there.

"Dark brown eyes, high cheekbones, smallish nose, now she has pushed back the bonnet hat, dark reddish-brown hair," Ethel intoned. I kept taking photographs pointing the camera toward the area where Ethel said the ghost was standing. The pictures did not show anything special, but then Ethel was not a photography medium, someone who has that particular phase of mediumship. I asked Ethel to assure the woman we had come in friendship and peace, to help her resolve whatever conflict might still keep her here. I asked Ethel to try to get the woman's name. Ethel seemed to listen, then said, "I like to call her Isabelle, Isabelle ..."

"How is she connected to the house?"

"Lived here."

I suggested that Ethel inform the woman we wanted to talk to her. Earnestly, Ethel then addressed the ghost, assuring her of no harm. Instead of being comforted, Ethel reported, the woman just kept on crying.

We asked the ghost to come with us as we continued the tour of the house; we would try and have her communicate through Ethel in trance somewhere in the house where she could be comfortable. Meanwhile Ethel gathered further psychic impressions as we went from room to room.

"Many layers here ... three layers ... men fighting and dying here ..." she said. "Strong Indian influence also ... then there is a small child here ... later period ... the men have guns, bleeding ... no shoes ... pretty far back ... Adam ... Joseph ... Balthazar ... war victims ... house looks different ... they're lying around on the floor, in pain ... some kind of skirmish has gone on here."

I decided to chase the lady ghost again. We returned to the living room. Ethel picked a comfortable chair and prepared herself for the trance that would follow.

"I get the names Hattie ... and Martin ... not the woman at the window... early period ... connected with the men fighting ... not in house, outside ... Golay? Go-something ... it is their house. They are not disturbed but they give their energy to the other woman. Someone by the name of Luther comes around. Someone is called Marygold ... Mary ... someone says, the house is all different."

I decided to stop Ethel recounting what may well have been psychic impressions from the past rather than true ghosts, though one cannot always be sure of that distinction. But my experience had taught me that the kind of material she had picked up sounded more diffuse, more fractional than an earthbound spirit would be.

"Abraham ...," Ethel mumbled and slowly went into deep trance as we watched. The next voice we would hear might be her guide, Albert's, who usually introduced other entities to follow, or it might be a stranger—but it certainly would not be Ethel's.

"It's a man. Abram ... Ibram ..., " she said, breathing heavily. I requested her guide Albert's assistance in calming the atmosphere.

Ethel's normally placid face was now totally distorted as if in great pain and her hands were at her throat, indicating some sort of choking sensation; with this came unintelligible sounds of ah's and o's. I continued to try and calm the transition.

I kept asking who the communicator was, but the moaning continued, at the same time the entity now controlling Ethel indicated that the neck or throat had been injured as if by hanging or strangulation. Nevertheless, I kept up my request for identification, as I always do in such cases, using a quiet, gentle vocal approach and reassurances that the pain was of the past and only a memory now.

Finally, the entity said his name was Abraham and that he was in much pain.

"Abraham ... Eben ... my tongue!" the entity said, and indeed he sounded as if he could not use his tongue properly. Clearly, his tongue had been cut out, and I kept telling him that he was using the medium's now and therefore should be able to speak clearly. But he continued in a way that all I could make out was "my house."

"Is this your house?"

"Yes ... why do you want to know... who are you?"

"I am a friend come to help you. Is this your house?"

"I live here ..."

"How old are you?"

No answer.

"What year is this?"

"Seventy-eight ... going on ... seventy-nine ..."

"How old are you?"

"Old man ... fifty-two ..."

"Where were you born?"

"Massachusetts ... Lowell ..."

"Who was it who hurt you?"

Immediately he became agitated again, and the voice became unintelligible, the symptoms of a cutout tongue returned. Once again, I calmed him down.

"What church did you go to?" I asked, changing the subject.

"Don't go to church much ...," he replied.

"Where were you baptized?"

"St. Francis ... Episcopal."

I suggested the entity should rest now, seeing that he was getting agitated again, and I also feared for the medium.

"I want justice ... justice ...," he said.

I assured him, in order to calm him down, that those who had done him wrong had been punished. But he would have none of it.

"They fight every night out there ..."

Again, I began to exorcise him, but he was not quite ready.

"My daughter... Lisa ... Elizabeth ..."

"How old is she?"

"Thirteen ... she cries for me, she cries for me, she weeps ... all the blood ... they take her, too ..."

"Where is your wife?"

"She left us in misery. Johanna ... don't mention her ... she left us in misery."

"What year was that?"

"This year. NOW..."

"Why did she leave you?"

"I don't know."

"Where did she go?"

"I don't know."

And he added, "I will go to find her ... I never see her ..."

"What about your father and mother? Are they alive?"

"Oh no ..."

"When did they die."

"1776."

The voice showed a definite brogue now.

"Where are they buried?"

"Over the water ... Atlantic Ocean ... home ..."

"Where did your people come from?"

"Wales ... Greenough ..."

Further questioning brought out he was a captain in the 5th regiment.

"Did you serve the king or the government of the colonies?" I asked.

Proudly the answer came. "The king."

When I asked him for the name of the commanding officer of the regiment he served in, he became agitated and hissed at me ...

"I am an American citizen ... I'll have you know!"

"Are you a patriot or a Tory?"

"I will not have you use that word," he replied, meaning he was not a Tory.

I went on to explain that time had passed, but he called me mad; then I suggested I had come as a friend, which elicited a bitter reply.

"What are friends in time of war?"

I explained that the war was long over.

"The war is not over ... I am an American ... don't tempt me again ..."

Once again I pressed him for the name of his commanding officer and this time we received a clear reply: Broderick. He was not infantry, but horse. We were finally getting some answers. I then asked him for the names of some of his fellow officers in the 5th regiment.

"All dead ..." he intoned, and when I insisted on some names, he added, "Anthony ... Murdoch ... Surgeon ... my head hurts!"

"Any officers you can remember?"

"Matthew ..."

I asked, what battles was he involved in.

"Champlain ... Saint Lawrence ... it's bad, it's bad ..."

He was showing signs of getting agitated again, and time was fleeting.

I decided to try to release the poor tortured soul, asking him whether he was ready to join his loved ones now. Once again he relived the wars.

"He won't come home again ... Hatteras ... fire ... I'm weary."

I began to exorcise him, suggesting he leave the house where he had suffered so much.

"My house ... my tongue ... Indians," he kept repeating.

But finally with the help of Ethel's spirit guide Albert, I was able to help him across. Albert, in his crisp voice, explained that one of the female presences in the house, a daughter of the spirit we had just released, might be able to communicate now. But what I was wondering was whether a disturbed earthbound spirit was in the house also, not necessarily a relative of this man. Albert understood, and withdrew, and after a while, a faint, definitely female voice began to come from the medium's still entranced lips.

"Ella ..." the voice said, faintly at first.

Then she added that she was very happy and had a baby with her. The baby's name was Lily. She was Ella, she repeated. When I asked as to who she was in relation to the house, she said, "He always came ... every day ... William ... my house ..."

"Where is he? You know where he went?"

There was anxiety in her voice now. She said he left St. Valentine's Day, this year ... and she had no idea what year that was.

Who was Willie? Was he her husband?

This caused her to panic.

"Don't tell them!" she implored me. The story began to look ominous. Willie, Ella, the baby ... and not her husband?

She began to cry uncontrollably now. "Willie isn't coming anymore ... where is he?"

What was she doing in the house?

"Wait for Willie ... by the window ... always by the window. I wait for him and take care of Lily, she is so sweet. What I can do to find Willie?"

I began to exorcise her, seeing she could not tell me anything further about herself. Her memory was evidently limited by the ancient grief. As I did so, she began to notice spirits. "There is my Papa ... he will be very angry ... don't tell anyone ... take me now ... my Papa thinks we are married ... but we have no marriage ... Willie must marry me ..."

She cried even harder now.

"Andrew... my husband ..."

Once again I asked Albert, the guide, to lead her outside, from the house. It wasn't easy. It was noisy. But it worked.

"She is out," Albert reported immediately following this emotional outburst, "but her father did find out."

"What period are we in now?"

"The eighteen-something."

"Is there anything in the way of a disturbance from the more recent past?"

"Yes, that is true. An older lady ... she does not want to give up the home."

Albert then went on to explain that the woman at the window who had been seen had actually been used in her lifetime by the earlier entities to manifest through, which created confusion in her own mind as to who she was. Albert regretted that he could not have her speak to us directly. Andrew, he explained, was that more recent woman's father. Both women died in this house, and since the earlier woman would not let go, the later woman could not go on either, Albert explained.

"We have them both on our side, but they are closer to you because their thoughts are on the earth plane, you can reach them, as you are doing."

After assuring us and the owners of the house that all was peaceful now and that the disturbed entities had been released, Albert withdrew, and Ethel returned to herself, as usual blissfully ignorant of what had come through her mediumship.

Two of the ladies mentioned earlier, who had been connected with the house and the phenomena therein, had meanwhile joined us. Mrs. Anthony Brooks, a lady who had been sleeping in one of the bedrooms with her husband two years prior to our visit had this to say.

"I had been asleep, when I was awakened by ruffling at the back of my head. I first thought it was my husband and turned over. But next thing I felt was pressure on my stomach, very annoying, and I turned and realized that my husband had been sound asleep. Next, my cover was being pulled from the bed, and there was a light, a very pale light for which there was no source. I was very frightened. I went upstairs to go to the bathroom and as I was on the stairs I felt I was being pushed and held on tightly to the banister."

I next talked to Mrs. Mildred Haynes Noyes, who had been able to identify the ghostly lady at the window as being the former resident, Mrs. Bell. Everything she had told the Brighams was being reiterated. Then Ken Brigham himself spoke, and we went over his experiences once more in greater detail.

"I was standing in front of the fireplace, painting, and at that time there was a door to that bedroom over there which has since been closed up. It was a bright morning, about eleven o'clock, the doors were open, windows were open, my wife Doris was upstairs at the time, I was alone, and as I stood there painting, I glanced out and there, standing in the doorway, *was a woman.* As I was glancing at her I thought it peculiar that the neighbors would simply walk through my house without knocking.

"She stood there simply looking at me, with her arms folded, a woman who was rather short, not too heavy, dressed in a flowerprint housedress, cotton, she had on glasses and wore flat-heel Oxford shoes, all of this in plain daylight. I did not know what to say to this woman who had walked into my house. I was about to say to her, What could I do for you? Thinking of nothing more to say than that, and with that—she was gone. I raced back to the hall, thinking this little old lady had moved awfully fast, but needless to say, there was no one there. I said nothing to anyone, but several weeks later, during the summer, both my wife and I were awakened several times during the night by a very chilly breeze coming into the bedroom. That was one of the bedrooms upstairs. Neither of us said anything but we both sat up in bed and as we did so, we watched a little light dance across the wall! We are very isolated here, and there was no light from the outside whatsoever. This continued for the next year.

At this point it was decided that Mrs. Brigham would tell her part of the story.

"The first summer that we had the house," Mrs. Doris Brigham began, "I was sitting here, about five in the afternoon, my husband was upstairs, and my son was outside somewhere. I was alone and I was aware that someone was here, and on this white doorway, there was a solid black shadow. It was the profile of a woman from top to bottom, I could see the sharp features, the outline of the glasses, the pug in the back of her head, the long dress and shoes—all of a sudden, the shadow disappeared, and a cold breeze came toward me, and it came around and stood in back of my chair, and all of a sudden I had this feeling of peace and contentment, and all was right with the world.

Then, all of a sudden, the cold air around my chair, I could feel it moving off. Then, practically every night in the room upstairs, I was awakened for several years in the middle of the night, by a feeling of someone coming into the room. But many times there would be the dancing lights. We moved into another bedroom, but even there we would be awakened by someone running their fingers up my hair! Someone was pressing against me, and the same night, a neighbor was in the house, and she told us the same story. Footsteps of someone coming up the stairs. A feeling of movement of air. A black shadow on the ceiling, and then it disappeared. Often when the children were sick, we felt her around. It was always strong when there were children in the house."

I wondered whether she ever felt another presence in the house, apart from this woman.

Mrs. Brigham replied that one time, when she did not feel the woman around, she came into the house and felt very angry. That was someone else, she felt.

I decided it was time to verify, if possible, some of the material that had come through Mrs. Meyers in trance, and I turned to Ken Brigham for his comments.

"It has been one of the most astounding experiences I have ever had," he began. "There are several points which no one could know but my wife and myself. We did a considerable amount of research back through the deeds of the house. This only transpired a few weeks ago. I had been excavating up out front, preparing some drains, when I came across some foreign bricks, indicating that there had been an extension to the house. This was not the original house, the room we are in; there was a cottage here built for Continental soldiers, at the end of the revolutionary war.

"These cottages were given to Massachusetts soldiers, in lieu of pay, and they got some acres up here. This house has been remodeled many times, the most recent around 1870. The town here was formed around 1775; the deeds we have are around 1800. Several things about the house are lost in legend. For example, down there was a brook called Mutiny Brook. There was a mutiny here, and there was bloodshed. There were Indians, yes, this was definitely Indian territory. At one time this was a very well settled area; as recently as 1900 there were houses around here."

I realized, of course, that this was no longer the case: the house we were in was totally isolated within the countryside now.

"The original town was built on this hill, but it has disappeared," Mr. Brigham continued, and then disclosed a strange coincidence (if there be such a thing!) of an actual ancestor of his having lived here generations ago, and then moving on to Canada.

"We only just discovered that at one time two brothers with their families decided to share the house and remodel it,"

Brigham continued his account. "But one of them died before they could move in. Much of what Mrs. Meyers spoke of in trance is known only locally."

"What about the two women Mrs. Meyers described?" I asked. "She mentioned a short, dark-haired woman."

"She was short, but had gray hair when I saw her," Mr. Brigham said. "A perfectly solid human being—I did not see her as something elusive. We only told our son about this recently, and he told us that he had heard footsteps of a man and a woman on the third floor."

"Anything else you care to comment on?"

"Well, we have the names of some of the owners over a period of time. There were many, and some of the names in the record match those given by Ethel Meyers, like Eben."

"When Mrs. Meyers mentioned the name Isabelle," Mrs. Brigham interjected, "I thought she meant to say Alice Bell, which of course was the former owner's name—the woman at the window."

"One thing I should tell you also, there seems to have been a link between the haunting and the presence of children. One of the former owners did have a child, although the neighbors never knew this," Ken Brigham said. "She had a miscarriage. Also, Lowell, Massachusetts, is where these Continental soldiers came from; that was the traditional origin at the time. Maine did not yet exist as a state; the area was still part of Massachusetts. One more thing: both Mr. and Mrs. Bell died without having any funerals performed. She died in a nursing home nearby, he in Florida. But neither had a funeral service."

"Well, they had one now," I remarked and they laughed. It was decided that the Brighams would search the records further regarding some of the other things that Ethel had said in trance, and then get back to me.

Mr. Brigham was as good as his word. On August 21, 1967, he sent me an accounting of what he had further discovered about the house, and the history of the area in which it stands. But it was not as exhaustive as I had hoped even though it confirmed many of the names and facts Ethel had given us in trance. I decided to wait until I myself could follow up on the material, when I had the chance.

Fortunately, as time passed, the Brighams came to visit my wife Catherine and myself in August of the following year at our home in New York, and as a result Ken Brigham went back into the records with renewed vigor. Thus it was that on August 20, 1968, he sent me a lot of confirming material, which is presented here.

Ethel Meyers's mediumship had once again been proved right on target. The names she gave us, Bell, Eben, Murdoch, Blackguard, Willie, Abraham, why there they were in the historical records! Not ghostly fantasies, not guesswork ... people from out of the past.

August 20, 1968
Dear Hans,

It was good hearing from Cathy and we did enjoy visiting with you. I presume that just about now you're again on one of your trips, but I promised to forward to you some additional information that we've gathered since last summer. Enclosed is a chronology of the history of the house as far as we've been able to trace back. Early this summer (the only time we made it up to Maine) we spent hours in the York, Maine, Registry of Deeds, but the trail is cold. Deeds are so vague that we can't be certain as to whether or not a particular deed refers to our property. We are, however, convinced by style of building, materials, etc., that the back part of our house is much older than thought originally—we suspect it goes back to the mid-1700s.

Although I haven't included reference to it, our

272

reading of the town history (which is extremely gar-
bled and not too accurate) indicates that one of the
Willard boys, whose father had an adjoining farm,
went off to the Civil War and never returned,
although he is not listed as one of the wounded, dead,
or missing. If memory serves me right, he was simply
listed as W. Willard ("Willie"?). Now the "ghost" said
her name was "Isabel"; unfortunately, we can find no
records in the town history on the Bell family,
although they owned the house from 1851 to 1959
and Eben Bell lived in the town from 1820–1900! This
is peculiar in as much as nearly every other family is
recounted in the Town History of 1874. Why? Could
"Isabel" be a corruption of the Bell name, or perhaps
there was an Isabel Bell. Checking backwards in a per-
petual calendar it seems that during the mid-1800s,
Tuesday, St. Valentine's Day, occurred on February
14, 1865, 1860, and 1854; the first seems most logical
since the others do not occur during the Civil War—
which ended on [May] 26, 1865!

Some of my other notes are self-explanatory.

Another question of course concerns the term
"Blackguard" for our particular road and hill. An
archaic term that connotes "rude"—note also that the
map of 1850 does not show a family name beside our
house ... this could be because the property was
between owners, or it could be that the owners were
"rude"—which also could account for the lack of reference in Town History to the Bell family. It's an interesting sidelight.

Now, to more interesting pieces of information for
you: 1) we've finally decided to sell the house and it's
just like losing a child ... I'm personally heartbroken,
but I'm also a realist and it is ridiculous to try to keep

it when we can't get up there often enough to maintain it. We have a couple of prospective buyers now
but since we're not under pressure we want to make
sure that any new owners would love it like we do and
care for it.

2) And, then the strangest ... Doris was going
through some old photographs of the place and came
across a color print from a slide taken by a guest we
had there from Dublin, Ireland. And, it truly looks like
an image in the long view up the lane to the house.
Three persons have noted this now. Then, on another
slide it looks as though there were a house in the distance (also looking up the lane) that is only 1 ½ stories
in height. We're having the company photographer
blow them up to see what we will see. I'll certainly
keep you posted on this!

Well, it all adds up to the fact that we did a lot
more work and learned a lot more about the place ...
nearly all of which correlates with Ethel's comments.
But as a Yankee realist, I'm just going to have to cast
sentiment aside and let it go.

Drop us a line when you get a chance.
Sincerely yours,
"Willie left on Tuesday, St. Valentine's Day."

Two points should be made here regarding this story.
Ethel Johnson Meyers had many phases or forms of mediumship, but despite her fervent belief that she might also possess the ability to produce so-called extras, or supernormal
photographs, she never did during my investigations. What
she did produce at times on her own were so-called sco-
tographs, similar to Rorschach effects used in psychiatry; they
were the result of briefly exposing sensitive photographic
paper to light and then interpreting the resulting shapes.

But genuine psychic photography shows clear cut images, faces, figures that need no special interpretation to be understood, and this, alas, did not occur in this case when I took the photographs with my camera in Mrs. Meyers's presence.

After the Brighams had sold the Maine property, they moved to Hampton, Virginia. Ken and Doris looked forward to many years of enjoying life in this gentler climate.

Unfortunately, exactly two years after our last contact, in August of 1970, Ken slipped and injured an ankle, which in turn led to complications and his untimely and sudden death.

As for the restless ones up in Maine, nothing further was heard, and they are presumed to be where they rightfully belong.

The following research material, supplied by the late Mr. Ken Brigham, is presented here to give the reader a better feel for the territory and times in which this took place.

Brigham's documentation:

1. Roberts, Kenneth, *March to Quebec*, Doubleday, 1938, p. 32. Listed in the King's Service: Thomas Murdock.
2. Carpenter, Allan, *Enchantment of America—Maine*, Children's Press, 1966, p. 27—85 years of Indian warfare, more than 1,000 Maine residents killed, hundreds captured; by year 1675, there were about 6,000 European settlers in what is now Maine.
3. Smith, Bradford, *Roger's Rangers & The French and Indian War*, Random House, 1956, p. 5—Indians began to slaughter them when they marched out of Fort William Henry to surrender—women and children and men (1757); p. 6—Robert Rogers of New York raised company of rangers in 1755, by 1758 had five companies. Ebenezer Webster came from his home in New Hampshire; p. 46—mentioned Colonel Bradstreet; p. 176—Ebenezer, 1761, returned east to Albany as Captain and then to New Hampshire where

he married a girl named Mehitable Smith ... pushed northward with men under Colonel Stevens and settled on 225 acres at northern edge of town of Salisbury. Later fought in revolutionary war.

Oxford County Registry of Deeds
(References: Book 14, p. 18; Bk. 25, p. 295; Bk. 49, p. 254; Bk. 67, p. 264; Bk. 92, p. 158; Bk. 110, p. 149; Bk. 117, p. 268; Bk. 187, p. 197; Bk. 102, p. 135; Bk. 240, p. 477–478; Bk. 260, p. 381)

1805 Abraham (or Abram) Whitney sold to Nathan Jewell

1809 Nathan Jewell sold to William Monroe (part of land and the house) (1/9/09)

1823 Jonathan Stone bankrupt and sold to Peter Gerry (house), Thaddeus Brown and Josiah Shaw (5/19/23)

1836 Peter Gerry sold to Moses M. Mason (6/14/36)

1848 John Gerry sold to Daniel Billings (5/27/48)

1895 Semantha Bell sold to Caroline Bell (3/4/95)

1940 Edna Culhan (daughter of Caroline Bell) sold to Irving and Alice Bell (11/7/40)

1956 Alice Bell transferred to Archie and Ethel Bell (10/12/56)

1959 Archie and Ethel Bell sold to K. E. and D. M. Brigham (1/59)

Bk. 3, p. 484, Feb 7, 1799
Isaac Smith of Waterford for $800 sold to Nathaniel Geary of Harvard, Lot 2 in 6th Range (southerly half). Deed written February 7, 1799, but not recorded until September 24, 1808. (m. Unice Smith) (See notes 1 & 2)

Vol. 3, p. 99, Jan 6, 1800 (Fryeburg)
Nathaniel Geary and Betey Geary, his wife, sold to Peter Geary for $400 westerly end of southern half of Lot 2 in 6th Range. Notarized in York, January 6, 1800. On April

2, 1801 Betey Geary appeared and signed document which was registered on February 11, 1804.

Peter Gerry (or Geary) b. 1776—d. 6/16/1847
m. Mary (b. 1782—d. 3/16/1830)
m. Elizabeth (b. 1787—d. 5/1/1858)
   c. Mary (b. 1834 or 1804—d. 1844)
(see note 3) John C. (b. 1808)
Roland (b. 1810—d. 1842)
m. Maria Farrar (b. 1811—d. 1842)
Abbie (b. 1812—d. 1817)
Elbridge (b. 1815—m. Anna Jenness)

Bk. 92, p. 158, May 27, 1848
John Gerry sold for $100 (?) to Daniel Billings
Daniel Billings (b. 1780 Temple, Massachusetts)
   ... m. Sarah Kimball (b. 1786)
   ... c. Louise (m. William Hamlin)
Caroline (b. 1810—m. G. F. Wheeler b. 1810)
George C. (b. 1837—d. 1919)
   ... m. Rebecca Whitcomb, private F. Co., 9th Reg.—3
years svc. Civil War)
Maria (m. Calvin Houghton)
James R. (m. Esther Clark)
John D. (m. Esther Knowlton)
Miranda

Bk. 102, p. 135, Oct 14, 1851
Daniel Billings sold to William F. Bell of Boston and Timothy Bell for $1,400

Bk. 117, p. 268, Dec 24, 1858
William Bell of Waterford paid his father, William F. Bell, $800 for lot 2 in 6th Range

Bk. 187, p. 197, April 3, 1871
William Bell, "for support of self and wife," transferred to Timothy
C. Bell "homestead farm" and its parts of lots.

Bk. 240, p. 24, 1894
Timothy Bell left property to his wife Semantha Bell

Bk. 240, p. 477–78, Mar 4, 1895
Semantha Hamlin Bell transferred to Caroline Bell of Boston
Caroline Bell (b. 4/4/1848—d. 9/20/1926)
... m. T. C. Bell (b. 10/10/1829—d. 7/13/1894)
... m. J. B. Bennett

1905
Caroline Bell (d. 1905??) left property to her son Irving Bell, "her sole heir."

Bk.442, p. 133, Oct 30, 1940
Edna Bell Culhan (unmarried) of Cambridge, Mass. transferred to Irving and Alice Bell
Nov. 7, 1940
Irving Bell transferred to Edna Culhan "premises described in deed from Semantha to his mother Caroline Bell and he was her sole heir."

Bk. 560, p. 381, Oct 12, 1956
Archie and Ethel Bell inherited Lot 1 & 2 in the 5th Range and Lots 1 & 2 in the 6th Range from Alice Bell
Jan 1959
Archie and Ethel Bell sold property to K. E. And D. M. Brigham

Notes

1. According to Bk. 2, pp. 445–46: On December 20, 1802, Nathaniel Gerry (wife Betey) for $800 sold to David Whitcomb of Boston, Mass., Lot 2 in 6th Range. Deed mentions road running thru land. Registered 1807 and notarized and signed by Justice of the Peace Eber Rice.

2. According to Bk. 9, p. 467–8: On November 13,1810, David Whitcomb for $150 sold to Peter Gerry Lot 2 in the 6th Range, including "Gerry Road." Apparently both these transactions (notes 1 & 2) were concerned with the westerly end of the northern half of Lot 2 in the 6th Range.

3. John C. Gerry (b. 1808): m. Nancy Farrar (b. 1810—d. 1841), Nancy Sawin (b. 1819). He had an apothecary store in Fryeburg.

Interesting Notes

1. Local cemetery has gravestone of Hon. Lewis Brigham, b. 1816, d. 1866 (at Amherst, Mass).

2. Eben Bell, (b. 8/5/1820—d. 6/8/1900)

3. Richard and Samuel Brigham, and David Whitcomb, signed petition for incorporation on December 19, 1795.

4. Historical:
Waterford was in York County when it applied for incorporation (January 27, 1796).
Fryeburg (Pequawkett) was settled in 1763, Inc. 1777; in 1768 Fryeburg had population 300 plus.
November 17, 1796—Isaac Smith petitioned, with others, Massachusetts for incorporation. Document stated there were fifty to sixty families in "said plantation."
History of Waterford, p. 25—"and when the Indians attacked the growing settlements on the Androscoggin in 1781, and carried Lt. Segar and others into Canadian captivity, Lt. Stephen Farrington led twenty-three men over this trial

in hot, although vain pursuit of the savages."
(Lt. Nathaniel Segar had cleared a few acres in 1774. A few
townships, as Waterford and New Suncook [Lovell and
Sweden] had been surveyed and awaited settlers. p. 22)
Waterford, settled 1775, incorporated 1797; population
1790—150; 1800—535
"Spirit of 76" (Commanger/Morris, p. 605)—General
Burgoyne surrenders October 1777 ... General John
Stark agreed to work with Seth Warner because Warner
was from New Hampshire or the Hampshire Grants
(1777).
November 15, 1745—First Massachusetts Regiment, under
Sir William Pepperrell—8th company: Capt. Thomas
Perkins, Lt. John Burbank, John Gerry (single).
Civil War: "Fifth Regiment commanded by Mark H. Dunnill
of Portland." Fifth was engaged in eleven pitched battles
and eight skirmishes ere it entered on terrible campaign of
the Wilderness which was an incessant battle. It captured
6 rebel flags and more prisoners than it had in its ranks."
5. Local Notes:
a) Androscoggin Trail was the main Indian route from the
East Coast to Canada. Below our property, in the area of
Lot 3 in the 4th Range, it follows a brook called "Mutiny
Brook." The origin of the term used here is vague, but the
natives say Indians mutinied there during the French and
Indian Wars.
b) When the town was first settled, the pioneers built their
homes on our hill rather than the flat land and the only road
around Bear Lake was at the foot of Sweden and Blackguard
roads.
c) Our road is called by the archaic word "Blackguard" which
connotes villain. No one knows why.
d) The second floor of the house was constructed sometime
after the first; timbers are hand hewn to the second floor

and mill cut above. The house was rebuilt several times apparently; about 1890 or so two brothers and their families intended to live there but one died before taking residence. Also, foundations of an earlier building were uncovered near the back door.

THE TEENAGERS AND
THE STATEN ISLAND
GHOST

I have received a great many letters from people between the ages of twelve and eighteen who had a serious, often very inquisitive interest in extrasensory perception. Sometimes they had a case of their own to report.

Such was the case when I first heard from Carolyn Westbo, who lived on Staten Island. It seemed that her aunt, Mrs. Carol Packer, had lived in a house on Staten Island where a poltergeist had also taken up residence. Poltergeists are ghosts who like to make noises or move objects around.

Carolyn's aunt no longer lived at the house. I asked the new owners, a family by the name of Goetz, for permission to visit.

What I liked about Carolyn Westbo, who was seventeen and very serious, was that she herself was doubtful about her experiences and wondered if they weren't all due to imagination or, as she put it, "self-delusion." But deep down she knew she was psychic, and had already accepted this knowledge.

"When were you at the house on Henderson Avenue the

last time, Carolyn?" I asked.

"The last time I was at the house was in January of 1965," she answered. "My aunt was in the process of moving out, and the house was in an uproar. I stood against the wall and watched the proceedings. My left side was turned to the wall, and I was reminiscing about the wonderful times I had had on New Year's Eve, and somehow smiled to myself. All of a sudden, my *right side*, the right side of my head, felt very depressed and a feeling of great despair came over me. I felt like wringing my hands and was very distraught. It only stayed with me a few moments, but I had the distinct feeling of a woman who was very worried, and I could almost feel something or someone pressing against the right side of my head. And then I saw a mist, in the large downstairs dining room of the house."

"A mist? What sort of mist?"

"It had a shape, rather tall and thin. It did not have a face, and looked kind of ragged. *But I did see hands wringing.*"

Carolyn had told her aunt about her uncanny experience, even though she was afraid she would be laughed at. Her own family had pooh-poohed the whole thing, and Carolyn did not like to be laughed at, especially when she *knew* she had seen what she had seen. But her aunt did not laugh. She, too, had observed the misty shape when she was alone in the house, yet she had always felt great comfort with the ghost, whoever it was.

It was then that Carolyn learned about the poltergeist on Henderson Avenue. Objects were moving by themselves, her aunt admitted, such as things falling from a table and other objects that hadn't been touched. On one occasion she heard a loud crash downstairs—the house had three stories—and found a freshly baked pie upside down on the floor. She had placed it far back on the shelf in the pantry. Pots and pans around the pie had not been touched, and no trucks were passing by outside that might account for the vibration that could have caused the pie to fall. There had been nobody else in the house at the time. The aunt, Carol Packer, then lives in upstate New York. She had never accepted the idea of a ghost, and yet could not offer any explanation for the strange happenings in the house.

"Have you had other experiences of a psychic nature?" I asked the young girl.

"Nothing really great, only little things, such as knowing what my teacher would ask the next day, or what people were wearing when I talk to them on the telephone or dream about them. I see things happening and a week later or so, they do happen."

Carolyn and her aunt had looked into the history of the house. They found that three families prior to Mrs. Packer's stay in the house, a woman had dropped dead on the front porch. They never knew her name or anything else beyond this bare fact.

There the matter stood when our little expedition consisting of Sybil Leek and myself, book editor Evelyn Grippo, and CBS newscaster Lou Adler and his wife, arrived at the Victorian structure where the ghost was presumably awaiting us. Mr. Adler brought along a CBS radio car and an engineer by the name of Leon, who we almost lost on the way over the Verrazano Bridge. It was a humid Sunday evening in May of 1965. Fifteen people had assembled at the Goetzes' to celebrate some kind of anniversary, but I suspect they were very curious about our investigation as an added attraction. We could hear their voices as we mounted the steep wooden steps leading to the house from Henderson Avenue, a quiet street lined with shade trees.

While the CBS people set up their equipment, I politely put the celebrants into the front room and collected those directly concerned with the haunting around a heavy oak table in the dining room on the first floor of the sturdy old house.

284

Carolyn Westbo, her younger sister Betsy, Mr. and Mrs. Goetz, their son, a married daughter, Mrs. Grippo, the Adlers, and I formed a circle around the table. I had asked Sybil to wait in another room, where she could not possibly overhear a single word that was said in the dining room. Afterwards, skeptical reporter Lou Adler admitted that "unless she had some sort of electronic listening device by which she could listen through walls, or unless you and Sybil set this up to trick everybody—there is no alternative explanation for what occurred this evening." Needless to say, we did not use electronic devices. Sybil could not hear anything, and neither she nor I knew anything of what would happen later.

As soon as Sybil Leek was out of earshot, I started to question the witnesses among those present. Carolyn Westbo repeated her testimony given to me earlier. I then turned my attention, and my microphone, to Betsy Westbo.

Betsy had been to the house a number of times. Had she ever felt anything unusual in this house?

"One time I walked in here," the serious young girl said in response. "My mother and my cousin were in the kitchen downstairs, in the rear of the house, and I walked into the hall. It was dark, about sunset, and I suddenly felt as if someone were staring at me, just looking at me. I was sure it was my cousin, so I asked him to come out. He had played tricks on me before. But he wasn't there, and I went into the kitchen, and he had not left it at all."

"Any other experiences bordering on the uncanny?" I asked.

This 15-year-old girl was calm and not at all given to imagination, I felt, and she struck me as mature beyond her years.

"The time my aunt moved out, I was here, too. I felt as if someone were crying and I wanted to cry with them. I was just walking around then, and it felt as if someone were next to me crying and saying, 'What's going to happen to me?'"

Betsy had also had psychic experiences in her young life. Not long before in her family's house, just down the street from the haunted house her aunt used to call home, Betsy was asleep in bed around 11 pm, when she awoke with a start.

"I heard a screech and a dog yelping, as if he had been hurt. I was sure there had been an accident, and we looked out the window, but there was nothing, no car, no dog."

"What did you do then?"

"We couldn't figure it out," Betsy answered, "but the very next evening, again at eleven o'clock, we heard the same noises— my sister was with me in the room this time. We checked again, and this time there was a dog. I had seen the entire accident happen, *exactly as it did, twenty-four hours before!*"

"Amazing," I conceded. "Then you are indeed clairvoyant."

Mrs. Mariam Goetz, a pleasant-looking, vivacious woman in her middle years, had been the lady of the house since February of 1965. She had not seen or heard anything uncanny, and she felt very happy in the house. But then there was this strange business about the silver—

"My silver spoons disappeared, one by one, and we searched and searched, and we thought someone was playing a prank. Each blamed the other, but neither Mr. Goetz, nor my son, nor my young married daughter, Irene Nelson, who lives with us, had hidden the spoons. The wedding gifts were displayed in Grandmother's room upstairs, including some pretty silver objects. One evening, after about a week of this, we discovered in each bowl—a silver spoon! Of course we thought Grandmother had been playing a trick on us, but she assured us she had not."

The rest of the spoons turned up in the drawers of the room, carefully hidden in many places. Although the grandmother was quite aged, she was in good mental condition, and the Goetzes really had no proof that she hid the spoons.

"Irene, my married daughter, had come to sleep with me several nights, because she hadn't felt very secure in her own bedroom," Mrs. Goetz added.

Mrs. Irene Nelson was a young woman with dark eyes and dark hair, not the dreamer type, but rather factually minded and to the point. She had been in the house as long as her parents, four months to the time of my investigation.

Had she noticed anything unusual?

"Yes," the young woman said. "One night I was sitting in the kitchen at the table, with two friends of mine, and as we sat there and talked, some screws were falling to the floor from the kitchen table, by themselves, one by one. My friends left. I got up to gather my things, and the table collapsed behind me. One of its legs had come off by itself. But the table was not wobbly, or any of the screws loose, just before we used it, or we would have noticed it. There was nobody else in the house who could have loosened the screws as a prank, either."

"And poor Grandmother can't be blamed for it, either," I added. The octogenarian did not get around very much any more.

"Anything else?" I asked, crisply.

"One night, about four in the morning," Mrs. Nelson said, "I woke up with a sudden start and I opened my eyes and could not close them again. Suddenly, I felt pin-prickles all over my body. I felt chilly. I felt there was someone in the room I could not see. I heard a strange sound, seemingly outside, as if someone were sweeping the sidewalk. This was in my bedroom directly above the living room. The feeling lasted about ten minutes, and I just lay there, motionless and frightened. I had several bad nights after that, but that first time was the worst."

"Have you ever felt another presence when you were alone?"

"Yes, I have. In different parts of the house."

The house, along with the building next door, was built at the turn of the twentieth century. It was Victorian in architec-

287

ture and appointments. Heavy wooden beams, many small rooms on the three floors, high ceilings, and solid staircases characterized the house on Henderson Avenue.

It was time to bring Sybil Leek into the dining room and start the trance.

Had anything happened to her while she was waiting outside in the kitchen? Sybil seemed somewhat upset, a very unusual state for this usually imperturbable psychic lady.

"I was standing by the refrigerator," she reported, "and the kitchen door opened about two inches. It disturbed me, for I did not want anyone to think I was opening the door to listen. There was someone there, I felt, and I could have easily gone into trance that moment, but fought it as I never do this without you being present."

Imagine—a ghost too impatient to wait for the proper signal!

"I wanted to run, but restrained myself," Sybil added. "I never moved from the spot near the refrigerator. I was terrified, which I rarely am."

We sat down, and soon Sybil was in deep trance. Before long, a faint voice made itself heard through Sybil's lips.

"What is your name?" I asked.

"Anne Meredith." It came with great difficulty of breathing.

"Is this your house?"

"Yes ... I want to get in. I live here. I want to get in!"

"What's wrong?"

"I ... have ... heart trouble ... I can't get up the steps."

Sybil's breathing was heavy and labored.

"How long have you lived here?"

"Thirty-five."

"What year did you move in?"

"Twenty-two."

"Were you alone in this house?"

"No ... James ... these steps ... James ... son."

"What is it you want?"

"I can't stay here ... want to get in ... the steps ... can't get to the door ... *door must be opened.*"

"How old are you?"

"Fifty-two."

"Where did you go to school?"

"Derby ... Connecticut."

"Your father's name?"

"Johannes.

"Mother's?"

"Marguerite."

"Where were you baptized?"

"Derby ... my lips are sore ... I bite them ... I have pain in my heart."

I started to explain her true status to her.

"You passed out of the physical life in this house," I began. "It is no longer your house. You must go on and join your family, those who have passed on before you. Do you understand?"

She did not.

"I have to get up the stairs," she mumbled over and over again.

As I repeated the formula I usually employ to pry an unhappy ghost away from the place of emotional turmoil in the past, Sybil broke out of trance momentarily, her eyes wide open, staring in sheer terror and lack of understanding at the group. Quickly, I hypnotized her back into the trance state, and in a moment or two, the ghost was back in control of Sybil's vocal apparatus. Heavy tears now rolled down the medium's cheeks. Obviously, she was undergoing great emotional strain. Then the voice returned slowly.

"I want to come in ... I have to come back!"

"You died on the steps of this house. You can't come back," I countered.

"Someone's there," the ghost insisted in a shaky voice. "I have to come back."

"Who is it you want to come back to?"

"James."

I assured her James was well taken care of, and she need not worry about him anymore.

"Don't leave me outside, I shall die," she said now.

"You *have* died, dear," I replied, quietly.

"Open the door, open the door," she demanded.

I took another tack. Suggesting that the door was being opened for her, I took her "by the hand" and showed her that someone else lived here now. No James. I even took her "upstairs" by suggestion. She seemed shocked.

"I don't believe you."

"This is the year 1965," I said.

"Fifty-five?"

"No, sixty-five."

There was disbelief. Then she complained that a dog kept her up, and also mentioned that her mother was living upstairs.

What was the dog's name?

"Silly dog ... Franz." A dog named Franz was unusual even for a ghost, I thought. Still, people do like to give their pets strange names. The Goetzes had named their aged spaniel Happy, and I had never seen a more subdued dog in my life.

Why was she afraid of the dog? I asked the ghost.

"I fall over him," she complained. "My heart ... dog is to blame."

"But this happened in 1955, you say."

"Happened *today*," she answered. To a ghost, time stands still. She insisted this was 1955. I strongly insisted it was 1965. I explained once more what had happened to her.

"Not dead," she said. "Not in the body? That's silly."

Unfortunately, very few ghosts know that they are dead. It comes as a shock when I tell them.

"I'm going upstairs and neither you nor that dog will stop me," she finally said resolutely.

I agreed to help her up the stairs.

"Lift me," she pleaded.

Mentally, we opened the door and went upstairs.

"Where is my mother?" she said, obviously realizing that her mother was not there. I explained she had died. The truth of the situation began to dawn on Anne Meredith.

I took advantage of this state of affairs to press my point and suggest her mother was awaiting her outside the house.

"May I come back sometime?" the ghost asked in a feeble voice.

"You may if you wish," I promised, "but now you must join your mother."

As the ghost faded away, Sybil returned to her own body.

She felt fine, but, of course, remembered nothing of what had come out of her mouth during trance. Just before awakening, tears once more rolled down her face.

I thought it rather remarkable that Sybil, in her trance state, had brought on a female personality who had died of a heart attack on the outside steps leading to the house. Sybil had no way of knowing that such a person actually existed and that her death had indeed taken place some years ago as described.

What about the names Anne Meredith and James?

Carolyn Westbo checked with the lady who had owned both houses and who lived in the one next door, a Miss Irving. Quite aged herself, she did not recall anyone with the name of Anne Meredith. By a strange coincidence, her own first names were Anne Adelaide. Derby, Connecticut, exists.

Checking church registers is a long and doubtful job at best. Finding a record of Anne Meredith would have been wonderful, of course, but if I didn't find such a record, it didn't mean she never existed. Many tenants had come and gone in the old house atop the hill on Henderson Avenue. Perhaps Anne and Meredith were only her first and middle names.

Time will tell.

Meanwhile, it was to be profoundly hoped that the hand-wringing lady ghost of Staten Island need not climb those horrible stairs any longer, nor cope with dogs who had no respect for ghosts—especially ghosts who once owned the house.

HOLLYWOOD NOT-SO-CONFIDENTIAL: EVEN ORDINARY CITIZENS HAVE GHOSTLY EXPERIENCES

*N*orth Beachwood Drive in Hollywood was an average street. Most of the houses on this particular block are two or four-family houses divided up into apartments. Farther up the street was one of the major motion picture studios, but the block in question was rather quiet and not at all ghostly in appearance. The C. family moved into apartment No. 4 in one of the houses on the 1200 block in 1963. Mr. C. was an artist, and they had a four-year-old daughter at the time. The apartment was the only one at the top of a stairway, and anyone coming up those stairs would be a member of the C. family or someone paying them a visit.

Shortly after the C.'s had moved into their new apartment, they noticed some rather unusual things. After they had settled in the new place and started paying attention to the surroundings, they became aware of a strange phenomenon occurring every night between eight and nine P.M. *Someone was walking up their stairs.* At first only Mrs. C. paid attention to it. Clearly those were the footsteps of a very old person having difficulty ascending the stairs. The footsteps were deliberate and loud, slowing down and then picking up speed again. After a while they stopped, but no one was heard coming *down* the stairs again. This went on for several evenings in succession.

Mrs. C. realized that there was no one actually coming up the stairs, and she wondered if she was hallucinating. She therefore did not mention it to her husband. A few days passed. One evening, again at the same hour, her husband suddenly looked at her and said, "Quiet, I hear something." Both C.'s then clearly heard the same slow footsteps coming up their stairway. This time, however, they jumped up and tore the door open. There was no one there. Mr. C. immediately ran down the stairs as quickly as he could and looked around the corner and up and down the block, but there was no one to be seen. Mrs. C. then confessed to her husband that she had heard the same noises several nights in a row.

They decided to lie in wait the following night. Sure enough, between eight and nine P.M. someone unseen tried to come up their stairs, and when they ran out to look, there was no one about. They were puzzling as to what to do about this phenomenon when their neighbor, Peggy V., decided to spend a night with them. Her daughter and the C.'s daughter were playmates. That night, everyone was fast asleep—Mrs. V. on the couch in the living room and the C's in their bedroom when an uproar woke them between two and three A.M. What woke Mrs. C. was an incessant scream coming from Mrs. V. As soon as she could be calmed down somewhat, Mrs. V. explained that she had been awakened by the sound of someone brushing his teeth and gargling in the bathroom. Puzzled as to who it might be, Mrs. V. had sat up on the couch. To her horror she clearly heard the dining room chairs in the dark apartment being pulled from the table, people sitting down on them, glasses being used and silverware tinkling, and muffled conversation. Since she knew very well that there was no one but herself and the C.'s in the apartment at the time, she screamed in absolute horror, unable to understand what was happening.

In conversation the following morning, Mrs. C. discovered that her neighbor had some occult interest in the past and was apparently "mediumistic." The C.'s themselves were not hostile to the idea of ghosts. Both of them were slightly interested in the occult and had a few books on the subject in their library. Mr. C. had always felt that ghosts were indeed possible, although he had never thought of having some of his own in the place where he lived.

The next day Mrs. C. went to see the owner of the building. After some hesitation, the landlady, Mrs. S., admitted that the previous tenant of their apartment had committed suicide in it—as a matter of fact, in the very bed in which the C.'s were now sleeping. That was quite enough for the C.'s. They decided to move from the apartment. When Mrs. S. was told of their determination to live elsewhere, she gave them an argument. "The old lady was a wonderful person," she exclaimed. "It is not a shame to commit suicide." Tactfully Mrs. C. explained about the phenomena they had witnessed.

Mrs. C. had had no ESP experiences either before or after living in the apartment on Beachwood. Nor had she any desire to again experience anything like it. One ghost was quite enough for her.

At the time that I knew her, Polly Blaize was a lady in her early fifties, filled with the joy of life and spilling over with the excitement of many experiences with the world of spirits. She came from a distinguished old New England family; many of her ancestors were either passengers on the *Mayflower* or early colonial dignitaries, and she counted two American presidents, Franklin Pierce and John Tyler, among her near relatives. Of Scottish background, she left New England at an early age to come to Hollywood, where she worked briefly for Warner Brothers. An early marriage proved a failure but left her with two small children. After a succession of various administrative jobs, she eventually remarried in 1965. Her husband was a design engineer working for NASA. Polly—or as she was more formally known, Pauline—lived with her husband in one of the beach communities south of Los Angeles in those days, but the experiences I am about to relate happened to her when she lived in and around Hollywood.

In 1924, not long after she had moved to California with her parents, Polly became friendly with a young boy named Billy Bennett. They were teenagers together when their families lived across from each other on Highland Avenue in Hollywood. Billy lived in an apartment that was part of a row of one-story apartments of the court type. The apartments have long since been leveled. His mother was then a famous screen star by the name of Belle Bennett, best-known for her starring role in the 1925 version of *Stella Dallas*.

Time passed, and Pauline was married. Her marriage did not last very long, and she found herself at age twenty with the responsibility for two small children, a one-year-old daughter and a two-year-old son. One night she was in bed, fully awake, when she heard the shrieking sounds of what seemed to her like a flock of birds. The window was open and she heard the birds coming through it, hovering around her with the sound of beating wings. The sound was so loud she could barely hear the human voice in the midst of this flock of birds. There was nothing to be seen, but the voice was that of Billy Bennett. "Beware of people who can hurt you, I still love you; I am ever near to protect you," the voice said, over and over. All this time she could see absolutely nothing but the darkness of the room.

Only a few days before the incident, Billy had died suddenly at the Presbyterian Hospital in Hollywood. His warning proved to be accurate indeed. For many years Mrs. Blaize lived almost as a recluse, until she met her second husband and married again, this time with happier results.

But the incident that has etched itself most deeply into her memory took place in 1935 when her daughter was five years old. They had just moved into a one-bedroom apartment on Cheremoya Avenue in Hollywood. It consisted of a living room and a bedroom, and between the two rooms was a dressing room large enough to contain a chest of drawers, a counter, and a large dressing mirror. About a week after they had moved into this apartment, Polly was suddenly awakened by the sound of what seemed to her like a heavy thud. It sounded as if a human body had dropped, followed by what sounded like a body pulling itself across the living room floor, from the dressing room area halfway to the kitchen, which was located on the other side of the living room. At first Polly paid no attention to these odd sounds, but when they repeated themselves exactly in the same manner at exactly the same time night after night, she became alarmed. Much later, she learned that her little girl was just as much aware of these sounds as she was.

Polly decided to make some inquiries of the landlady. The latter, named Beatrice Scriver, listened to the account of the nightly disturbances and then turned white. Since everyone in the building, which contained eight apartments, seemed to be familiar with the story, there was nothing for Mrs. Scriver to do but to let Polly in on the secret.

Prior to Polly's moving into the apartment, the place had belonged to a woman and her nineteen-year-old son. The young man was a successful athlete and had high hopes for a professional career. Suddenly he was informed that he would have to lose one of his legs because of severe illness. After his doctors had given him this verdict, the young man returned home and in front of his dressing room mirror shot himself to death. He fell to the floor, his body hitting it near the dressing-room door. Not quite dead, he pulled himself into the living room, pushed himself up on one elbow, and then dropped again to the floor, only to try to pull himself up again. He did this several times in an effort to reach his mother, who was then in the kitchen. Because she had the water running, she had not heard the shot through the closed door.

Polly shuddered. Mrs. Scriver had described the exact sounds she had heard night after night in her apartment. But there was still another sound she wanted an explanation for. It sounded to her as if a basket were being pulled along the floor. The landlady nodded grimly. The young man's body had been taken out of the apartment in a basket, down the back stairs and to the morgue.

But that was not the end of the story by any means. Being spiritually attuned, Polly realized she had to help release the young man from his sufferings. Quite obviously, she argued, he did not realize what had happened to him. (In the intervening time, the young man's mother had also passed away.)

Polly thanked the landlady for the information and went back to her apartment. Her eyes fixed themselves on the dark rug on her living room floor. Turning the carpet back, she noticed a large brown stain and realized that it was made by the young man's blood. That was all the proof she needed. That night she waited until the sounds started up again. Speaking in a soft voice, she then called him by name.

"Your mother has gone ahead of you and is waiting for

you; do not keep her waiting any longer," she said, pleading with the unseen presence. There was only silence.

Several nights in a row she spoke the same words, and finally there was a sound in answer to her pleading. She was seated in a chair near the spot where he had died when she suddenly heard a long, drawn-out voice as if called to her from far away, saying, "Mama—help me." The voice sounded hollow, as if it were coming from some distant place, but she heard it clearly and responded. For a while the sounds continued. Polly did not give up; she kept repeating her plea, asking the young man to reach out to his mother so that he could be free from the unhappy surroundings where he had died. Ultimately the message got through to him, and just as suddenly as the phenomena had entered Polly's life, they stopped. With a sigh of relief Polly Blaize realized that she had successfully freed the ghostly young athlete.

Lise Caron and her husband Leo moved to Los Angeles in 1965. The family had originally lived in Paris, but the two older daughters, named Liliane and Nicole, had decided to strike out on their own and go to the United States. They liked it so much they induced their parents to follow them. Thus Mr. and Mrs. Caron and the third daughter joined the two girls in Los Angeles in a house at El Centro Avenue in the 1200 North block. A cluster of houses in the Spanish style was arranged around a narrow courtyard, open on one side toward the street. The landlord occupies the house at the bottom of this cluster of houses, and the apartment that was to be the home of the Carons was the first one on the right.

Liliane had been married a short time before her parents' arrival in Los Angeles and had moved out, leaving Nicole the sole occupant of the apartment. Nicole had decided that the place was too small for three additional people and had therefore rented a small single apartment close by, intending to leave her former apartment to her parents and their youngest daughter.

When Lise Caron arrived at the house, she had a good impression of it. The street was quiet, the house, though old, seemed in good condition, and she felt that they would be happy in it. The apartment itself consisted of a good-sized living room separated from the dining room by a folding door.

At the time of their arrival, the dining room had been transformed into a bedroom for Martine, the youngest daughter. Between the dining room and a short hallway stood a chest of drawers. On top of the chest a candle was burning. Surprised, Mrs. Caron turned to her daughters, asking why they were burning a candle. The answer was an evasive one, but Lise was too tired from the long journey to pay much attention to it. Thus, when Nicole implored her mother to leave the candle in its place, she nodded and went on to other things. To the right side of the hallway was a bedroom in which stood two beds separated by a night table with a lamp on it. To the left of the hallway was the bathroom, and in front of the dining room door was the kitchen door. This kitchen door would swing with a particular noise as it went from one side to the other. In every room there were flowers and green plants helping to create a happy impression. The Carons were so happy to be together again after the long separation that they lingered over their dinner. It was late when they decided to go to bed.

Mr. and Mrs. Caron went to their bedroom, while Martine closed the folding door between bedroom and living room. She then went to bed in her makeshift bedroom in the living room.

Almost as soon as Mr. Caron lay down, he was asleep. Mrs. Caron was still in the bathroom when she suddenly received the impression that there was someone observing her. Turning around, she saw no one. She continued with her chores, but again received the distinct impression that someone was standing at the bathroom door staring at her. Turning around again, she said, "Is that you, Leo?" But a look into the bedroom convinced her that her husband was fast asleep. She decided to see whether Martine might have gotten up and come in to see her.

Martine was still up, and when her mother came over to her she seemed to have a strange look on her face. "What is wrong?" Mrs. Caron asked her daughter.

"I don't feel comfortable here," the girl said, and explained that she had a strange feeling of a presence. Mrs. Caron did not wish to upset her youngest daughter, so she made light of this, at the same time opening the folding door to change the atmosphere of the room. The only light came now from the flickering candle, and that too helped to create a somewhat spooky impression. But since everyone was tired, she did not want to make an issue of it and decided to find out about the candle later. Then she returned to bed. But, as soon as she had lain down, she again had the feeling of another presence.

But the next few days were too exciting to leave room for worry about the impressions of that first night, and in the end she ascribed her strange feelings to the need for adjustment to new surroundings.

Unfortunately, the impressions continued night after night. A few days after their arrival she woke up to the noise of the kitchen door swinging. She thought that her husband had gone to the kitchen to get a drink. But a glance at his bed showed her he had not. A little later, she awoke again to see someone standing between their two beds. She thought her husband had gotten up, but to her surprise saw that he was fast asleep. In fact, she could see right through the strange person standing between the two beds. She sat bolt upright, her heart pounding, looking straight ahead at the apparition. At that moment, the stranger vanished into thin air.

She woke up her husband and told him what had happened. Quickly he put on his coat and ran around to the out-side of the house, thinking an intruder had somehow gotten into the apartment. But there was no one about.

The next morning she decided to talk about this with her older daughters. It was then that she received an explanation for the strange goings-on and the flickering candle on the dresser. When the two young women had first rented the apartment, they too had the feeling of a presence with them. At first they had been rather scared by it, but after some time they ignored the unusual impressions, preferring to live with whatever it was that was disturbing in the atmosphere rather than look for a new apartment. This had gone on for some time, when one night they were aroused by the noise of the kitchen door opening. Both women woke up simultaneously, fastening their eyes upon the darkness of their bedroom. There between the two beds stood a man. Their first thought was that a burglar had gotten into the house. As they jumped from their beds the apparition vanished. A quick check of doors and windows disclosed that none of them was open, nor was there anyone outside. Several days later Liliane heard the same noise again. Bravely she opened her eyes and saw a white apparition close to Nicole's bed. Again she sat up in bed, and the apparition vanished. She was not sure, but the second apparition might have been that of a woman. After that the two women decided they needed the help of a medium and went to see famed clairvoyant Brenda Crenshaw. Mrs. Crenshaw, wife of newspaper writer James Crenshaw, had been a practicing medium in the Hollywood area for many years and had an impeccable reputation for honesty and accuracy. After a few minutes the two girls were told that the medium saw the problem surrounding them quite clearly.

It appeared that a young couple had committed suicide in the apartment some time before. On checking this they found the information to be correct. From that moment on they decided to place a candle in the apartment and to pray for the unfortunate ones every day, in the hope that they might find peace. With their daily prayer becoming part of the routine, they managed to continue living in the haunted apartment.

Mrs. Caron wasn't exactly ecstatic about the idea of continuing to live with the ghostly couple. On the other hand, she thought that perhaps she might release them. She promised herself to stay calm should anything further occur. Her opportunity came a few nights after her conversation with her daughters. She woke up again to the sound of the kitchen door opening by itself. Slowly Mrs. Caron looked up and saw a young man standing between the two beds, close enough to be touched. He was standing near her husband's feet. Mrs. Caron could see him very clearly. He was a short man, with curly hair, but since his back was turned toward her she could not see his face. She estimated that he was between thirty and thirty-five years old. He stood there without moving, as if transfixed. Mrs. Caron hoped that he would turn around so she could see his face, but he did not. After a while the apparition started slowly to vanish, until it was completely gone. He never returned to the apartment visually, but his influence could still be felt for a long time after this incident.

Continuing their prayers for the release of the unhappy couple, the Carons nevertheless felt that their apartment was not exactly a happy one and decided to move just as soon as they could find another place.

I spoke to Mrs. Caron in 1970 and found that all was well in their new place. She had no idea as to what had happened to the apartment on El Centro Avenue but readily supplied me with additional information about the landlord. In October of 1972 I drove to the house on El Centro Avenue in the company of Paula Davidson and her brother.

Walking about in front of the apartment, Paula felt nothing in particular. As for me, I felt rather depressed at the sight of this cluster of houses, which somehow reminded me of something out of Hollywood's past, but that may have been due to my knowledge of the incidents just described. Bravely I rang the doorbell. A dark-haired middle-aged lady opened the door, peering out at me, wondering what I wanted. I explained that I was writing a book about Hollywood, not saying that I meant *haunted* Hollywood. I asked the lady whether she knew anything about the background of her apartment.

"I am sorry I can't help you," she replied politely. "I have been living here only two years."

"Is there anything special that you might have observed during those years?" I asked.

The lady shook her head and smiled rather wryly. "Nothing really. Except that I've been very unhappy here. I've had nothing but bad luck ever since I moved into this apartment. I haven't the vaguest idea why."

Anyone who thinks that such experiences are rare and happen only to the imaginative or perhaps those who are "believers" just doesn't know his facts. I have hundreds upon hundreds of parallel cases in my files, all of them reported by sane, sensible and rational people from every social and economic level. These incidents occur in new houses as well as in old ones.

Take the case of Mrs. Barbara McDuffa, a lady who was then living in West Los Angeles. She had gone through a harrowing and, to her, inexplicable experience that preyed on her mind until she could find some sort of explanation for it. She needed a "rational" explanation, because otherwise there was the suggestion that she had perhaps imagined the whole thing or that there was something wrong with her powers of perception. Eventually she heard of my work and telephoned me when I was on the Gil Henry radio program in L.A. We talked about the matter, and I assured Mrs. McDuffa that there was nothing wrong with her mind, her eyes or her hearing. It just happened that she had moved into a haunted apartment.

In the late sixties, Mrs. McDuffa, her mother, and her son David moved into a brand-new, never before-lived-in apartment on Roscoe Boulevard in Panorama City, a community at the end of Van Nuys, which in turn borders on North Hollywood. Up to that time Mrs. McDuffa scoffed at the supernatural or the notion that there might be ghosts or haunted apartments. If anyone had mentioned such possibilities to her, she would have thought him insane or jesting.

The first night after they had moved into the new apartment, they went to bed fairly early, because there remained much work to be done in the morning. It was a warm night and Mrs. McDuffa couldn't sleep. She decided to get up and open the bedroom window. As she started for the window, she suddenly perceived a tall figure of a man, wearing an overcoat and hat, standing in the closet doorway at the foot of the bed. Mrs. McDuffa had left the closet door open, but there wasn't anything in it as yet since they hadn't unpacked their things. When she saw the figure she rushed for the light switch. As soon as the light went on the figure disappeared. For a moment Mrs. McDuffa was stunned, but then she assumed that she had had an hallucination and went back to bed.

The following night she was awakened from a deep sleep by the sound of footsteps on the carpet. As she was trying to get her bearings, she noticed that her mother had been awakened by the same noises. It sounded as if someone were walking on the carpet, shuffling his feet, yet there was no one to be seen. The two women exchanged experiences but eventually put them out of their minds, since there was a great deal of work to be done in the apartment, and no one had much time to think about such matters as the supernatural.

The footsteps, however, continued for several nights. They were now joined by a tapping sound on the window of the bedroom. Since there weren't any shutters or trees or bushes or anything else near the window that could have caused this noise, they were puzzled. Worried that the unseen phenomena might upset the little boy, the ladies then put the boy's bed into their room and shut the door of the other room at night. Still thinking that it might be a prowler or some other physical force, they pulled a dresser up in front of the door so that no one could enter. The door of the bedroom opened into a little corridor. There was no direct access to either the windows or the entrance door of the apartment. That night, as if in response to their new security measures, the closed bedroom door started to rattle. The doorknob moved as if someone were trying to get in. The force rattling the door was so strong that only a wind of close-to-hurricane force could have caused it. Nevertheless, it was totally quiet outside the house; none of the windows were open, and there was no natural explanation for the rattling sound or the movement of the doorknob. The women had to conclude that they had been "blessed" by a ghost.

One day Mrs. McDuffa was combing her hair in her bedroom. Suddenly she felt a pressure on her shoulder and then felt something brushing her cheek as if an unseen person had passed very close by her. She turned around, but again there was no one to be seen. Shortly after this experience she heard the noise of a glass being put down as if someone had taken a drink of water in the kitchen. There was no one in the kitchen at the time. Several days after this experience, Mrs. McDuffa, now fully aware that there was something strange going on in their apartment, went to bed, turning on the bedside lamp in order to read. The moment she had turned it on, the lamp went out by itself. Three times Mrs. McDuffa turned it on, only to see it go out of its own volition. She checked the bulb, but it worked perfectly in other lamps. The next day she called in an electrician and had the switch examined as well as the lamp. He could find nothing wrong with either. That night she turned the lamp on again and nothing went wrong with it. Apparently her unseen visitor had decided to leave things well enough alone for that night.

A few days after this experience, Mrs. McDuffa was getting ready to go to work. It was a dark, rainy morning, and as she shut the door she looked back toward the apartment. A bright light shone across the living room as if the sun were shining in. Both her mother and her son saw the same thing and looked at her in amazement. There was no way such a light could have appeared in her living room.

One evening everyone had gone to bed; the hall light was left on and the door between the two bedrooms stood open. Mrs. McDuffa was looking toward the open bedroom door when she suddenly became aware of two roundish shapes made of a white, cloud-like substance. It seemed to her to resemble in a vague way the outlines of a human figure, but no details could be seen. As she observed this apparition in a state of shock mingled with fascination, the whitish shape slowly drifted into the second bedroom and disappeared.

But that was the end of the trail as far as Mrs. McDuffa was concerned. The following day she made arrangements to move. They had lived at the apartment for less than three months. Since she had lived in many places before without encountering anything unusual, Mrs. McDuffa became convinced that she had somehow stumbled upon a very haunted apartment. She had no idea who the apparition might be, nor did she make any inquiries with the landlord. All she wanted was to get out of the place, and fast.

John K. was twenty-six years old, lived in Hollywood and worked as a freight cashier at a steamship company. "I don't quite know where to begin," he said when he contacted me in May of 1971. He explained that he felt he was being harassed by reincarnation memories or by someone he thought was in some mysterious way connected with his personality. Since I am always on the lookout' for "evidential" reincarnation cases, I was naturally interested. In October of the same year we met at the Continental Hotel in Hollywood. Mr. K. turned out to be a slight, quiet-spoken young man, far from hysterical and not particularly involved with the occult. Gradually I pieced his amazing story together and discovered what lay at the base of his strange and terrifying experiences.

John K. was born in a small town in the Ozarks with a population of only forty-two people. The house he was born and raised in was quite old, built before the Civil War. His family lived there until he reached the age of twelve, when they moved to another small town in southwestern Arizona. There his father was employed by the government on a nearby Army base. At the age of twenty, Mr. K. dropped out of college and headed straight for Los Angeles, where he had lived ever since.

His first twelve years in the Ozarks were spent on a farm with five brothers and two sisters. The family lived a very primitive life. There was no indoor plumbing; heat was provided by a coal stove, and each Saturday night the entire family would take turns bathing in the same tub of water. At first there was no electricity in the house. For the first three grades, Mr. K. went to a one-room schoolhouse. "Our teacher was very young and had not yet finished her college education but was permitted to teach us anyway."

Mr. K. explained, "The reason I am relating all of my earlier surroundings to you is to point out the fact that the first twelve years of my life I lived a very isolated existence." Until he reached the age of ten, Mr. K. had not seen a television set; entertainment in his family consisted mainly of playing cards and talking. He attended the local Southern Baptist Church, into which he was duly baptized; however, after the family left the farm they dropped out of organized religion.

From an early age John K. received the impression of a presence that no one else could see. None of his immediate family had ever been out of the country, yet he was aware of the presence of a French lady whose name, he came to know, as Jacqueline. When he mentioned the presence of this woman to his family he was laughed at and told that he had a fantastic imagination, so he stopped talking about it. At an early age he also developed the ability to dream of events that later happened *exactly* as seen in his dreams. These prophetic dreams did not forecast great events but concerned themselves with everyday matters. Nevertheless, they were upsetting to the boy. He never remembered his dreams, but when the event became objective reality he started to shiver and realized he had seen it all before. This, of course, is called *deja vu* and is a fairly common ESP phenomenon. He could not discuss his dreams with his family, since psychic experiences were not the kind of thing one could talk about in the Ozarks in the early 1950s. But he hated to stay in the house alone; he had a terrible fear of darkness and of the house itself.

One afternoon when he was ten years old, he happened to be in the house alone, upstairs in the back bedroom. All of a sudden he knew there was a presence there, and the most horrifying fear swept through him, as if he were being choked to death. The walls seemed to vibrate, and he heard a loud sound for which there did not seem to be any natural explanation. Eventually he was able to break out of his terror and flee down the stairs.

There was something else that seemed strange about John K. from an early age on. He could never relate to men and felt completely at ease only with women—his grandmother, his mother, and his older sister. When he was very young, he began playing with his older sister, six years his senior, and enjoyed playing girls' games tremendously. He would never join his brothers in boys' games. He loved wearing long flowing dresses, fashions of an earlier time that he had found in the attic. Whenever he wore these dresses, he felt completely at ease and seemed to have a rather sophisticated air about him. The strange thing was that he insisted on wearing only those dresses of an earlier period of history; the shorter dresses of the current era interested him not at all. At those times he felt as though he were another person.

It was during those early childhood days that he first became aware of Jacqueline. Especially when he played with his sister, he felt that he was sexually just like her. He continued to wear dresses around the house until the time he started to school. Often when he came home from school he would go upstairs and put on his dresses. Finally, his father became aware of the boy's tendency and threatened to send him to school wearing a dress if he didn't stop, so John stopped. However, the impression of a female life inside him and the desire to wear long dresses persisted.

"Needless to say," Mr. K. explained in complete frankness, "I was not the average run-of-the-mill boy, and I turned out to be very effeminate and was teased constantly by my schoolmates." Rejected by the other boys, he began to turn within himself and did not bother to explain his ideas to others. Although he had never traveled outside the area surrounding his native village, he began to feel very emotional about France, particularly Paris. "I somehow seemed to have fond memories of a life of many human pleasures, a life of a woman who was very aware and felt a need to express herself totally," John K. explained, adding that he knew by that time that Jacqueline, whoever she might have been, had led the life of a prostitute. He thus had a sense of heavy religious condemnation, of being a wicked sinner with the threat of hell hanging over him.

When the family finally moved to Arizona, he thought that perhaps some of his agonies would subside. But the conflict between his present surroundings and the world of Jacqueline increased almost daily. At the age of fourteen he felt that since he could not belong to this world he might as well kill himself and return to where he really belonged. He wrote a farewell note to his mother, the only one to whom he could relate at the time, his sister having married and his grandmother having grown old and feeble. In the note he told his mother that he was going to return to where he belonged, that he felt he had come from another planet and it was time for him to go back. He then ran a rope over one of the rafters in his room, put a chair under it, and placed the noose around his neck, ready to jump. Then, fate intervened in the person of one of his mother's friends who had stopped by unexpectedly. Since his mother was asleep, John had to answer the door. The visit lasted a long time, and by the time the lady had left he was no longer in the mood to take his own life.

From then on he did rather well in school, although most people thought him too shy and introverted. He never dated girls, since he felt himself female. But he did make friends with one particular boy and remained close friends with him for ten years. Later, the boy moved to Los Angeles. When John K. dropped out of school in his junior year of college, he came to Los Angeles and moved in with his friend. At the time he was twenty years old. He still felt like a female and was still continually aware of Jacqueline.

It was then that John became involved in the homosexual world and had the first sexual experience of his life. Whenever he had sexual relations, he felt strongly that he was fulfilling the part of the woman.

About six months after he came to Los Angeles, he started to have terrible dreams. One night when he was totally awake he suddenly saw a woman standing at the foot of his bed. She was wearing a long nightgown and had long hair and was smiling at him. She seemed to float just above the floor. At first

John thought that it was his imagination and passed it off as a silly dream. The next night the same thing happened. He realized the apparition wanted to tell him something. Strangely enough, he wasn't particularly frightened. The third night the apparition returned, and her smile had turned into a frown of deep sorrow. She returned the following night, and this time her face showed utter terror. Deep veins stood out on her face, her eyes were bloodshot, and her mouth grinned hideously.

She returned once again the following night, and this time her entire head had been torn off, and blood was spilled all over her beautiful flowing gown. John was fully aware of the utter torment of her soul. That same night something grabbed hold of his arm and forcibly yanked him out of bed and onto the floor. He screamed for help from his roommate, who was in the next room, but the young man had no compassion for his condition and yelled out for John to shut up or he would have him committed.

After this incident John thought he was going mad and wondered to whom he could turn for advice.

A few months passed. He was still living in Hollywood with the same roommate but by this time was a prostitute himself. He had gone to college and found himself a good job, but he had had a strong urge to become a prostitute, and so followed it. Whenever he engaged in these activities he felt a very deep satisfaction. Also at this time he resumed wearing female clothes, and since his roommate was a make-up artist by profession, he would do the make-up for him. John would never go into the streets in this array; he would wear these clothes only at home. His friends began to call him Jackie, for Jacqueline.

Whenever he put on the clothes, John became another person. The first time he saw himself in complete make-up and female clothing he felt that Jacqueline had won at last. He now felt that she had taken total possession of him and that he was cursed for life.

"It was not a simple case of transvestitism or going in female drag," John explained, "It was a complete soul satisfaction on my part, and when Jacqueline came out she controlled me completely. She was very strong and I was very weak."

It finally reached the point that when John came home at night he would dress up in female clothing and spend the entire evening in this manner. He even slept in evening gowns. He removed all the hair from his body and delighted in taking baths and dousing himself with perfumes. This went on for two years, until John felt that something had to be done about it. He realized something was wrong with him.

About that time another friend introduced him to Buddhism. For three years he practiced the Buddhist religion, and through it, he was able to find many answers for himself that had eluded him before. Because of his devotion to Buddhism, Jacqueline finally left, never to return again. A new male image began to emerge slowly but surely as a result of his Buddhist practices, and once again he was able to relate to the environment around him and find a reason for living.

Through a friend, John received my address. He contacted me in the hope I might hypnotize him and regress him to an earlier life in which he might encounter Jacqueline. John was firmly convinced that his predicament had been due to an unfulfilled reincarnation problem, and that perhaps through hypnosis I might put him further on the road to recovery.

"I never felt fulfillment during my pre-Buddhist sexual contacts while portraying Jacqueline," he told me, "but it did satisfy my Jacqueline personality completely. But she is totally gone now and a new John is emerging—one who is not afraid of the dark anymore and who can live alone and stand on his own two feet, and who is very optimistic about the future."

Although neither John nor his immediate family had had any interest in or knowledge of occult practices, this was not entirely true of others in his background. An Aunt Mary had been a practicing witch, had owned many books dealing with witchcraft of the fifteenth and sixteenth centuries?it had been a sore subject in the family. Nobody dared talk about her. But she had died before John was born, and all knowledge John had of his Aunt Mary was secondhand. Nevertheless, there had been ESP talents in the family on his father's side, mainly messages from dead relatives, though John was never able to obtain any details. In his family the occult was something not suitable for family conversation.

After Jacqueline had left John, he kept having ESP experiences unrelated to his ordeal. They were not world-shaking experiences, but they did convince him that his ESP faculty had remained unimpaired by the hold Jacqueline had exercised upon him for so many years. A short time before our meeting there had been a steamship strike and he was laid off. He was wondering if he should get another job outside the steamship industry when he had a strange dream. In the dream he saw his boss at the steamship company coming out of his office and saying to someone, "Call John K. back to work." At the same time he saw the number 7 flash through the dream. Upon awakening he remembered every detail. On September 7 his boss came out of his office and told an aide, "Call John K. back to work," and, as foreseen in the dream, he returned to his former position.

I was rather interested in his continuing ESP experiences since I had begun to wonder whether Jacqueline was indeed a reincarnation memory or perhaps something else. We proceeded to begin hypnotic regression. I first took John K. down to age twenty, when he remembered every detail of his life. He even remembered the names of his best friends and what was on his desk at the time. I then took him back to age twelve and his life in Missouri. In each case he even knew his exact height at the time. He knew the names of the nearest neighbors, how many children they had and even the name of their dog. Satisfied that he was deeply in the third stage of hypnotic regression, I then took him back beyond the threshold of birth into an alleged earlier life. I worked very hard and very gradually to see whether we could locate some other personality that had been John K. in a previous lifetime, but he saw nothing. I then asked him to look specifically for Jacqueline.

"Do you know who she is?" I asked.

"She is someone who doesn't like me."

"Is she a real person?"

"Yes."

"Have you ever lived in France?"

"No."

I then took him as far back as the Middle Ages, fifty years at a time, in case there were other incarnations. When we got to the year 1350, he said he felt very strange and put his hands upon his chest in a gesture I interpreted as religious. But there was no recognition of another person. I then took him, step by step, back into the present, finally awakening him, and then inquiring how he felt. Since John was a good hypnotic subject, he remembered absolutely nothing of what he had said during hypnosis.

"Do you feel different from the way you felt fifteen minutes ago?" I inquired.

"Well, I had a headache before I came; I don't have a headache now."

He felt well rested and satisfied with himself. Jacqueline had not put in an appearance, as she would have if she had been part of John K. I then explained to the young man that his ordeal had not been caused by reincarnation memories or an unfulfilled earlier lifetime. To the contrary, he had been victimized by an independent entity, not related to him in any way, who had somehow sought him out to serve as her medium of expression in the physical world. Jacqueline, the French prostitute, whose choice of clothes indicated that she had lived in the nineteenth century, wanted to live in this century through another body. For reasons of her own she had chosen a male body for her experiment.

If there was any reincarnation connection between the two, it remained obscure. There is, of course, the possibility that John K. had been in another life someone close to Jacqueline, in her time, and had since reincarnated while Jacqueline had not, and that the woman attached herself to John K. just as soon as she could after his birth into the present life. I myself tend to favor this theory. It was unfortunate that this earlier John K. could not be rediscovered either consciously or in hypnosis. But if this earlier incarnation had led a fully satisfactory life, the need to retain traces of memory would not be there.

In the case of Jacqueline, her inner conflict between what she was doing and the religious pressure exerted upon her must have been the compelling factor in keeping her in a time slot, or, rather, suspended in time, preventing her from reincarnating herself. In her predicament and frustration she needed to express herself through someone in the present, since she could not herself go on and be someone else. Deprived of her medium, Jacqueline perhaps had found an avenue of escape into the next stage of existence, not to be heard from again.

When it comes to seeing the ghosts of celebrities, all sorts of people are likely to imagine they are in touch with their favorite movie star, when in fact they are merely expressing a wish fulfillment. In such cases, however, there exists a real attachment, an admiration for the personality involved. Frequently the people who have such fantasies are fans who have never met the star in question but wish they had.

Not so with attractive Doris Danielson, a Texas divorcee whom I met in Houston, after she had requested my help in clearing up the mystery of her psychic experiences. At that time in her thirties, she worked as a secretary.

"Miss Danielson, have you ever had any interest in psychic phenomena since you have grown up?" I began my questioning.

"No, I haven't."

"Have you had any experiences whatever that you might classify as psychic besides the one we are about to discuss?"

"No."

"When did this phenomenon take place?"

"It was in March of 1957. I was about to be discharged from the Air Force and was staying with a friend, Roger Smith, overnight. His house was in Trenton, New Jersey. I had been a stewardess, and I was planning to leave for New York to try to get into modeling. This happened the night before I left.

"I woke up for some reason in the middle of the night and crawled to the edge of the bed on my hands and knees. I asked myself, why did I wake up? I couldn't think of any reason. Then I looked at the door—it appeared to be getting brighter! Then a circle formed in the middle of the door. It was red. The circle started coming toward me. And inside the circle was *James Dean's head.*"

"Had you seen his face before?"

"I'd seen him in the movies, but I had no particular interest in James Dean; I simply thought he was a good actor. But I never thought about him. The only parallel in my life was that my boyfriend at the time resembled James Dean somewhat in his likes and dislikes, such as motorcycles, speed, and all that."

"Did he *look* like him?"

"Not really."

"How long did the image last?"

"I don't know, but I kept thinking if I stared at it long enough it might disappear. I did, but instead it floated across the room, and only then did it disappear. It came from the door and floated toward me as I was sitting on the bed. Just a head in a circle."

"Did it speak?"

"No."

"Was there any form of movement?"

"I can't remember any form of movement. His hair was very curly. Suddenly, it was gone. I sat there and pinched myself to make sure I was awake. When it was gone I really became scared, and I prayed."

"Have you had any similar experiences before or after?"

"No. The only other experience I had was after I had moved to Houston. I was married then, and my husband had gone on guard duty and was to be away for two weeks. Two days after he was gone, this happened. I had just turned out all the lights and gone to bed. I heard somebody come down the hallway. I thought it might be my husband coming back, although I wasn't expecting him. He was the only one who had a key. I said, 'Bob, is that you?' But there was no answer. Then I felt someone come right into the bedroom and stand by my bed. The springs of the bed creaked as if someone were sitting on it. I shot out of the bed on the other side and ran to the bathroom, where I turned on the lights. There was nobody in the bedroom."

"Was the house in any way connected with a tragedy?"

"No. It was a brand-new house when we moved in."

"Did the footsteps sound like a man's or a woman's?"

"I had thought it was my husband coming home, but I don't know how I *could* have heard footsteps, because there was a rug on the floor."

"Had you seen any James Dean movies since the first incident?"

"No."

One can only surmise that the late actor recognized Doris as a potential communicator, but somehow never got his message across the veil.

PIPELINE TO THE
BEYOND

*A*s I have said in my previous books, ghost hunting is fruitless without a good medium to serve as spokesman for the unhappy ones in the in-between world.

Genuine mediums are few and far between. By that I don't mean to imply that the majority of psychics are fraudulent. They are not. But there are a good number of people who are neither frauds nor really efficient mediums; they are gifted with a degree of ESP or with psychic powers, but are not able to channel them properly and constantly into directions where their abilities can be used for the obtaining of scientific evidence.

Some spiritualists are genuine and some are not, and only a handful of those who are not genuine are dishonest. In most cases known to me, the medium who fails to give evidence is merely incapable of doing so and does not realize it. Occasionally, a medium will build up what he or she obtains through psychic means, to make it sound better than it is. And a few are genuinely great instruments between the physical and psychic worlds.

Dealing with hauntings as I do, I naturally place the highest value on trance mediumship, since it gives me an immediate, clear-cut entry into the world of the ghost. When the ghost speaks to me through the entranced medium, I can pose questions and get answers directly and under my own control.

On the other hand, I have always worked with creditable clairvoyants, people who sense events and things and are able to describe them often very precisely. My aim is information, regardless of the manner in which it is obtained, but it is information that is unknown to me, the medium, or those present at the time it is given to me that I desire. I want information I can check out. By obeying simple safety rules of evidence, I am able to dismiss any unfriendly allegations of coincidence, mind-picking, previous knowledge and other forms of alternate explanations for what I have come to accept as genuine psychic material.

California teems with metaphysics and its practitioners of various persuasions. I give them all a wide berth, for the realm of religious philosophy is incapable of objective proof by reasonable scientific standards. Then there are the psychic readers and professional mediums, none of whom had attained a world reputation to date, except perhaps Sophia Williams, the great voice medium, and she was no longer working, I was told.

I found a man named Zenor well spoken of in Hollywood, although I could not get to see him. The "church directory" of any spiritualistic magazine is full of advertisements of psychics, some of which may indeed be talented people.

I had occasion, however, to meet a few of the non-professional mediums who had not seen fit to commercialize their gifts—not that doing so is necessarily bad. Everybody has a right to choose the way in which to make a living, and if the charge for a psychic reading is modest, it seems to me a fitting way to work for a livelihood and yet do something of value— provided one is scrupulously honest in one's readings and does not allow interpretations or the desire to please to interfere with the results!

One of those who impressed me particularly by her sincerity was an unassuming middle-aged lady by the name of Maureen Petersen. I first heard of her in 1960 and met her in person three years later, when she drove all the way from her home in Turlock, California, to meet us.

What had made her come forward was a haunted house she once lived in; like so many others who reach me, she thought her instance might be of interest to me in my quest for ghosts.

Mrs. Petersen's stay at the old house in Healdsburg, about two hours north of San Francisco, took place back in 1920, but her memory was remarkably fresh about it.

When she was fifteen years old, her family moved into this ordinary-looking house on Tucker Street, a house without either an attic or a basement, with all rooms being on one level. Immediately both her mother and Maureen became aware of strange goings-on in the house. Being psychic had been handed down in the family for the third generation then, and they took it all in their stride.

Night after night, they heard the sounds of running water in the kitchen sink, although the faucets were off; the sound of light switches being turned on and off, dishes rattling in the cupboard, chairs being pushed around, and finally a sound resembling that of the crash of a heavy object falling. This was accompanied by heavy, masculine footsteps of one or more men, and lasted several hours, always starting and ending at the same time each night!

At first it was only her mother who awoke because of the disturbances and Maureen often slept through them. Her father never heard anything unusual, not being psychic. Whenever she was awakened by the noises, Maureen's mother investigated all rooms, only to find everything dark and nothing amiss.

Soon the young girl also heard it. The first time she

thought her father had gotten up for some reason and was causing the disturbances in the kitchen. But he was fast asleep all that time.

Maureen shared a bedroom with her sister and it adjoined the dining room where the activities seemed to center. She decided to brave it out and usually the noises ceased after a while.

One night the heavy footfalls came toward her bedroom door, however, and her heart almost stopped beating. Then they stopped abruptly at the threshold.

At this point Maureen's father decided to make some inquiries about the background of the house. It was then that the family discovered their home had been a meeting place for a group of men who used it, as Mrs. Petersen so delicately put it, "to drink and carouse in."

They decided to move out and kept their mouths shut. But the next tenant was no luckier. When they returned to the house sometime later, their successors complained about the very same phenomena that had driven them away.

Although her parents had long ago passed away, Maureen's sister Rose still lived in Santa Rosa and her brother Myron was in San Francisco. Both were witnesses to the unearthly phenomena at the time, and her sister, now Mrs. Rose Hatch, recalled the incidents quite clearly.

But what interested me in the case of Mrs. Petersen was not just another haunted house, of which I know a large number already, but her mediumship. We chatted about her experiences when she met with me in Hollywood.

A native of Colorado, Maureen grew up with the belief in the supernatural all around her, for both her mother and maternal grandmother had been gifted psychics. As a matter of fact, her own daughter also had the gift, apparently passed down through the female line of the family.

While still in her teens, Maureen acquired the ability to

foretell the future, and on one such occasion informed her astonished family that she would marry a poor farmer and move back to Colorado with him. The family at this time was living in California. Then she turned to her sister Rose and predicted that she would marry a professional man and live well. Many years later, both predictions came true. Maureen married a poor farmer and moved to Colorado with him, and Rose settled down with a dentist.

After her first husband passed on, Mrs. Peterson married her present husband and returned to California.

The incidents of paranormal nature in her life were numerous during those years. Take, for instance, the time she was walking to a neighbor's house with her little girl, Mardelle.

"Something's happened at home, we must go back," she suddenly screamed, and they retraced their steps at once. At home they found her little boy Melvin had been attacked by a neighbor's dog.

Or the time she needed some dental work done and found herself unusually reluctant to enter the dentist's office. The treatment was painful and she ascribed her foreboding to her fear of pain. But when she returned for additional treatment the next day, she found that the ceiling had collapsed over the dentist's chair.

Soon Maureen developed the gift of automatic writing, that is, letting a psychic force use her arm and send messages through her in this manner. Voices which she feels are spirit friends guide and protect her and often warn her of impending danger. Often she had been able to heed these warnings and prevent the worst.

I asked Mrs. Petersen to tell me of some of the more remarkable incidents of this kind.

"Once, my second husband, Gilbert, and I were hundreds of miles away on a trip when I was told to turn back, as one of my children needed me. We started home and, as soon as we arrived, went to the home of my daughter, Mardelle Adams. She was alone with her children. She was in premature labor and had been unable to locate her physician. Phoning from a neighbor's house, I was able to engage another, and we took her to the hospital an hour before the birth of her child.

"One day I had a dream which was not a dream but a warning.

"I saw my sister, Rose Hatch, in a car in great danger. Very upset, I told my family but didn't write my sister, fearing to frighten her. A card arrived telling me she was on vacation. When I saw her, she said that on this trip her foot had accidentally jammed against the accelerator and the car came within inches of going over a bridge into a deep canyon with the whole family in it. This same day her husband barely saved her from drowning in a whirlpool in a strange river."

But Mrs. Petersen's traffic with the netherworld did not confine itself to such dreary things as warnings of impending doom or dangers. Many of her ESP experiences show the close contact she was apparently able to maintain with the non-physical world for all these years.

Having a gifted medium as an outlet, a person to manifest through, must evidently mean a great deal to discarnates, for they seem to show their gratitude for this service by giving Mrs. Petersen "a hand" in many mundane matters as well as spiritual counsel.

Again I requested that she select some of these experiences and tell me about them in her own words. There was no hesitancy in her voice as she related her brushes with the uncanny.

"Six years after my first husband passed away, a relative, Joyce M., received a message by automatic writing that he would appear to me within three days. Three days later I awoke and noted, through closed lids, that it was light. Then

I saw a book with open pages appear above the foot of my bed. As I tried to make out the printing in it, it disappeared and my husband appeared. He looked young and handsome and very real. He soon disappeared, and right afterward I felt his kiss on my lips as plainly as I ever felt it in life. I was definitely awake.

"After losing my husband, I was grieving and felt a great need to visit my sister, but lacked the money for a bus ticket. One morning I was walking to town, and, before leaving, remarked to my mother that if I found the money on the sidewalk I would visit my sister. I found just a little more than the needed amount on the sidewalk. It hardly seems a coincidence, since I have never found money on a sidewalk before or since.

"I have seen apparitions or thought forms quite often. On a number of occasions, I have seen my husband returning home, when he was nowhere near and didn't return for some time. I used to see my first husband the same way. Once I saw my husband Gilbert on his bicycle. I was in the yard and only a few feet from him. He turned his head and looked at me but said nothing. I went inside and he disappeared, and didn't arrive until some time later. He wasn't near the house when I saw him.

"My mother and I were shopping and went on separate errands, agreeing to meet at the car. Returning, I saw her in the back seat. I glanced away a moment as I stepped to the front of the car. My mother had disappeared. When she did come she said she had wanted very much to return to the car at the time I saw her there.

"While writing a friend in England, a spirit came to me. He identified himself as John Bennet and gave other identification. He named a son and said he wanted to get in touch with his relatives in England. I had never heard of this man but my English friend had mentioned the son in letters. I wrote her, Mrs. W., and her letter verified the information in the message, including the name, and confirmed that this man had recently died."

I made a note to take Mrs. Petersen to a haunted house sometime—not the one she knew so well, perhaps, but one about which she knew nothing whatever. That way, her mediumistic powers could be tested to a larger degree.

One of the difficulties with mediums is the reception they get from their families or friends when their peculiarities are discovered. Until we can educate the "non-believers" that being psychic is not so bad as having a dreaded disease, we cannot very well expect people to come forward and talk about these experiences as freely as they should.

Anatomy of a ghost? Many people have questioned me about the apparent inconsistencies between the various forms in which ghosts make themselves known.

Sometimes, the form is merely a light or ball of light moving about. This in my opinion is the concentrated life force within the personality when that personality does not wish to make itself known or be identified as someone who had lived in the body. Sort of a lazy type of ghost!

White mists, whitish outlines of bodies or amorphous white clouds, sometimes almost human in shape, sometimes not, also occur. But most apparitions are of people wearing clothes and appearing very much "alive" in the physical sense. They are two-dimensional generally in that you can walk through them and they will dissolve instantly when challenged.

But occasionally the dead appear as solid bodies, so solid they are mistaken for the living. In my estimation they can accomplish this amazing feat by surrounding their thought forms with a plastic matter drawn from the living in the house and/or built up by concentration of their own energies to the required densities. This plastic substance, sometimes referred to as ectoplasm, and in an earlier period as teleplasm, varies in density from smoke to solid "flesh." It is equally capable of instant dissolution. All the personality inside this "mantle" has to do is interrupt the thought and suggest dissolution. I have come to these seemingly outlandish conclusions of what the dead can do only after many years of careful study and thousands of cases involving apparitions.

There is no real inconsistency between these ghosts— merely a difference in method and intensity of desire to make oneself known to the physical world!

Perhaps a good case in point is the psychic world of a twenty-three-year-old housewife in Ontario, California. Mrs. Walter W. hesitates to discuss her gifts with the neighbors for fear of being ridiculed or considered odd. With me she knew she would find understanding, so she communicated freely.

At 21, she had left home and had struck out on her own. Her parting from her mother had not been without emotional upsets and she found herself rather under a strain at the time she rented an apartment. Immediately she felt "bad vibrations" at the place. She explained her feelings by her general mood, but in her heart she knew that this would not hold water. Especially not as an explanation for the sound of footsteps and of the front door opening and closing by itself, without any visible visitor around!

Soon she heard footfalls also on her porch at night and felt herself being watched. One night she could not ignore it any longer and looked up. There in the doorway of the bedroom, leading in from the living room, was a fog-like translucent substance hanging in the upper portion of the doorway. Not believing her eyes, Mrs. W. assured herself it was all in her head and tried to sleep. But the feeling of the presence grew stronger. She felt sure "it" was very close to her now. Finally, she opened her eyes again. The substance was hanging directly over her head a few feet from her face! She screamed and buried her head in the pillows.

The next morning she was calmer, but the "mist" reappeared again and again. She left the lights on at night, but the feeling of a presence persisted. But, the rent was low and she hated giving up such a convenient flat.

Then another apartment directly across from hers became available and she moved into it. No more white mist, no more presence. Whatever it was had stayed in the haunted flat.

In old houses such as this, where people come and go frequently and few questions are asked, tragedies can remain undiscovered for long periods, or even forever. Mrs. W. was sure the ghost merely wanted to confide in her, but she just was not ready to be the channel for his plea.

THE GHOST WHO REFUSED TO GO

*O*ne of the most spectacular cases I reported in *Ghosts I've Met* concerned the hauntings at a house on Ardmore Boulevard, Los Angeles.

The house itself, barely thirty years old, was being plagued by the noises of a wild party going on at night, during which apparently someone was killed, by footsteps where nobody was seen walking and by other uncanny noises, including voices resounding in the dark, telling the current owners to get out of *their* house!

I had been to this house several times and brought Maxine Bell, a local psychic, on one occasion. That visit proved memorable not only because of material obtained by Ms. Bell, in semi-trance, which proved accurate to a large degree, but because of my own photographic work.

Left alone in the most haunted part of the house, I took at random a number of black and white pictures of a particular bedroom which of course was empty, at least to my eyes.

On one of the pictures, taken under existing daylight conditions and from a firm surface, the figure of a young woman dressed in a kind of negligee appears standing near the window. As my camera was double exposure proof and both the film and the developing beyond reproach, there was no other rational explanation for this picture. Since that time, I have succeeded in taking other psychic photographs, but the "girl at the window" will always rank as one of my most astounding ones.

The whistling noises, the popping of a champagne bottle in the dark of night followed by laughter, the doors opening by themselves, and all the other psychic phenomena that had been endured by the owner of the house, Helen L., for a long time would not yield to my usual approach: trance session and order to the ghost to go away. There were complications in that Miss L. herself had mediumistic talents, although unsought and undeveloped, and there was present in the household a sister who was disabled, which is often the sources of energies with which poltergeist phenomena are made possible.

Nevertheless, when we left the house on Ardmore Boulevard I had high hopes for a more peaceful atmosphere in the future. For one thing, I explained matters to Miss L., and for another, I suggested that the garden be searched for the body of that murder victim. We had already established that a fight had actually occurred some years ago in the house, observed by neighbors. It was entirely possible that the body of one of the victims was still on the grounds.

In July of 1964 the noises resumed, and thuds of falling bodies, footfalls and other noises started up again in the unfortunate house. Quite rightly Helen L. asked me to continue the case. But it was not until the spring of 1965 that I could devote my energies toward this matter again.

All I had accomplished in the interim was a certain lessening of the phenomena, but not their elimination.

On March 14, 1965, Helen L. communicated with me in a matter of great urgency. For the first time, the ghost had been seen! At 3 A.M. on March 13, her mother had been awakened by strange noises, and looking up from the bed, she saw the figure of a man beside the bed. The noise sounded to her as if someone were tearing up bed sheets. Frightened, the old lady pulled the covers over her head and went back to sleep. Helen L. also heard heavy footsteps all over the house that same night. Needless to say, they had no visitors from the flesh-and-blood world.

"Are you going to be here in April? Help!!" Helen L. wrote. I answered I would indeed come and bring Sybil Leek with me to have another and, hopefully, final go at this ghost. But it would have to be in June, not April. During the first week of May, Helen awoke on Sunday morning to hear a man's voice shushing her inches away from her pillow. She could hardly wait for our arrival after that. Finally, on June 28, I arrived at the little house with Sybil to see what she might pick up.

"I know there is a presence here," Sybil said immediately as we seated ourselves in the little office that was situated in back of the bedroom where most of the disturbances had occurred. I turned the light out to give Sybil a better chance to concentrate, or rather, to relax, and immediately she felt the intruder.

"It is mostly in the bedroom," she continued. "There are two people; the man dominates in the bedroom area, and there is also a woman, a young girl."

I decided Sybil should attempt trance at this point, and invited the ghost to make himself known. After a few moments, Sybil slipped into a state bordering on trance, but continued to be fully conscious.

"Morton," she mumbled now, "there is something terribly intense … have a desire to *break* something … Morton is the last name."

I repeated my invitation for him to come forward and tell his story.

"The girl goes away," Sybil intoned, "and he says he comes back to find her. And she isn't here. He was going to celebrate. He must find her. Wedding party, celebration ... for the girl. She wasn't happy here; she had to go away. This man is a foreigner."

"You're right." The booming voice of Helen L. spoke up in the dark across the room. Evidently Sybil had described someone she recognized.

"Jane Morton," Sybil said now, flatly, "something to do with building, perhaps he had something to do with building this house ... he's an older man. Jane ... is young ... I'm trying to find out where Jane is ... that's what *he* wants to know ... I will tell him it didn't matter about the party ... she would have gone anyway ... she hated the old man ... this man fell ... head's bad ... fell against the stable ..."

"Did he die here?" I pressed.

"1837," Sybil said, somewhat incongruously, "1837. Came back ... went out again, came back with people, was drunk, hurt his head, left hand side... ."

Despite my urging, the entity refused to speak through Sybil in trance. I continued to question her nevertheless.

The ghost's name was Howell Morton, Sybil reported, although I was not sure of the spelling of the first name, which might have been Hawall rather than Howell.

"He came here to do some building; someone was accidentally killed and buried in the garden ..."

"Who buried this person?"

"Boyd Johnson ... Raymond McClure ... Dell ... Persilla ..." The voice was faltering now and the names not too clear.

"Is the girl dead too?"

"Girl's alive... ."

"Is there anyone dead in this house outside of Morton?"

"Morton died here."

"Who was the figure I photographed here?"

"Jane ... he wants to draw her back here ... but I think she's alive ... yet there are things of hers buried ..."

Sybil seemed confused at this point.

"Meri ... Meredith... ." she said, or she could have said. "Married her." It just was not clear enough to be sure. Morton and some of his friends were doing the disturbing in the house, Sybil explained. He died at the party.

"There was violence outside," Sybil added and Helen L. nodded emphatically. There was indeed.

"Drunk ... four o'clock ... he died accidentally ..." Where is he buried in the garden, Helen L. wanted to know, anxiously.

"Straight down by the next building," Sybil replied. "It wasn't built completely when he died."

Later we all went into the garden and identified the building as the garage in back of the house.

But Helen was not yet ready to start digging. What would the neighbors think if we found a body? Or, for that matter, what would they think if we didn't? There we left it, for her to think over whether to dig or not to dig—that was the question.

I returned to New York in the hope that I would not hear anything further from Helen L. But I was mistaken. On July 5 I heard again from the lady on Ardmore Boulevard.

Her other sister, Alma, who lived in Hollywood but had stayed at the house on Ardmore on occasion, called the morning after our visit. It was then that she volunteered information she had been holding back from Helen L. for two years for fear of further upsetting her, in view of events at the house. But she had had a dream-like impression at the house in which she "saw" a man in his middle years, who had lived in a lean-to shack attached to the garage.

She knew this man was dead and got the impression that he was a most stubborn person, difficult to dislodge or reason with. What made this dream impression of interest to us, Miss

L. thought, was the fact that her sister could not have known of Sybil Leek's insistence that a man lay buried at that very spot next to the garage! No shack ever stood there to the best of Helen L.'s knowledge, but of course it may have stood there before the present house was built.

Also, Helen reminded me that on those occasions when her mother and sister slept in the garage, when they had company in the main house, both had heard heavy footsteps coming up to the garage and stopping dead upon reaching the wall. Helen L.'s mother had for years insisted that there was "a body buried there in the garden" but nobody had ever tried to find it.

Nothing more happened until May 8, 1966, when Sybil Leek and I again went to the house because Helen L. had implored us to finish the case for her. The disturbances had been continuing on and off.

With us this time was Eugene Lundholm, librarian and psychic researcher. Trance came quickly. Perhaps Sybil was in a more relaxed state than during our last visit, but whatever the reason, things seemed to be more congenial this time around.

"I'm falling," her voice whispered, barely audible, "I'm hungry ..."

Was someone reliving moments of anguish?

"Who are you?" I demanded.

"Can't breathe... ."

"What is your name?"

"Harold ..."

He had great difficulties with his breathing and I suggested he relax.

"Kill her ..." he now panted, "kill her, kill the woman ..."

"Did you kill her?"

"NO!"

"I've come to help you. I'm your friend."

"Kill her before she goes away... ."

"Why?"

"No good here ... where's he taken her? Where is she?"
The voice became more intelligible now.

"What is her name?"

"Where is she ... I'll kill her."

"Who's with her?"

"Porter."

"Is he a friend of yours?"

"NO!"

"Who are you?"

"Harold Howard."

"Is this your house?"

"My house."

"Did you build it?"

"No."

"Did you buy it?"

Evidently my questioning got on his nerves, for he shouted,
"Who are *you?*" I explained, but it didn't help.

"Too many people here ... I throw them out ... take those
people out of here!"

Strangely enough, the voice did not sound like Sybil's at
all; it had lost all trace of a British flavor and was full of anger.
Evidently the ghost was speaking of the revelers he had found
at his house and wanted them out.

"His friends ... take them away ... she brought them ...

"While you were away?" He was somewhat calmer now.

"Yes," he confirmed.

"Where were you?"

"Working."

"What do you do?"

"Miner."

"Where do you work?"

"Purdy Town." He may have said Purgory Town, or some-

335

thing like it.

"What happened when you came home?"

Again he became upset about the people in his house and I asked that he name some of them.

"Margaret ..." he said, more excited now. "Mine ... twenty-five ... I came home ... they were here ... too many people ... party here...."

"Did you hurt anyone?"

"I'm going to kill her," he insisted. Evidently he had not done so.

"Why?"

"Because of him." Jealousy, the great ghost-maker.

"Who is he?"

"Porter."

"Who is he?"

"He took my place. Eric Porter."

"What year is this?"

It was high time we got a "fix" on the period we were in.

"Forty-eight."

"What happened to you ... afterwards?"

"People went away ... Porter ... outside ... I want to go away now ..."

It became clear to me that the girl must have been killed but that a shock condition at the time of the crime had prevented this man from realizing what he had done, thus forcing him to continue his quest for the girl. I told him as much and found him amazed at the idea of his deed.

"Why did he follow me ... he followed me ... then I hit him in the guts ..."

"What did you do with him then?"

"Put him away."

He became cagey after that, evidently thinking I was some sort of policeman interrogating him.

"I watch him," he finally said. "I look after him ... in the garden. I won't let him in the house."

I asked him further about himself, but he seemed confused. "Where am I?"

He asked me to leave the other man in the garden, in the ground. He would never go away because he had to watch this other man.

"Margaret comes back," he said now. Was there a foursome or were we dealing with more than one level of consciousness?

"Keep him away from her," the ghost admonished me.

"I will," I promised and meant it.

I then told him about his death and that of the others, hoping I could finally rid the house of them all.

"She'll come back," his one-track mind made him say. "I'll wait till she is in bed and then I'll kill her."

I explained again that killing the other man wouldn't do any good since he was already dead.

"My head's bad," the ghost complained.

"You cannot stay at this house," I insisted firmly now.

"Not leaving," he shot back just as firmly. "My house!"

I continued my efforts, explaining also about the passage of time.

"Forty-eight ..." he insisted, "I fight ... I fight ..."

"You've been forgiven," I said and began the words that amount to a kind of exorcism. "You are no longer guilty. You may go."

"Carry him," he mumbled and his voice weakened somewhat. "Where is she? Who'll clean up?"

Then he slipped away.

I awakened Sybil. She felt fine and recalled nothing. But I recalled plenty.

For one thing, it occurred to me that the ghost had spoken of the year 'forty-eight, but not indicated whether it was 1948 or 1848, and there was something in the general tone of the voice that made me wonder if perhaps we were not in the wrong century. Certainly no miner worked in Los Angeles in 1948, but plenty did in 1848. Eugene Lundholm checked the records for me.

In the 'forties mines sprang up all over the territory. In 1842 Francisco Lopez had discovered gold near the San Fernando Mission, and in 1848 a much larger gold deposit was found near Sacramento.

In 1848 also was the famous gold strike at Sutter's Mill. But already in the early 1840's mining existed in Southern California, although not much came of it.

After we went back to New York, Helen L. reached me again the last week of July 1966.

Her mother refused to leave the house, regardless of the disturbances. Thus a sale at this time was out of the question, Miss L. explained.

Something or someone was throwing rocks against the outside of the house and on the roof of their patio—but no living person was seen doing it. This, of course, was par for the poltergeist course. Just another attention-getter. Loud crashes on the patio roof and nobody there to cause them. Even the neighbors now heard the noises. Things were getting worse. I wrote back, offering to have another look at the haunted house provided she was willing to dig. No sense leaving the corpus delicti there.

But on September 18 Miss L. had some more to tell me. Rocks falling on the driveway behind the house brought out the neighbors in force, with flashlights, looking for the "culprits." Who could not be found. Nor could the rocks, for that matter. They were invisible rocks, it would seem.

This took place on numerous occasions between 6:15 and 7:30 P.M. and only at that time. To top it off, a half ripe lemon flew off their lemon tree at Miss L. with such force that it cracked wide open when it landed on the grass beside her. It could not have fallen by itself and there was no one in the tree to throw it.

I promised to get rid of the lemon-throwing ghost if I could, when we came to Los Angeles again in October. But when I did, Miss L.'s mother was ill and the visit had to be called off.

I did not hear anything further about this stubborn ghost. But the area was populated in 1848 and it could be that another house or camp stood on this site before the present house was erected. There was a brook not far away. So far, neither Mr. Morton nor Mr. Howard had been located and Jane and Margaret were only ghostly facts. A lot of people passed through the house when Miss L.'s family did not own it, and of course we know nothing whatever about the house that preceded it.

One more note came to me that helped dispel any notion that Helen L. was the only one bothered by the unseen in the house on Ardmore.

It was signed by Margaret H. Jones and addressed *To Whom It May Concern*. It *concerned* the ghost.

"Some years ago, when I was a guest in Miss L.'s home at Ardmore Boulevard, in Los Angeles, I heard what seemed to be very heavy footsteps in a room which I *knew* to be empty. Miss L. was with me at the time and I told her that I heard this sound. The footsteps seemed to advance and to recede, and this kept up for several minutes, and though we investigated we saw no one. They ceased with the same abruptness with which they began."

I fondly hoped the manifestations would behave in a similar manner. Go away quietly.

But on October 6, 1967, Helen L. telephoned me in New York. She had spent a sleepless night—part of a night, that is.

Up to 4 A.M. she had been sleeping peacefully. At that hour she was awakened by her cat. Putting the animal down, she noticed a strange light on her patio, which was located outside her bedroom windows. She hurriedly threw on a robe and went outside.

In the flower bed on her left, toward the rear of the garden, she noticed something white. Despite her dislike for the phenomena that had for so long disturbed her home, Helen L. advanced toward the flower bed.

Now she could clearly make out the figure of a woman, all in white. The figure was not very tall and could have been that of a young girl. It seemed to watch her intently, and looked somewhat like the conventional white bed sheet type of fictional ghost.

At this point Miss L.'s courage left her and she ran back to her room.

The next morning, her eyes red with exhaustion, she discussed her experience with her aged mother. Until now she had been reluctant to draw her mother into these matters, but the impression had been so overpowering that she just had to tell *someone.*

To her surprise, her mother was not very upset. Instead, she added her own account of the "White Lady" to the record. The night before, the same figure had apparently appeared to the mother in a dream, telling her to pack, for she would soon be taking her away!

When Helen L. had concluded her report, I calmed her as best I could and reminded her that *some* dreams are merely expressions of unconscious fears. I promised to pay the house still another visit, although I was frankly weary of the prospect: I knew full well that you can't persuade a ghost to go away when there may be a body, once the property of said ghost, buried in a flower bed in the garden.

After all, a ghost's got rights, too!

ARE THERE SUCH THINGS AS "LIVING" GHOSTS?

s my investigations of psychic phenomena mounted in number and importance, it became increasingly clear to me that ghosts and spirits and human beings must all have something in common: if a living person can turn into a "dead" spirit or ghost, then that which survives must already have been contained within mortal man. We are as much spirit in our lifetime as we'll ever be.

I also noticed an amazing analogy between certain sleep and dream states and death—as reported by those claiming to be surviving entities speaking through entranced mediums.

The seat of personality seems encased within a temporary frame called the physical body. Under certain conditions, the personality (or soul, if you want to be religious-minded) can emerge from the "box" and behave independently of it. This is called astral travel, or out-of-the-body experience. Here the separation is temporary and still under the control of the traveler—the sleeper. At death the separation is permanent and the personality, the inner self, leaves the "box" behind, rising to a new and freer existence in what Dr. Joseph Rhine of Duke University has called the world of the mind and what I prefer calling the non-physical world.

But there are cases where a ghost appears and on checking it is found that the one whose ghost it is still alive and kicking. Are there such things as "living ghosts"?

Many years ago, Mrs. L. lived in a small oil town in Oklahoma. Her husband was a drilling contractor and their lives were ordinary lives without a trace of the uncanny. One morning Mrs. L. awoke to the sound of a buzzer that preceded the sounding of the hour on her alarm clock. She opened her eyes and noticed it was 7 A.M., or rather five minutes before the hour. In direct line between her eyes and the wall was a chest of drawers. Between the chest and the window there was some space, and as her eyes fastened on that area, she became aware of a figure standing there. It was her husband, staring straight at her. However, she noticed that the apparition ended at the knees where the figure faded out. He wore his usual tan pants, but she also noticed a white shirt with purple stripes. What puzzled her about this shirt was the fact that it was at this moment neatly tucked away inside the chest of drawers.

Now the figure of her husband started to fade away, slowly, from the bottom on up. By the time the apparition had fully dissolved, the clock chimed the hour—seven o'clock.

Mrs. L. got up quickly and opened the chest of drawers; there was the shirt. Before she realized what she was doing she had torn the shirt to bits!

A short time after, Mr. L. was involved in an explosion at the oil rig where he worked. He was blown into a wheelhouse and knocked unconscious. Everything around him was on fire, but he came to just in time to grab a plank and kick it out of the wheelhouse, and thus make his escape.

At the time she saw her husband's "ghost," Mrs. L. was sure he was alive. She was equally convinced that it was a kind of warning. If she hadn't destroyed the telltale shirt and if he had worn it that fatal day, would he have been able to save himself? A tantalizing question.

"Haven't seen a ghost now for about two years," confided the lady from New Britain, Connecticut, who had come to hear my lecture at the college.

It turned out she had seen ghosts galore before that date, however. Mrs. Lillian D. had a husband, a daughter, and a lot of common sense. And she was very psychic, like it or not.

The first time anything unusual happened was in 1957. She had just fed the baby her bottle and fallen asleep, around midnight. Suddenly, she awoke to see what she thought was her husband standing beside her bed. It was 2 A.M. When she asked him what he was doing, standing there like that, he did not answer. So Mrs. D. reached over and switched on the light. There in bed beside her was her husband, sleeping peacefully.

When she explained to him that she had just seen him standing near her bed, he thought she had had a nightmare. But she had no doubt about it—she knew she had been awake. What she did not know at the time was that she had just undergone an experience of bi-location. Mrs. D. encountered the "living ghosts" again, some time after her husband had passed away unexpectedly. A friend of hers had left her and she had gone to bed. In the middle of the night she saw his apparition standing by her bed. He was very much alive at the moment she saw him, perhaps still thinking of their evening together.

In November 1966 she saw an apparition of a man she could not recognize at the time. Again it was in the very heart of the night, around 1 A.M.

Several months later she met this man and became friendly with him. Obviously he had been alive at the time she saw his apparition—but how could one explain this link, since she had not yet encountered him, nor he her, except by prevision on her part.

"Regular" ghosts—that is, of dead people—were nothing new to her, of course. Take her favorite uncle, Harry, for instance. Five days after the family had buried him, there he stood on the right side of her bed. All the "living ghosts," projections of people still in the body, had always appeared on her *left* side. Moreover, the living ones were in color while Uncle Harry wore a plain white suit. When she switched the lights on, he melted away like the others.

Mrs. D. feared ridicule so she had not seen fit to talk about her experiences. She also had had out-of-the-body experiences of her own when she found herself soaring out onto rooftops and trees. And the incident she remembered most vividly was her neighbor's funeral. While the proceedings went forward in the customary manner, she noticed the neighbor sitting on a wall near the casket, laughing and looking over the mourners.

Projections of living people, or "Phantasms of the Living," as the author Sidgwick has called them, occur when a person's thoughts are so strongly engaged at a distance that part of their personality travels with them. If the person on the other end of the "line" happens to be receptive, that is, a psychic person "in tune" with the sender, reception of an image or even a voice may result. And yet, by nature, the ghosts of the living and the ghosts of the dead have much in common. Both prove by the sheer weight of the evidence—numerous as these cases are— that man possesses an indestructible inner self which is capable of breaking through the conventional limits of time and space.

But apparitions of the living and ghosts of the dead have a common frontier in the type of ghost that refuses to accept the facts of afterlife. These people are aware that they are not what they used to be but persist in their habits in what was formerly their world. In a way, they too are psychotic in the sense every ghost is disturbed, but their aberration is more refined, more sophisticated than that of the "run of the mill" specter unable to recognize its own demise.

A young lady that we shall call Miss K., a New Englander, had lived with her psychic experiences without too much concern. So what if several relatives had dropped in on her at the precise moment of their deaths? Distance had no bearing on these visitations. Miss K. was in Rhode Island once and the dead left this world in Philadelphia, but the twain met in Miss K.'s bedroom at the very instance of death.

In 1962 the young lady moved into an old house in town, along with her parents and a brother. Two weeks after they had installed themselves Miss K. was startled to find another person in the house, a person who could not be accounted for as a visitor or otherwise. The woman was clearly visible in the downstairs bedroom, so clearly, in fact, that Miss K. had a good chance to look at her carefully. Her stern face was what struck her strongly, and she wore a plain, dark dress with high neck and a thin strip of lace at the throat. Her steel-gray hair was pulled back severely from her face. The woman was of medium height, very slight build, and seemed elderly.

After this initial experience when Miss K. saw the woman for several seconds before she disappeared, the ghostly occupant of the house returned a number of times. Soon she would show up all over the house, day or night, meeting the family at the top of the stairs and always looking them over before "allowing" them to pass, then descending the stairs herself. Miss Kennett's mother also saw her, so much so that it became a daily routine for her to see the ghost woman in her kitchen first thing every morning.

The stern expression on her face never changed and though the family accepted their "house ghost," the dogs and cats did not and kept out of her way.

345

Miss K. made some discreet inquiries about their house. She was able to trace the apparition to a former owner of their house, a Mrs. Frances F. The lady evidently felt the house was still hers, and the downstairs bedroom in which she first appeared to Sharon K. was indeed her former bedroom. What were strangers doing in *her* house? What sort of people are going up *her* staircase? Look at it from the ghost's point of view, if you please.

I daresay that at least one percent of all those who die either unhappily or with some unfinished business on their minds may stay behind in what was for so long their proper home.

Ghosts are the personalities of people who died tragically, it is true, but this death need not be sudden.

Lingering suffering, mental or physical, can result in the same type of phenomenon.

My files are bulging with such cases, verified properly and containing the eyewitness—or sometimes ear witness—reports of reputable people.

Neither are the ones clinging to their former abodes spirits in the sense that all of us turn spirit at death, if death occurs normally and is accepted by us as such.

The natural order of things is to leave one's physical surroundings at the time the physical body is left behind.

Those refusing to leave are therefore in violation of this rule and become like fish out of water: of spirit "matter," yet within the physical world, they are part of neither one.

The stay-behinds are a real problem only when they become so filled with hatred for those succeeding them in their former homes that they attempt to drive them out, by whatever means are at their command.

Thus the *Poltergeist* or physical phenomena stage is reached, when frightening movements of objects, noises and other manifestations occur and convince the living that theirs is not a safe place to be. Unfortunately people are filled with fears of the Unknown. They often do give in and move out, leaving the stay-behind dead in command. In so doing, they condemn the stay-behinds to a far worse existence than being dead—an in-between state where no progress is possible.

Until people became used to my ideas of contacting the stay-behinds through trance mediums, there was really little they could do: either stay and endure the shenanigans, or leave and let the stay-behinds have the house, or perhaps rent it to some other tenant with thicker skin.

Not everybody is psychic in the same degree. The majority of people are so insensitive they may not even notice a stay-behind. But a substantial minority do get impressions of them ranging all the way from a mere "uneasy feeling of a presence" to full sight of the dead one. This is why not everybody experiences the presences by merely walking into a place plagued by stay-behinds. One cannot request a command performance by the stay-behind just so one can prove that he or she is always there. They are, having no other place to go to.

Often enough, they frequent a certain room or even a favorite piece of furniture. Having imparted much of their personal aura or magnetism to the object through long years of bodily contact with it, they naturally are drawn to it both by sentimental memory and by automatic attraction. If a stranger sits in their favorite chair, quite rightly the stay-behind will deeply resent the intrusion. To the stay-behind the living are the intruders in *his* world, not the other way round. He neither comprehends nor cares to know that things have changed through his death.

It is futile to walk into an old house in the hope of encountering a "ghost," just because the house has been lived in for a long time and perhaps has seen many and varied emotional scenes, or even violent death or struggle.

What the sensitive person might feel in such a place would be an impression of past events rather than participants in them.

On the other hand, some such houses do have ghosts or stay-behinds in them. But then one should rather expect someone among the living, sooner or later, to have an experience of an objective kind, an experience of either seeing or hearing the stay-behind. I, for one, would never investigate a house unless and until several reputable people reported to me that they had indeed had an unusual firsthand experience in the house in question.

Miss K. and her family had long accepted the former owner as one of their people. They were not overjoyed with her, but they understand why she was there. And if she looked out for them and the safety of their house, then having Mrs. F. around wasn't so bad after all!

Because the people involved in the following story were all prominent in New England society, I do not mention their names. Suffice it to say that I have them, and the story, to the best of my knowledge, is absolutely true.

Miss S. had a winter home on Manhattan's East Side and a summer home in Massachusetts. All her life she had partaken of the supernatural, be it in little warnings or larger incursions from the so-called dead.

Once, she was shopping at Bloomingdale's when she felt a sudden and inexplicable urge to visit her aged uncle who lived in New York's Washington Square. She tried to reason it out, saying to herself that the time of day was already too late for such a visit and that she should go the next morning, but the urge within her got the upper hand.

When she reached her uncle she found him happily smoking his pipe and in good spirits. He was an elderly gent and was almost blind. Miss S. was sure that she had given in to a foolish impulse, but she went to take her coat off and hang it in the nurse's room. When she returned to her uncle, she saw that the bowl of his pipe had just caught fire and was blazing away, and he was not at all aware of it. Within moments, she managed to put out the fire. Had she not been there at the time, surely the uncle would have perished.

Years ago, Miss S. bought a summer home in Massachusetts from a friend, Mrs. R. Built originally in 1904, the house had had four prior owners. Neither lady recalled anything unusual about the house until one summer day, when they experienced something they could not explain by ordinary means. The house had a rear patio in back of the living room, in direct line with the front door and the steps leading up to it. That day, they and some friends clearly heard some heavy footsteps coming up the front steps. Miss S. got up and hurried to see who it was, but found no one.

At first Miss S. dismissed it as some sort of practical joke, but she soon learned differently. Over the years, the steps would return, mainly in July and August, and always between noon and 3 P.M. Other phenomena included banging noises coming from an empty workshop once used by a former owner, and the clicking sound of a light switch being turned on—but no light.

It became difficult to "explain" these happenings to the maid and various visitors, but Miss S. steadfastly refused to accept the supernatural explanation, although she knew what it was.

Finally, the matter came to a head. Miss S. had been ill and her doctor was coming to see her?this was in the days of doctor's house visits. Since she was expecting him, she was sitting on the back patio facing the front door. The doctor happened to be a cousin, and when she heard footsteps coming up the front steps she rose to greet him.

To her surprise it was not her cousin who appeared at the front door, but a strange man she had never seen before. He was a thin, elderly man in a Palm Beach suit and a panama hat. Miss S. rushed to the door as fast as her feet would carry her, but he stepped sideways and just disappeared. She looked everywhere but there was no trace of the stranger. This experience so unnerved her she decided to discuss the apparition with her neighbors. It was then that she learned the story of the house. The man she had seen was indeed well-known in the community?it was Mr. B., who had died in 1940. Up to 1939 the house had been owned by the P.'s, husband and wife. Mr. P. was an economist at a leading eastern university. At the time, it was common knowledge in the community that a love affair had been going on between Mr. P. and Mrs. B., also dead now. The ghostly visitor was Mr. B., the husband, looking for his wife at his neighbor's house.

What convinced Miss S. that this was indeed the case, was her friend's experience when she bought the house from the economist's wife. Overly anxious to sell the house, Mrs. P. took a sum below its actual value, and left everything in the house behind—even personal items such as the family Bible. Surely the house must have had bad memories for her, and she wanted to get out as quickly as possible.

Well, Miss S. was not one bit amused. The prospect of having the ghost of the deceived husband dropping in on her unannounced did not please her at all. She took her Bible and said a few prayers in the firm New England manner that was part of her character. She followed this up with a request that Mr. B. should get his rest and not drop around again.

Either Mr. B. realized that the family scandal had better be forgotten now that he didn't have a ghost of a chance to do anything about his rival, or Miss S.'s direct approach worked.

Except for some tapping at her bedroom window in the late 1960s, she did not hear any unusual noises again. And the tapping might have been *someone else*. After all, Miss S. was a receptive person.

THE WOMAN ON THE TRAIN

*he night train gave one more shrill whistle, then pulled out of Vienna's spanking new Western Station. By the next morning, it would be in Zurich, Switzerland. One could make the same journey in an hour by air, but then how many mountains and lakes can one look at from 10,000 feet up? So there were always enough people who preferred the night train, enough at any rate to make the train continue as it has for all these years. It was a good train, as trains go, far cleaner and better than American trains. The sleepers were comfortable and the dining cars served good food, and the soup did not come up and meet you half way to your face the way it did on some of the rickety American diners.

Now the train was running at a faster pace, leaving Vienna's sprawling suburbs behind. After it passed *Huetteldorf-Hacking*, the so-called *Vorbahnhof*, or advance station, for Vienna proper, it became an express train and the clickety-clack of the rails turned into a smoother faster ride. Travelers could now settle back into their cushioned seats and enjoy the ride. True, the landscape would not be interesting until after Tulln, but by then darkness would be setting in. But the early morning glory of seeing the mountains out of the train windows around 6 A.M. would amply compensate for the dark portions of the voyage. The Zurich Express wasn't as glamorous as the famed Orient Express but it was no less classy, and the railroad made every effort to keep their clientele from leaving for the airlines. Even to the extent of placing perfume containers in the washrooms and flowers in the compartments. Let the Penn-Central try that!

One of the travelers beginning to relax was a diminutive redhead with large, dark eyes and the unmistakable air of show business about her. She was well dressed, to be sure, but in a manner and style just a trifle too showy for the ordinary Vienna *hausfrau* or even the elegant lady of the world. There was nothing cheap about her clothes or manner, but she seemed rather self-assured, too much so to be just another wife or sister traveling to Zurich by herself. Her luggage took up almost all of the available space, leaving very little for any other traveler if she had shared her compartment. As it was, she was alone, luckily, and having the sleeping compartment all to herself contributed immeasurably to her sense of comfort at this moment.

Rita Atlanta used the fading moments of the day to reflect on the weeks past. She had just ended a successful engagement in Vienna, two months of full houses in the nightclub where she was employed with her specialty act. Her specialty? Rita is a striptease dancer, one of the best in this somewhat "old-fashioned" field in this day of extremes—like topless dancers and bottomless chorines. But Rita, despite the fact she takes her clothes off in public, was a lady. She had once been married to an American officer of high rank who had met her in Germany. Far from asking her to give up her occupation, he insisted she continue with it. It did not sit well with the general, but the enlisted men loved it, and her performances were always sellouts.

Ultimately, her husband passed away, and Rita began to divide her year between her European engagements and her comfortable trailer stationed near Boston. Her son was growing up and going to school, and Rita's life was pretty orderly and peaceful. She came from a good Austrian family and grew up among people to whom the horrors of war and occupation were only too familiar.

Somehow she had forgotten about those horrible years and only now and then did something remind her about them as she traveled across Europe now.

Since childhood Rita had shown a remarkable degree of extrasensory powers. She was aware of the death of a relative long before it became known and she knew when someone would soon pass away by merely looking at him. This ability she found far from welcome, but it stayed with her, like it or not. Then, when she moved into a trailer near Boston, she soon discovered that she had also inherited a ghost. She was repeatedly awakened at three in the morning by the specter of a large man in a wide-brimmed hat, staring at her from the foot of her bed. Later, it was discovered that a car had run over a man nearby.

Show business people often like to talk about the unknown, and she often found herself regaling her friends in the dressing rooms with her experiences. She formed many a friendship because of her special "gift," and though she viewed all this with mixed emotions, she knew she had to live with it all her life.

Now that her summer season had ended and she could look forward to a good engagement in the fall, she had decided to take some time off and visit a friend of many years at her home at Locarno, Switzerland. Susan West had been ill two years prior to this visit, but a successful operation for cancer had apparently halted the spread of the disease, and she had been declared cured. Thus her friend welcome the idea of Rita's visit, as she had never felt better in her life.

Outside the train window, the landscape started to become more interesting even as the light faded. The hills of the Wachau Valley clearly etched themselves against the skyline and the Danube nearby gave one the feeling of a truly romantic journey. Rita turned the overhead lights low and settled back for a while. Then the monotonous sound of the rails affected her and she felt herself tiring. She undressed and got into bed, turning the overhead lights out and the bedside lamp on. But she was not quite ready for sleep. To begin with, in her profession one does not go off to sleep until very late at night, and the habit pattern had made early bedtimes very difficult for her. Then, too, the brisk October air outside made her feel alive and she decided to read a little before turning the lights off.

She had bought some magazines at the Western Station and now she went through them, always hoping to find perhaps a picture or mention of herself somewhere—an occupational habit most show business people have.

After about twenty minutes of this, she felt sleep reaching out to her, and she dropped the magazines. She turned off the light and prepared herself for sleep. Within a few minutes, she was fast asleep.

All of a sudden, she woke up. Outside, it was quite dark now and the train was very quiet. She had no idea how long she had slept, but it must have been several hours by the way she felt. Still, she was wide-awake and began to wonder why she had suddenly awakened. She turned her head and looked away from the bed into the compartment. Even though there was no moon, enough light from reflected surfaces streamed into the window to let her see the outlines of everything in the small room. There, in front of her bed, was a woman she had never seen before in her life, kneeling on the floor before her.

With a jerk, she sat up and stared at the figure. Stunned by the intrusion, all she could think of was how the woman could have gotten into her room. The woman was kneeling with her hands raised over her head, looking upward. Rita saw her face, the face of a dark complexioned woman with dark hair, perhaps of Latin ancestry. The woman's expression was one of sheer terror as if something horrible was about to be done to her!

Rita found herself scared out of her wits, her heart pounding to her teeth, and yet unable to move. Then she started to find her way to the light switch to turn on the lights. It took her several seconds, which seemed like hours to her, to find the switch and turn it.

When the light flooded the compartment, the apparition was gone. Quickly Rita tried the door, but it was locked securely, just as she had left it prior to retiring. There was no way in which the woman could have gotten into the compartment, if she had been of flesh and blood. But Rita knew from her previous experience in the trailer that she was not confronted with a human being. "Do trains harbor ghosts too?" she wondered and then the thought hit her that this had something to do with her friend Susan.

It did not seem to make sense, but she could not shake the feeling that the ghostly woman was someone connected with her friend, who had come to warn her of impending doom for Susan.

Perhaps it was a ghost, someone killed in this compartment, she tried to reason, but to no avail. Her inner voice told her it was not.

The entire incident cast a sad spell over her otherwise pleasant trip, but eventually she went back to sleep and arrived in Zurich somewhat more composed.

She changed trains and took the train to Bellinzona where her friend and prospective hostess was to meet her and take her the rest of the way to a little town outside of Locarno, where she lived. When she saw Susan in Bellinzona, Rita's fears vanished. Her friend looked radiant and quite obviously was in good health. In fact, she looked years younger than the last time she had seen her. She had changed her hair to red and it looked good on her. The two women embraced, and the bright southern sun quickly made Rita forget the horrible experience on the train to Zurich.

They traveled together now to Locarno, and to while

away the time, or perhaps out of an inner compulsion to be reassured somehow, Rita told Susan about the apparition on the train. But she did not mention her own fears that it had some foreboding concerning her friend.

"I hope it has nothing to do with me," Susan said, as if reading her thoughts. Rita immediately assured her that it didn't, and couldn't.

"How could a ghost on a train have any possible connection with you here in Locarno?" she reasoned, but her friend was not relaxed.

"I don't know," she said and then they changed the subject. Soon afterward they arrived at her apartment in Tenero, near Locarno, and the afternoon and evening was spent talking over old times and plans for the future. When it was time to go to sleep, Rita was given a bed in her friend's living room. Her hostess slept in the bedroom of the apartment.

The place was pretty and new and Rita immediately took a liking to it. She was looking forward to her visit now, and the experience on the train went even further into the background.

She read for a while, as was her custom, then she turned the light out and lay quietly in the dark, waiting for sleep to come and blot out her conscious thoughts.

As she was slowly drifting off to sleep, deliberately avoiding any recollections or reflections upon her experience on the train, she felt herself surrounded by an unseen presence. She blamed her unfamiliarity with her surroundings, the long journey, and the excitement of the trip for her nervousness. But it did not help much, the feeling of an ominous presence in the room persisted.

After a while, it seemed to her as if someone were watching her from all over that room, someone she could not actually see but whom her keen senses felt very much present. She wasn't even sure whether it was one person or several, because the feeling seemed to drift over her from all sides.

It was a very bad night and she hardly slept at all, but she did not wish to alarm her hostess, so she said nothing of it at break-fast the next morning. Instead, at the first opportunity, she went into town and bought sleeping pills, the strongest she could get.

That night, she was drowsy almost at once, due to the drug in the pills. She still felt the presence however, just as strongly as the first night. Only, because she had taken the pills, she did not care, and fell asleep.

Two days after her arrival, she met Mrs. Recalcati, a neighbor of Susan's. Somehow the conversation turned to the psychic world and ghosts in particular, and to her surprise Rita discovered that the lady was not hostile to the possibility that such things did indeed exist.

Encouraged by this open-minded attitude, Rita confided in the neighbor, telling her of her ghostly encounter on the train and of the uncanny sensations in the apartment afterwards.

"I have the feeling Susan is going to die," she added, some-how unable to hold back her dreary thoughts.

The neighbor woman was at first horrified, but then she nodded. "Susan hasn't been well of late," she remarked and Rita shuddered. She had only seen the radiant joy of the reunion of two old friends after many years.

The five days allotted to her visit passed quickly. She returned to Vienna and her own apartment. It was good to spend a night in a room without an unseen presence staring at her from out of the dark.

For the first two days, she just rested—rested from a vaca-tion. Then she confided in a close friend, Elfie Hartl, what had occurred on the train and in Locarno.

Soon after, she returned to America for her usual Christmas holiday with her son, and again discussed what had happened with some of her American friends. But after that, the matter was dropped and not discussed again. Rita was busy living her daily life and the less she had to do with psy-chic matters, the better from her own point of view.

357

This was not entirely possible, as the ghostly manifestations in her trailer never ceased. But she had taken her 3 A.M. "visitor" for granted by now and was not unduly disturbed by him any longer. After all, he was dead and she knew that it did not concern herself or anyone close to her. If he wanted to visit her trailer for some strange reason, that was all right with her. She had often thought of changing her residence or moving the trailer elsewhere, but it was a lot of trouble to go to on account of a ghost. Besides, she had made friends in the trailer camp, and her boy was in school nearby.

Meanwhile the demands for her act were as great as ever. The "girl in the champagne glass," as she was known, had added an oriental act to her original routine, and as a belly dancer she was in almost greater demand than as a striptease artist. There are hundreds of small clubs in the United States using this type of talent and Rita had a busy winter season, traveling about the country.

Somehow, word of her preoccupation with the occult had gotten around, perhaps because she liked to talk about it on occasion with fellow performers. Agents and managers would proffer their palms and ask to be "read" as if Rita were some kind of carnival gypsy. Rita, of course, refused but did not bother to explain the difference between a casual psychic reader, and a person genuinely possessed of ESP and a serious interest in that which she did not want, but nevertheless found present within her.

Still, inadvertently, she sometimes told friends what she felt about them only to find out later that it had all come true the way she had so casually mentioned it. It did not give her any sense of pride in her psychic accomplishment. To the contrary, she kept asking herself, what is the matter with me? I don't want to see ghosts; I don't want to tell people's fortune or misfortune—I just want to be left alone by the forces that cause all this.

She could handle the freshest of hecklers when performing her act, and quench the rudest remark, if necessary. But this was different. How can you deal with something you don't see or hear, something within you?

One day in Baltimore, she was sitting in her dressing room backstage at a local club. It was an icy February day of 1968 and business had been good despite the cold weather. Perhaps because of it, she reasoned, men wanted to see a pretty girl undress. She had some time to kill between performances, and her son had forwarded her mail to her from Boston.

As she casually went through the stack of fan mail, she noticed an unfamiliar stamp. It was a letter from Locarno. Quickly, she tore open the envelope. The letter was from Susan's son. She had died on January 7 of that year. As she put the letter down, she kept seeing her red-headed friend in her mind, how lifelike and joyous she had been during their last get-together.

Then, with a shudder, she felt herself think of the woman on the train again, and all at once Rita knew that this was someone connected with Susan's death. But why had she been chosen to receive this warning and not Susan herself? Was she the "telephone between worlds" for all her friends and should she have told her friend about the warning after all? "No," she said to herself, "no," it would have spoiled the last few happy months she had on earth. With a sigh Rita put the letter back with the others and prepared herself for the next performance.

Rita often returned to Vienna, but the night train to Zurich was out of bounds to her. Perhaps there were ghosts on airplanes too, but at least the flight to Zurich only took an hour.